K. Garrett

£ 2.50

EDWARDIAN WORTHING

Eventful Era in a Lifeboat Town

ROB BLANN

Published in England by

Rob Blann, 349 Tarring Road, Worthing, West Sussex, BN11 5JL
to benefit the
Royal National Lifeboat Institution

All rights reserved. No part of this publication may be reproduced, transmitted
or used in any form by any means – graphic, electronic or mechanical,
including photocopying, recording, taping or information storage and retrieval
systems or otherwise – without the prior permission of the Publisher.

© copyright Rob Blann 1991

1st Edition 1991

British Library Cataloguing in Publication Data
Blann, Rob
Edwardian Worthing – eventful era in a lifeboat town
1. West Sussex, (England). Social life. History, 1901-1914
I. Title
942.2680823

ISBN 0-9516277-1-6

The painting, by Worthing artist Ted Bennett, reproduced on the front cover
was commissioned for this book, and depicts the Worthing lifeboat *Richard
Coleman* being launched on service to the distressed barque *Andrac* on
6 August 1912. The view from Worthing Pier clearly shows the magnificent
Kursall, now the Dome Cinema with an uncertain future.

Typeset by MGN Graphics, 67 Victoria Road, Worthing
Photograph scanning by Michael Gorton Design, Wordsworth Road, Worthing
Printed by Hillman Printers (Frome) Ltd., Frome, Somerset

Foreword

Raymond Baxter

It was in the early 1970s, as I recall, that undergraduate humour suddenly found expression in a spate of graffiti which appeared all over the country. Some of it was mildly outrageous: much of it was, by any standards, witty. One of my favourites on a wall behind University College, Oxford, read 'Nostalgia is not what it used to be!'

Whatever he or she was, the author of that little gem was certainly no prophet. During the last 20 years, nostalgia has become a thriving industry as seen in the revival of interest in classic boats, cars and aeroplanes, steam locomotives, toys and games – and, of course, lifeboats. Half of the RNLI stand at the 1991 London Boat Show consisted of the reconstruction of a Lifeboat House of 100 years ago.

This fascination for days gone by is encapsulated accurately and charmingly in every single page of this book. From it we learn, for example, that in 1903 the owner of the eight heavy horses employed to drag the lifeboat on its masssive carriage to the beach and into the surf received the considerable sum of £3 4s (three pounds and four shillings), for a protracted standby.

Long before the advent of television and home entertainment we are reminded that thousands of people would travel into Worthing from miles around to enjoy the innocent fun of the annual regatta, complete with its greasy pole competition (boys under 15 only) and the fiercely contested racing between fishermen and their craft.

And in year after year of this detailed history we are also reminded of the unfailing gallantry of generation after generation of lifeboatmen prepared to put their lives at risk in order to rescue their fellow men in peril at sea.

Much, much has changed in the succeeding years. What has remained unchanged since its inception to this day is the spirit of the RNLI and those who man and serve its lifeboats.

RAYMOND BAXTER
Vice President &
Committee of Management, RNLI.

January 1991

The Borough Crest

'From the land wealth and the sea health'

Introduction

It is a privilege to be asked to write an introduction to this fascinating piece of history, planned, researched, written and published in Worthing by a man whose family has lived in the town for generations.

There are only a handful of books about Worthing's history but this is the second one written by Rob Blann. It carries on the history of the town where the first book ended, at the end of Victoria's reign and the beginning of the twentieth century.

"Edwardian Worthing" concentrates on the lives of those courageous men who manned the Worthing lifeboats, and spans the reign of Edward VII from his coronation to his death. It throws an interesting light on the importance, in the days before radio and television, of local participation in events of national importance like the coronation and the mourning of King Edward's death in 1910 and the part played in such events by the seafaring community, in particular the lifeboatmen.

The story makes compelling reading for one whose grandfathers, one a Borough Councillor and the other the leader of a small local fishing fleet, would undoubtedly have known Rob Blann's family in a town as small as Worthing then was.

Just to have collected in one volume so many rare and irreplaceable illustrations of old Worthing is an achievement in itself; they will fascinate anybody with an interest in Worthing and its lifeboatmen and I also found the useful and informative footnotes at the end of each chapter particularly interesting. I commend this book to you as a valuable contribution to the written history of the town.

COUNCILLOR HUGH BRADEN C.M.G.
Mayor Elect

March 1991

Acknowledgements

I sincerely thank the following for their many hours of selfless devotion in assisting me with this book:

    Eric Cockain
    Phil and Margaret Hayden

For their continued co-operation, I would like to thank:

    Terry Child
    Jeff Morris, honorary archivist, RNLI Enthusiasts Society
    Derrick Marshall Churcher
    Mrs. Arthur Wingfield and Alan Wingfield
    Bill Blann, my father
    Mrs. Mabel Foggett (nee Blann), my aunt
    Mrs. Gena Wilmshurst

Many of the postcards and photographs reproduced in this book are from my own collection. For those borrowed from other sources I would like to thank:

    Terry Child
    Derrick Marshall Churcher
    West Sussex County Council Library Service
    Worthing Museum
    Phil Hayden
    Mrs. Mabel Foggett (nee Blann), my aunt
    Mrs. June Roberts (nee Blann), my cousin
    Mrs. Ann Tugnett (nee Bashford)
    Mrs. Molly Wakefield and David Wakefield
    Mrs. Ida Wadey (nee Street)
    The National Maritime Museum

Contents

Foreword iii

Introduction v

Acknowledgements vi

List of illustrations x

Preface xvii

Worthing street map, c.1907 xxi

Chapter 1: Warm Welcomes   1901-2 1

    Four lifeboats paraded through the town, 7 Aug 1901
    The new *Richard Coleman* christened, 7 Aug 1901
    Demonstration by four lifeboats, 7 Aug 1901
    Annual Regatta held Aug 1901
    The first practice using the *Richard Coleman,* Sept 1901
    Boats and fishing equipment auctioned on the beach, 10 October 1901
    Largest catch of prawns, spring 1901
    Fisherman found dead at sea, 7 Aug 1901
    Worthing Branch RNLI AGM, 30 Jan 1902
    Worthing lifeboatmen feature in a national periodical, 1902
    Local Fisheries Committee, Jan 1902
    Surprise capture of a Kingfish, July 1902
    King Edward VII Coronation Parade, 9 Aug 1902
    Old folks' dinner, 9 Aug 1902

Chapter 2: On Film   1902-5 33

    Regattas, 26 Aug 1902, 28 Aug 1903 and Sept 1903
    RNLI Annual Meetings, 29 Jan 1903 and 10 Feb 1905
    Barquentine *Lizette* runs aground, 4 April 1903
    Completion of a land yacht, Sept 1903
    Fishing boats damaged in storm, 10 Sept 1903
    RNLI lecture, Dec 1903
    Film of Worthing lifeboat made for showing in picture houses, Jan 1904
    Worthing lifeboatmen at Kingston, 25 June 1904
    Sussex Sea Fisheries Committee, 10 Nov 1904
    Foundering of the barque *Liburna* and launching of the
       Richard Coleman, 15 March 1905

Chapter 3: One More Saved   1905-6 49

    A pleasure cruise goes wrong, 21 May 1905
    Regattas, Aug 1905, Sept 1905 and Aug 1906

Contents

Chapter 3 *continued*

    Lifeboat Sunday
    RNLI Annual Meeting
    Worthing Fishermen's Mutual Insurance Association, 1906
    Pleasure boating, 1906
    The passing of John Belton, the boatbuilder, 27 Nov 1906
    Worthing lifeboat crew in the Lord Mayor's Show, 1906
    Rescue in the Channel by the lifeboat, 10 Nov 1906

Chapter 4: The Watermen's Day   1907-8 65

    RNLI Annual Meetings, 28 Feb 1907 and 11 March 1908
    Anniversary remembrance service of the *Lalla Rookh* disaster, Nov 1908
    Fierce storm smashes fishing boat, 2 May 1907
    Body on beach reveals a lovelorn tale, May 1907
    Lifeboat Saturday at Kingston, 6 July 1907
    Demonstration of lifebuoys, 15 Aug 1907
    Belton & Co., boatbuilders, 1907
    The Regatta season of 1907
    The Shipwrecked Mariners' Society, 1907
    The Fishermen's Mutual Insurance Society, 1907
    Boatmen rescue passengers from capsized craft on Easter Sunday 1908

Chapter 5: Loyal Servants, Supporters & Subjects   1908 85

    Lifeboat Sunday, 19 July 1908
    Watermen's Regatta, 5 Aug 1908
    Swimmer disappears, July 1908
    Annual Regatta, 1 Sept 1908
    King Edward VII comes to Worthing, 12 Dec 1908
    Channel search by lifeboat, 10 December 1908

Chapter 6: Rejoicings & Laments   1909 101

    RNLI Annual Meeting, Feb 1909
    Boating party missing, March 1909
    Fishermen foil suicide attempt, April 1909
    Captain Collins and the *Skylark*, 22 June 1909
    The Fish Market, 1909
    Watermen's Regatta, 6 Aug 1909
    Worthing lifeboat exercise illustrated in a national newspaper, 24 Aug 1909

Chapter 7: Six Cheers for the King   1910-11 115

    The Theatre Royal radically altered, Dec 1909
    Mr. Seebold plans a multi-purpose entertainment complex, Dec 1909
    Worthing's seaweed features in a national newspaper, 1910
    RNLI Annual Meeting – new kapok lifejackets, 1910
    King Edward VII memorial procession, May 1910
    Lifeboat launch during funeral of Cox. Charlie Lee, 13 Oct 1910
    Fishermen's and Watermen's Benefit Association, 1910

Contents

Chapter 7 *continued*
        A record catch of fish, 1911
        A seaside drama, July 1911
        Drunk in charge, Sept 1911
        Storms wreak havoc, Nov 1911
        A message in a bottle, 1911
        A new landlord, Oct 1911
        Annual Regatta, 1911
        The Kursall opens, 1911
        King George V Coronation Parade, 22 June 1911
        Old Folks' Dinner at the Kursall, 22 June 1911

Chapter 8: A Vital Role   1912 143
        Innovative launching poles, 1912
        RNLI Annual Meeting at the *Warnes Hotel*
        Destructive storm blocks roads, 4 March 1912
        The great groyne debate, March 1912
        Lifeboat investigates distress rockets, 11 July 1912
        Italian sailors on the barque *Andrac* rescued by Sussex lifeboats, 6 Aug 1912

Chapter 9: A Severed End   1912-13 161
        Excessively bad weather threatens watermen's livelihoods, Aug 1912
        Annual Regatta, 3 Sept 1912
        Gale sweeps the country on Boxing Day, 1912
        RNLI Annual Meeting at the *Warnes Hotel*, 5 March 1913
        Pier destroyed by a great storm on Easter Saturday, 1913

Chapter 10: Pulling Together   1913-14 173
        Watermen's Regatta, 25 Aug 1913
        Worthing watermen spot waterspout, 15 Sept 1913
        RNLI Annual Meeting, 24 Feb 1914
        Lifeboatmen experiment with oil on rough sea, 3 March 1914
        The Lord Mayor of London travels to Worthing to open the
            rebuilt Pier, 29 May 1914
        Lord Mayor's Parade through the town, 29 May 1914
        Lunch at the *Warnes Hotel* to commemorate the Pier
            opening, 29 May 1914

Lists of names 191
        Mayors of the Borough
        Worthing Lifeboat Crews 1901-1914
        Worthing Fishermen's and Watermen's Benefit Association Committee
        Swimming Club Officers
        Built in the Edwardian Era
        Demolished in the Edwardian Era
        Guests at the Lord Mayor's Luncheon at *Warnes Hotel,* 1914

By the same author 194

List of 210 illustrations

Preface xvii
The *Henry Harris* at sea
Worthing lifeboat *Henry Harris* and crew at the lifeboat station

Chapter 1   1901-2 1
Worthing's Invitation
A promotional postcard
Jesse Belville Blann
The 1901 lifeboat procession in Liverpool Gardens. A sequence of 3 photos from the same spot:-
    1 The Littlehampton *James Mercer & Elizabeth* and Shoreham's *William Restell*
    2 The *Henry Harris*
    3 The *Richard Coleman*
The 1901 lifeboat parade in Montague Street. A sequence of 7 photos from the same spot:-
    1 Volunteer soldiers
    2 High-spirited youngsters
    3 Drummers
    4 Flautists
    5 Shoreham's *William Restell*
    6 Littlehampton's *James Mercer & Elizabeth*
    7 The *Henry Harris*
The *Henry Harris* parading past the lifeboat house, 1901
Littlehampton's *James Mercer & Elizabeth* passing Marlborough House, 1901
The *Henry Harris* and the *Richard Coleman*, 1901
The *Richard Coleman* passing the burnt-out Royal Hotel, 1901
The four lifeboats at the naming ceremony of the *Richard Coleman*, 1901
Coxswain Harry Marshall wearing lifeboat gear.
Naming ceremony of the *Richard Coleman*, 1901
Oars raised in salute at the naming ceremony, 1901
The four lifeboats entering the water, 1901
Littlehampton's *James Mercer & Elizabeth*
The *Richard Coleman*
The lifeboat display viewed from the Pier, 1901
The lifeboat display as seen from the landing stage, 1901
The *Henry Harris* awaiting transportation to London
Harry Marshall with the *Jolly Sailor*
The entrance to Worthing Pier
The *Richard Coleman* preparing to launch
Worthing Branch RNLI committee, 1902
Second Coxswain Bill Blann
The *Richard Coleman* horsed and crewed outside the lifeboat house, 1902
A closer shot of the above
West Parade viewed from the Pier
West Parade
Richmond Road homes decorated for the King Edward VII Coronation celebrations
Worthing Town Hall festooned for the celebrations
St. Paul's Church looking south
Beach House
A gilded goat-chaise

Illustrations

Chapter 2   1902-5 33
Climbing the greasy pole, 1902
The Bandstand in 1902
The *Richard Coleman* and carriage on the sands
Steve Wingfield senior
A motor omnibus at Worthing Railway Station
Coastguards with their galley at Lancing
A violent sea at Splash Point
The *Richard Coleman* just east of the lifeboat house in Marine Parade
The *Richard Coleman* being launched in a heavy sea
Worthing lifeboatmen at Kingston
The Catholic Church
South Street looking north towards the Town Hall
The *Richard Coleman* to the rescue
The *Liburna* stranded off Shoreham, 1905

Chapter 3   1905-6 49
The Paddling Pebble
Fred Marshall with holidaymakers on the *Jolly Sailor*
The wrecked steamer *Indiana*
The *Hotel Metropole*
The *Richard Coleman* inside the lifeboat house
The lifeboat house after 1905
Harry Marshall
A safe return for three young ladies
Worthing's *Britannia*
Steyne Gardens
The beach west of the Bandstand before 1907
A launch of the *Richard Coleman*
The *Richard Coleman* returning from exercise
A Worthing coastguardsman
Thomas Anderson and rowing boat
South Street
Warwick Street

Chapter 4   1907-8 65
Three Plums
Frozen sea
The lifeboat crew in front of the lifeboat house, 1907
The Marshalls' *Jolly Sailor*
Orme Road
Worthing lifeboat crew at Kingston, 1907
The lifeboatmen rowing out to sea
Belton & Co. boatbuilders
East beach
Oiling the tarpaulin
A NE view of the Bandstand
Turning the capstan
A goat-chaise on the promenade
Worthing from the sea end of the Pier
Jo Street junior
Chapel Road looking north
Colonnade House and the southern end of High Street

Illustrations

Chapter 4 *continued*

The *Stanhoe Hotel*
The Broadway

Chapter 5   1908 85
Henry Hayden
The *Richard Coleman* in Marine Parade
Youngsters on the beach
Inside St. Paul's Church
Outside St. Paul's Church
The Public Library and Museum
Three steamers at Worthing Pier
Sir Henry Aubrey-Fletcher
Holidaymakers
Paddling
The *Worthing Belle*
Motor & Cycle Carnival looking east, 1908
Motor & Cycle Carnival looking west. 1908
Motor & Cycle Carnival judging, 1908
The Arundel omnibus
Children's Carnival on Worthing Pier, 1908 (a)
Children's Carnival on Worthing Pier, 1908 (b)
King Edward VII at Worthing
Recovering the *Richard Coleman* at low tide
Hauling the *Richard Coleman* on carriage along the sands

Chapter 6   1909 101
Don't mind me, girls, I'm only a baby.
A family on holiday
The lifeboatmen wearing kapok life-jackets
The Parade east of the Pier
The *Steyne Hotel*
Regatta day
An omnibus on the seafront
Street entertainers
Relaxing in a shelter outside the Pier Pavilion
A return of the *Richard Coleman*
Worthing seafront
The Congregational Church
Christ Church

Chapter 7   1910-11 115
"Just as you are for ninepence!"
Beach Parade
The proclamation of King George V
Councillors joining the King Edward VII memorial procession
King Edward VII memorial procession at the bottom of Chapel Road
The procession in Chapel Road
The procession passing Worthing Lodge

Illustrations

Chapter 7 continued

Sailors on the *Barfleur*
Taking down the sails after beaching the *Richard Coleman*
On the rocks at low water
A fish auction
East Beach
The Parade after a gale, 1910
The *Warnes Hotel* entrance
Eel catching on marshland
Bill Blann junior and friend
The Kursall
The George V Coronation parade in South Street
Harry and Bert Blann
The Coronation parade in Chapel Road (a)
The Coronation parade in Chapel Road (b)
The Coronation parade in Chapel Road (c)
Worthing Church Lads' Brigade
The Boys Brigade
The Coronation Parade in Grafton Road
The Coronation procession in Marine Parade
Firing a 'Feu de Joie' on Coronation day
Old Folks' Dinner
Old Folks' Dinner
The Kursall Garden
Warwick Street

Chapter 8   1912 143
A Bathing Beauty
Pulling the *Richard Coleman* into the sea.
The *Warnes Hotel*
High seas lashing the Parade, 1912
The Bandstand shelter after the storm, 1912
Marine Parade flooded, 1912
The *Worthing Belle*
A NW view of the Bandstand
The Bandstand and its shelter as seen from the beach
The *Richard Coleman* on the seafront road
A whale thresher on the beach
A torpedo on the beach
The *Richard Coleman* being launched
The *Richard Coleman* under sail, 1912
People waiting on the Pier for the lifeboat to return, 1912
Return of the *Richard Coleman,* 1912
The barque *Andrac* towed by the tug *Stella*
Edwardian Humour

Chapter 9   1912-13 161
A witty and romantic Edwardian postcard
Launching the *Richard Coleman*
Rough sea at Splash Point

Illustrations

Chapter 9 *continued*

'Running the gauntlet' on Beach Parade
A high sea lashing the Pier
'Easter Island'
Montague Street
The Kursall and a capstan
Sightseers in the Pier wreckage
The Pier's remains, looking north
The Parade after the great storm, 1913
Storm-damaged Bandstand shelter, 1913
Wrecked wooden bungalows between Lancing and Shoreham, 1913 (a)
Wrecked wooden bungalows between Lancing and Shoreham, 1913 (b)
Broadwater Road

Chapter 10   1913-14 173
A 'style' much in favour at Worthing.
Aerial view of the 'Island Pier'
Crowds on West beach
Pier reconstruction (halfway)
Launch of the *Richard Coleman* using a temporary warp, 1914
Reconstruction of the Pier (last section)
Fixing new decking planks on the rebuilt Pier
Street decorations in Chapel Road and outside the Town Hall, 1914
Arrival of the Lord Mayor at the railway station, 1914
The Lord Mayor's parade by Broadwater Bridge
The Lord Mayor's parade in Chapel Road
The Lord Mayor's parade going past the Town Hall
One of the carriages in South Street
The Lord Mayor's parade in South Street (a)
The Lord Mayor's parade in South Street (b)
The opening of the new Pier
The procession along the new Pier
The procession outside the *Warnes Hotel*
The Royal Naval Ladies Orchestra
Worthing-by-the-Sea

To my daughter, Lisette

Preface

At the beginning of my first book – 'A Town's Pride: Victorian Lifeboatmen & their Community' – I detailed a tragic event that brought home to the people of Worthing how necessary it is to make proper provision for the saving of lives off our coast.

Longfellow's description of the sea summed up its unpredictable ferocity thus:

> The ocean old, centuries old,
> Strong as youth, and as uncontrolled!

A sea wild as this, took the lives of 11 of our fine fishermen soon after they put out in an ordinary beach boat to render assistance to the distressed East Indiaman *Lalla Rookh* in 1850.

Great Britain was deeply stirred by the magnitude of the tragedy, which left nine wives widowed and 47 children fatherless, and a magnificent sum exceeding £5,000 was quickly raised towards a relief fund.

Almost immediately, another fund was organised to pay for a self-righting lifeboat which subsequently came into service in 1853, and was housed at the top of Worthing's beach.

The National Lifeboat Institution received its royal charter in 1854 when Queen Victoria agreed to become the institution's first Royal Patron.

In 1858, disaster struck on Worthing's coastline again, when the *Mary Eliza* was hit by a sudden squall of exceptional strength while on a pleasure trip. Thirteen of its occupants, many of them children, were drowned.

Seven years later the Worthing lifeboat establishment was taken over by the Royal National Lifeboat Institution (RNLI). A new and improved lifeboat, the *Jane*, was built. At the same time, a new boat house was constructed in a side street some little distance from the sea (Crescent Road).

Admiral Hargood, and later his son, was the organising force behind both the operational and fund-raising activities of the Branch.

By this time, the Lifeboat Institution, which had been founded in 1824, ran 153 lifeboat stations around the U.K., and had been responsible for saving nearly 15,000 lives.

In 1868, the first significant rescue by the crew of the *Jane* resulted in saving, not only the six crew from the distressed brigantine *Hilena*, but also the ship itself.

One year later, following severe storms, Worthing lifeboatmen boarded a drifting fishing smack, *Active*, which belonged to a fellow lifeboatman from Selsey. After saving the fishing boat, the Worthing lifeboat also picked up a small upturned boat that belonged to a French ship, and landed it back at Worthing.

Drenched and exhausted sailors from the wrecked Spanish barque, the *Benvenue*, ended up on Worthing Pier one night in 1869, and were given food and blankets by locals.

To facilitate rescue work, a replacement lifeboat house was built on the seafront, and came into use in 1875. (The building is still there today.)

At the time of the great flood in 1877, the *Jane* brought in the drifting lugger *Harkaway* belonging to a Worthing fisherman.

Renamed the *Henry Harris*, the Worthing lifeboat successfully took off the crew of the distressed schooner *Theresa* in a violent sea during 1883.

Three years later, the *Henry Harris* was launched to aid a French barque and a Guernsey brig that had collided in the Channel.

After more than 20 years in service, comprehensively described in 'A Town's Pride', the veteran lifeboat was replaced by a further improved and slightly larger lifeboat, the *Henry Harris*, which was initially launched as the principal event in Worthing's celebrations to mark Queen Victoria's Golden Jubilee.

Active service was again called, when, in 1888, the coal ship *Albert H. Locke* ran aground off West Worthing. Ten were rescued.

The following year, another collision occurred, this time off Littlehampton, between the barque *Vandalia* and the steamer *Duke of Buccleuch*. The latter immediately sank. Wreckage and cargo from the *Vandalia* spilled along the coast until the barque itself finished up off Brighton.

In November 1891 the *Henry Harris* was launched not once but twice on the same day. Two vessels were driven ashore by howling gales: the *Capella* at West Worthing; and the *Kong Karl* at Lancing. For his outstanding leadership of the courageous lifeboat crew who battled against ferocious weather in monstrously rough conditions, Coxwain Charlie Lee was awarded the silver medal of the RNLI.

Fishing was a thriving industry at this time.

Worthing lifeboat *Henry Harris* photographed between 1892 and 1897 when Harry Marshall was 2nd coxswain.[1]

For Worthing watermen the big annual event of the year was the Regatta. But in 1893, when an outbreak of typhoid hit Worthing, this event was cancelled.

Following Fever Year, as 1893 was called, some novel events were staged to attract more visitors to this seaside town and to prove that the water was quite pure once again. One of those visitors, Oscar Wilde, who stayed here for some time, witnessed an unprecedented spectacle: a procession of four lifeboats on their carriages, from neighbouring stations, through the town and their subsequent racing on the sea.

Towards the end of 1894, the bodies of 14 shipwrecked sailors from the ill-fated steamship *Zadne* washed ashore on Worthing beach. Controversial rumours as to why the Worthing lifeboat had not been called out were eventually laid to rest at a public inquiry called by Worthing RNLI Branch Chairman, Harry Hargood, J.P.

During the following year of 1895, the *Henry Harris* saved a French captain from his foundering brigantine *Halcyon*, after his crew had abandoned ship some time earlier for the safety of a passing vessel. This same year, the Annual Regatta was dogged by bad weather, but this did not prevent local fisherman and coastguards from competing.

Worthing lifeboat crew, wearing oilskins, sou'esters and cork lifejackets, pictured
in front of the *Henry Harris* and the lifeboat house on the seafront.[2]

With most of its sails torn away by storm, the distressed barque *Ophir* was driven aground at Lancing, in 1896. Two of its crew were successfully taken off under horrendous conditions by the Worthing lifeboat, and, with great difficulty, the remainder were saved by the coastguards who made a breeches buoy from the beach.

Just eight days later, another ship ran aground, this time at West Worthing. It was the schooner *Flora Emily* laden with potatoes, and its crew of five were glad to be rescued by the Worthing lifeboat.

The following year, the *Henry Harris* and crew were prominent in a procession through the town centre which included the Duke of Cambridge, following his official opening of the new waterworks on the outskirts of the town.

Launched on a rescue mission in 1899, the *Henry Harris* was responsible for saving the crew of the drifting schooner *Prince Llewellyn*, which nearly smashed into the Pier.

The last errand of mercy for the *Henry Harris* was to the holed steamship *Indiana*, which had been rammed by another vessel, and which eventually ground to a halt in the shallows off Worthing. Scattering its cargo of fresh fruit along the beach, it quickly became known as the Orange Wreck.

Those of you who have read my first book will know of the difficulties and hazards faced by Worthing fishermen in pursuing their calling, in not only local waters but in distant seas, and how God-fearing attitudes, which were very strong among folk in the 19th century began to lessen a little towards the end of Queen Victoria's reign.

Hurricanes and storms are not new to Worthing. Storms, flooding and sea defences have always been part of life in this seaside town, and when well-to-do Worthingites were called upon, on many occasions, to aid working-class fishermen in their hour of need, we've seen how they rallied philanthropically.

The chronicle of the construction and extension of Worthing's Victorian Pier is a story in itself.

Happy times and sad times. Life went on for the folk of Worthing. Its population had increased fourfold, from 5,000 inhabitants in 1850 to just over 20,000 in 1901.

In this follow-on chronicle I continue to weave together the social and working histories of Worthing's fishermen and lifeboatmen. Intermingled are events connected with Worthing's beach.

I hope you enjoy reading this book as much as I enjoyed researching and putting it all together.

Footnotes

[1] Wearing their red woolly hats, blue jerseys, white trousers and cork lifejackets – dress reserved for a special festive occasion – the crew are accompanied by a bowler-hatted gentleman, possibly a branch officer. Coxswain Charlie Lee, with the heavily whiskered face is operating the rudder by pulling on the yoke lines running over his shoulders. To assist in steering the boat, the 2nd cox, standing in the stern, is using a sweep oar – an arrangement that was more often used in lifeboats on the east coast of England.

[2] In the middle is Mark Marshall, and to his right sits Bill Blann; standing far right is Harry Marshall with his brother Fred next to him. This photograph was probably taken after Coxswain Lee retired in 1897 and before the *Henry Harris* was replaced in 1901.

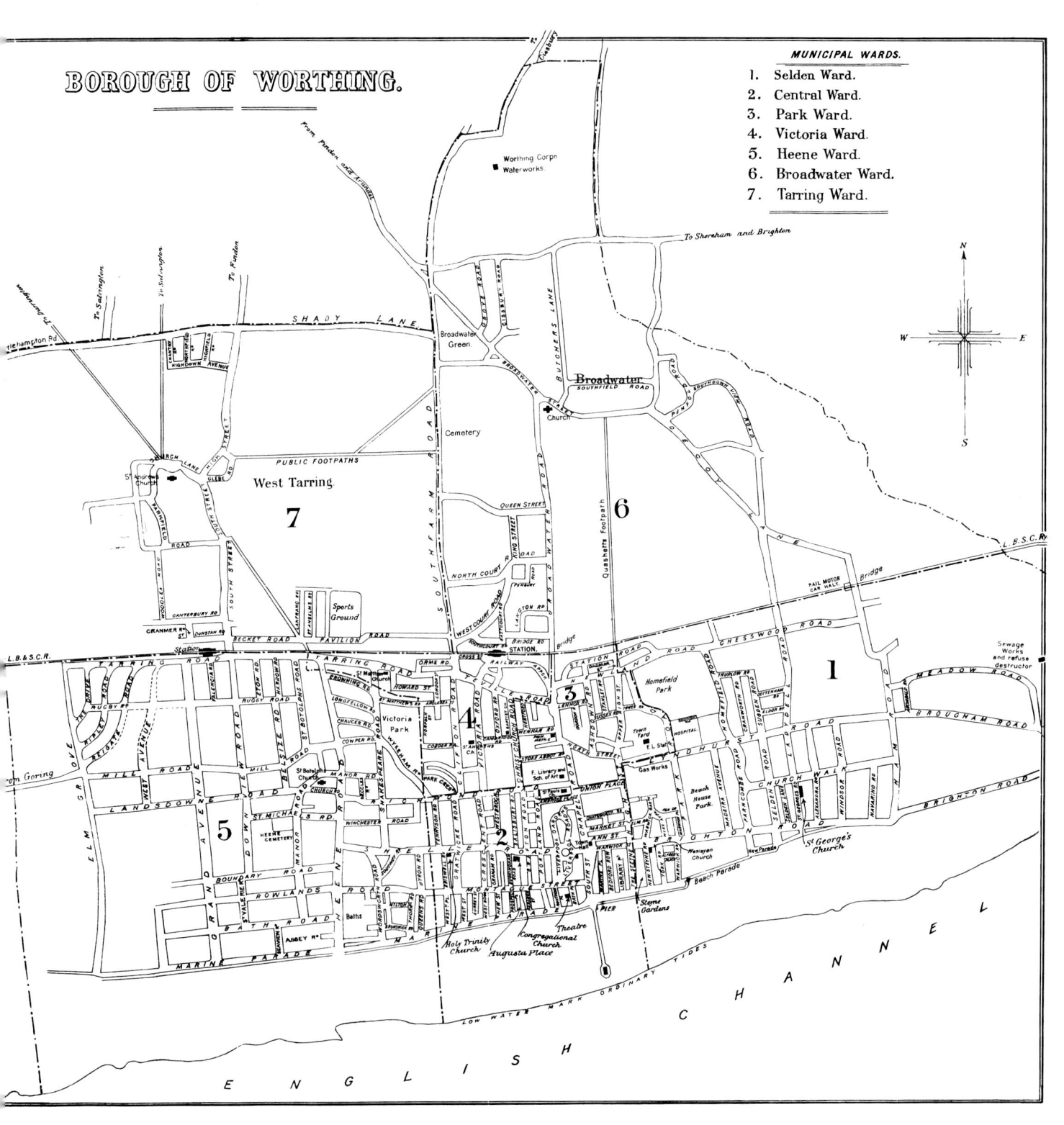

Worthing Street Map circa 1907

TO THE JADED LONDONER.

Worthing's Invitation.

Whene'er run down or weary,
  And longing for the sea,
Just come down South and see me—
  Quite welcome you will be.

In England you'll ne'er find a spot
  So balmy and so sweet;
It's nice and warm, but not too hot—
  Just wire what train to meet.

A lovely front, a season band
  That music sweetly plays;
The bathing—it is really grand,
  And will receive your praise.

And then upon a nice long pier
  You'll hear some music fine,
For there a Ladies' Orchestra
  Plays daily—rain or shine.

The yachts are very smart and trim,
  In which to take a sail;
So take a trip if in the whim,
  E'en if it blows a gale.

And if good fishing you desire,
  To pier head you should go;
To cater for your needs entire,
  Is Worthing's wish, you know.

The sands are safe, the boats are good,
  The Downs a splendid view;
When you return in *sunny* mood,
  You'll say my words are true.

So come to Worthing sunny,
  And lead a simple life;
Be free from care and worry,
  From London's toil and strife.

OWEN EDWARDS, *Author of "Sweet Summer," etc.*

Printed and Published by J. R. Keeley, 67, Chapel Road,
Copyright.]   Worthing.

An Edwardian postcard

Chapter 1

Warm Welcomes

1901-2

During the year 1901 a new age was dawning. Not only was it the beginning of a new century, the late Queen Victoria's middle-aged son, Edward, was about to succeed to the throne.

For residents in the town of Worthing another era in the lifeboat station's history was unfolding as the building of a new lifeboat to replace the 14 year old *Henry Harris* neared completion.

This modern 'pulling & sailing' lifeboat had been generously paid for by a Mrs. Birt-Davies Coleman through the RNLI. It was finished during the summer, in time for the naming ceremony, which had been arranged for 7 August 1901. A committee had been formed to make the necessary arrangements and to raise the estimated expense of £100 for the programme, which was to be a principal feature of the season and certain to attract a large number of holiday-makers and day-trippers to the town.

Two inviting girls promoting Worthing on an Edwardian postcard, posted in 1906, which depicts a Regatta west of Worthing Pier.[1]

This committee, whose chairman was the Mayor, Mr. F. E. Ovenden, included members of the Town Council as well as members of the lifeboat committee. It decided to hold a lifeboat demonstration similar to that held in 1894, including a procession, simultaneous launch of several lifeboats, and an illuminated promenade concert.

At the beginning of August special trains were laid on to transport an exceptionally large number of people wanting to visit the town. Thousands came to Worthing expecting to experience the fun and excitement of the celebrations surrounding the official launch of this new lifeboat.

In response to a request by the Mayor the appointed day was declared a public holiday, and virtually all the shops and businesses in the town closed at 2 p.m. Soon after, the lifeboat crews and others began taking up their allotted positions in the procession, which was being marshalled in Shelley Road.

Jesse Belville Blann, my grandfather, who was a young man of 21 had a wonderful time with his buddies. The high-spirited bachelors playfully teased young ladies whose eyes lit up watching the smart, uniformed soldiers taking up their positions in the parade with distinguished military discipline.

My grandfather, Jesse Belville Blann, as a young man of 21 in 1901, smartly dressed for his portrait.[2]

At about a quarter to three the magnificent procession moved off from Shelley Road, and made its way via Liverpool Gardens to Montague Street. Here, photographers hung out of first floor windows above the shops and captured some close-up shots of the procession of four lifeboats and military contingents passing almost beneath them in the narrow street.

Continuing into Rowlands Road, the great parade, led by the Borough Band and followed by several detachments from Volunteer Regiments together with their band, created an arousing, acoustic phenomenon with booming marching music echoing loudly between the closely-packed buildings.

Overcome with emotion as they watched the patriotic parade, some of the older men amongst the spectators stood to attention and saluted the passing soldiers.

Coxswain Harry Marshall dressed in lifeboat gear –
dark oilskin and sou'wester, cork lifejacket and heavy boots[2]

The 1901 lifeboat procession moving southwards along Liverpool Gardens from Shelley Road. A sequence of three photographs[3] taken from the same spot.

1   The Littlehampton boat *James Mercer & Elizabeth;* followed by Shoreham's *William Restell,* and in the distance Worthing's *Henry Harris.*

2   The *Henry Harris* pursued by the *Richard Coleman* is passing Lavender's drapery store at 32 Montague Street.[4] Liverpool Terrace is out of view on the left behind the dense foliage.[5]

3   Last in the line of procession, the new Worthing lifeboat, the *Richard Coleman*.
In the bow is Councillor Walter Butcher wearing a straw boater.[6]

The two kiosks and pay-box at the Pier entrance, a popular venue for bathchair men plying for hire.

The 1901 lifeboat parade moving westward along Montague Street past its junction with Buckingham Road[7]. A sequence of seven exposures taken from the same spot, the first four in quick succession.

1   Volunteer soldiers on their bicycles followed by some cheeky young lads.

2   The same high-spirited youngsters mimicking a detachment of Volunteers.

3   Drummers in the Volunteers' band

4   Flautists in the Volunteers' band.

5 At this point the photographer swung his camera round to the left to capture this shot of the Shoreham lifeboat *William Restell,* which had just passed by.

6 The Littlehampton lifeboat *James Mercer & Elizabeth.*

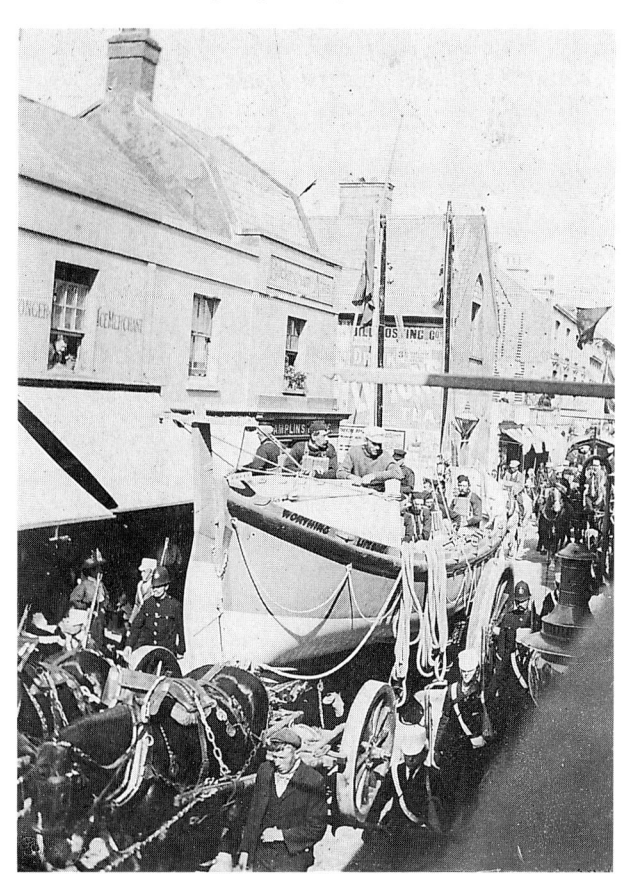

7 The old Worthing lifeboat *Henry Harris* followed by the new *Richard Coleman.*

The cortege turned left into Heene Road and left again into Marine Parade with contingents from 1,700 members of the Church Lads' Brigades, from five regiments camped two miles away at Goring, proudly marching along. This part of the procession was the one with which 2nd Coxswain Blann's[8] young son Bill, only nine years old, identified. He admired and even possibly envied the huge concourse of proud lads forming this enormous contingent. Young Bill's adrenalin ran so high as the seemingly never-ending brigade detachments marched by. But the climax for Bill, seeing his father high up in the lifeboat, was yet to come.

Huge crowds lined the streets to watch the passing procession, and flags fluttered gaily from many of the houses and shops along the main roads. Moving past the lifeboat house itself was truly ecstatic: for its unique lookout turret dominated a well-maintained building faced with knapped flints that had been built more than a quarter of a century ago. An annual repaint had just been completed according to the rules laid down by the RNLI. Head office allowed £2 10s. per year for the exterior of the wooden doors and windows to be finished in chocolate brown, and the whole of the inside of the boathouse in a practical stone colour.

7 August 1901. The old Worthing boat *Henry Harris* followed by the new *Richard Coleman* parading past the seafront lifeboat house whose roof turret can just be seen near the middle of the photograph above the bow of the *Henry Harris*.

As the parade moved by, one of the town's first lifeboatmen, Tom Blann, my great great grandfather, stood there with a feeling of pride. Vivid memories filled his mind, memories of the town's first lifeboat house, which had been little more than a flint barn built on top of the beach itself, just west of the present boathouse, a little less than half a century earlier. In those days, Tom would recall, if a distressed ship was downwind, the lifeboat would have simply been dragged down the beach and launched directly into the sea.

The number of people along the seafront was simply incalculable. Hordes of eager spectators stretched nearly a mile, from Heene Road to way beyond Steyne Gardens. Passing the levelled site at the corner of South Street, now surrounded by hoarding, where the *Royal Hotel* had commanded such an admirable view of not only the Pier but the Channel generally, seemed strange to the crews as they passed by, high up in their boats. The building had been gutted by fire earlier in the year, and was shored-up with scaffolding. Even though the shell was far from safe, sightseers ventured onto a balcony for a better view of the lengthy parade. One even risked climbing the scaffolding itself.

Four lifeboats were prominent in the parade: the Littlehampton boat, the *James Mercer and Elizabeth,* and the Shoreham boat, the *William Restell* from neighbouring stations; the old Worthing lifeboat *Henry Harris* and the new Worthing lifeboat itself, flying the Worthing Lifeboat Flag and the Union Jack. Three were each drawn on their carriages by six horses. The new one, which weighed three tons 15 cwt. plus the carriage, was pulled by eight horses. Having cost £826 to build, this new boat was of great interest to the crowds who closely scrutinised it at every opportunity.

Every lifeboat had a full crew aboard dressed in their familiar red hats and cork lifebelts. Tom was exceedingly proud of his two sons in the lifeboat service. Coxswain Bill Blann was in charge of the *Henry Harris* while Harry Blann, my great grandfather, crewed the new boat.

The crewmen of the *Henry Harris* were as follows: F. Collier, Fred and Mark Marshall, George Wingfield, Wm. Cousens, Frank Burden, George Newman, J. Groves, Wm. Wells and Jack Burgess.

In the new boat under Coxswain Harry Marshall were: Steve and Tom Wingfield, Jo Street, George Benn, George Belton, Harry Blann, Wm. Curvin, Arthur Marshall, J. Elliott, Fred Collins and Steve Bacon. Elevated in the bow of this new boat was Councillor Walter Butcher, who for many years had supplied the horses for pulling the lifeboat and carriage to launches, and who had acted as signalman on its return.

Each boat was accompanied by the military and members of the coastguard service; the procession turning left into the Steyne, left into Warwick Street, then left again, down South Street opposite the Town Hall, where an unusually large crowd availed themselves of a vantage point offered by its steps, into South Street before halting at the Pier.

It was nearly 3.45 p.m. when the head of the procession reached the Pier. On the east side a square enclosure, which had been cordoned off on the beach, filled with the coastguards, troops and the Church Lads' Brigade, while the four lifeboats, from stations on the coastal plain between the two rivers Arun and Adur, were drawn into the centre. The new boat occupied a place of honour near a small platform, which had been temporarily erected for the occasion, at the side nearest the Pier. The borough fire brigade assisted the police in keeping clear the entrance, instead of taking part in the procession as they had done on the previous Lifeboat Demonstration day some seven years earlier. The Mayor, Councillor F. E. Ovenden, wearing his robes and chain of office, and accompanied by other members of the town council, was accomodated in the arena.

Not least remarkable was the enormous multitude who had come to see the demonstration. Exhilarated people on Marine Parade and the Pier buzzed with excitement, while against the Pier entrance itself a dense crush of heads strived to glimpse the ceremony that was about to begin.

Not even when Worthing received its charter of incorporation on 3rd September 1890 — a day which held the previous record for the largest crowds — had so many people been in the town. Widespread interest aroused by the spectacle also surpassed that shown in the great Lifeboat Demonstration.

Throughout the afternoon the weather was beautiful as the sun shone gloriously. Even if people found the wind a little brisk it was ideal for a lifeboat launch. The sea, with its surface sparkling in the sunlight, swarmed with sailing and other craft.

In the presence of many of her relatives, the new lifeboat's lady donor accepted a lovely bouquet of flowers from the Mayor. Mrs. Birt-Davies Coleman then turned to Lieut. Keppel Foote, the RNLI District Inspector, and said that she had very great pleasure in presenting the boat to the Institution. At this point the vast array of smartly-dressed people surrounding the arena cheered.

Lieut. Keppel Foote, in accepting the gift, gratefully thanked her on behalf of the Institution. He went on to explain to his audience that this magnificent contribution represented less than half of what this noble lady had done for the Lifeboat Institution.

Many had not been aware that this benefactress had provided sufficient funds to enable a lifeboat to be always kept and maintained here at Worthing in memory of the late Richard Coleman. The crowds cheered again. This wonderful woman had actually donated all this money to the Worthing lifeboat as a mark of great respect, not only to her late husband, but also to the valorous Worthing lifeboatmen themselves.

Two photos taken within minutes of each other of the 1901 lifeboat procession passing the Marlborough House Boarding Establishment at the seafront end of Paragon Street.

1   The Littlehampton lifeboat *James Mercer & Elizabeth*, followed by Shoreham's *William Restell*.

He continued, assuring Mrs. Coleman that there was no better lifeboat committee than Worthing anywhere in the British Isles. He had been to Worthing so often, and had been treated with such kindness that he felt quite at home here. The principal characteristic of the committee members, he discovered, was that they possessed the proverbial tenacity of the British bulldog. Whenever they wanted improvements for their lifeboat or their Station they obstinately badgered the central lifeboat committee until they got them. Some years ago when the local committee had wanted a new carriage, the committee in London said no, but the Worthing committee, by their importuning, got the carriage all the same. Then again, a short time ago they thought they ought to have a new boat, and by their persistence they got Mrs. Coleman's philanthropic gift.

Addressing the crew of the new lifeboat, Lieut. Keppel Foote expounded upon the great work which had been done by the Worthing lifeboat, both under the previous coxswain, Charlie Lee,

2 The two Worthing lifeboats, *Henry Harris* and *Richard Coleman,* bringing up the rear of the parade.

and the present coxswain, Harry Marshall. When they had been called out of their homes at the dead of a wintry night to go to the assistance of a vessel in distress, they had 'hung on' until they had brought their men back to shore.

In reply, the Mayor said that the records of our Lifeboat Station showed that there was a need for a lifeboat here, and he could only say that so long as the boat remained at Worthing, they would never be short of willing hands and stout hearts to man her.

Mr. Harry Hargood, chairman of the Worthing RNLI committee of management, thanked Mrs. Coleman for her exemplary present, and welcomed the stationing of the new lifeboat at the town; and before proceeding further, asked the Mayor's Chaplain, the Rev. C. G. Coombe, M. A., to bless the boat and its anticipated rescue work. After an impressive prayer, the assembled crowd joined together in singing a well-known hymn for those at sea, 'Eternal Father Strong To Save', accompanied by the massed bands.

Then the Mayor escorted Mrs. Coleman to the carriage of the new boat, where the christening ceremony was performed with a bottle of water which she had brought specially from the River Jordan.

Breaking the bottle on the boat's rudder, Mrs. Coleman uttered in a subdued but quite audible tone, I name this boat the *Richard Coleman,* in everlasting remembrance of my beloved husband, and I wish her and her brave crew every success.

The emotive audience listening attentively to her every word remained silent for a few moments, reflecting on her last sentence. This benevolent widow had courageously come forward and played the leading role in this naming ceremony of a lifeboat which she hoped would be of valuable service in the years to come.

Standing with their oars tossed in a form of naval salute, all four lifeboat crews looked especially smart wearing their red woolly ceremonial hats.

The new *Richard Coleman,* passing the burnt out skeleton of the *Royal Hotel* at the corner of South Street, on its way to be officially named.

The four lifeboats taking up their positions for the naming ceremony of the *Richard Coleman,* which is itself in the centre of the photograph.

Suddenly, the peaceful silence was broken by the sound of a rocket fired by the coastguard as a signal to launch, and amidst enthusiastic cheering in a pulsating atmosphere the four lifeboats glided gracefully into the warm water. The Littlehampton boat was slightly ahead of the others, as several of the crew had literally jumped the gun and dipped their oars in the sea early. On the *Richard Coleman* itself, while Coxswain Harry Marshall was standing up shouting orders, Tom Wingfield was on hands and knees attending to something on top of the white-painted stern air chamber. Painted in the new colours of the Institution, a duo-tone of dark blue and white, the new boat stood out from the other three, whose liveries were still the 19th century regulation pale blue and white. Both the old and the new styles sported a standard vermilion-painted fender along each side of the boat.

The emotive audience listening to Mrs. Coleman naming the *Richard Coleman*, pictured right, in 1901.

Thousands of people remained on the seafront for some time to watch displays by the lifeboat crews. Celebrations continued with entertainment on the Pier and a water polo match at the Corporation Baths, before drawing to a close with an illuminated concert in Steyne Gardens.

Dozens of collectors with miniature lifeboat collecting boxes were successful in gathering a total sum of £50 12s.4d. throughout the day.

The novel *Richard Coleman,* official number ON 466, measured 35 feet in length and 8½ feet across the beam, slightly larger than the *Henry Harris*. The new boat, built by Thames Ironworks at Blackwall and again powered by ten oars, double-banked, and sail, was superior in many respects and had all the latest improvements. She had a drop keel based on a new principle which enabled the craft to sail much closer to the wind, water ballast tanks, and improved valve arrangements for automatically discharging any water. The mast was fitted with a device that could raise it instantly, known as a swinging or weighted mast. There was more room inside to accommodate people who had been rescued, and she was faster than the old boat. The new boat was again a self-righter with the traditional large air chambers at either extremity, which were sufficient to bear the entire weight of the lifeboat should she capsize. In this capsized position the heavy iron keel, which would be above the centre of gravity, would unbalance the equilibrium and right the craft.

The new lifeboat was kept in the boathouse, which meant that while the redundant *Henry Harris* was waiting to be transferred to London it remained parked on the south side of Marine Parade, marked by oil lamps at night. The old lifeboat was destined to be used in Saturday Lifeboat Demonstrations at inland towns, to raise money for the RNLI.

Taken at the same moment as the previous photograph, but viewed from the Pier, this shot clearly shows all four lifeboats and their saluting crews. From left to right: the *Richard Coleman, Henry Harris, William Restell* and *James Mercer & Elizabeth*.

Two weeks after the naming ceremony, the annual event of the season, the Worthing Regatta, was held on a brilliantly sunny day, 52 years after the first event of its kind was held in Worthing. By tradition several races were exclusively for Worthing watermen, that is fishermen and boatmen, most of whom were lifeboatmen. Their race for pair-oared boats entertained the spectators with Tom Wingfield's *I'm a coming* and George Belton's two boats, *Ivy* and *Florrie* competing.

In a similar race, but this time not outrigged, the Wingfields took all three prizes in a well-contested race: Tom Wingfield again, in *Lord Roberts*; Charlie Wingfield in *Primrose*; and George Wingfield in *White Rose*.

Most of the competitors wore the typical boatman's outfit of blue jersey and white trousers. It must have been extremely difficult to keep them clean.

The sailing race for Worthing watermen, was entered by F. Collier's *Princess May*, George Wingfield's *Lancashire Lass* and Harry Marshall's *Jolly Sailor*. Forty one year old Harry who was born in the town, at 11 New Street, was highly respected, for although fishermen were renowned for their drinking habits, Harry was different: he never touched a drop of alcohol. His vice was pipe smoking.

As the four lifeboats, glided gracefully into the water, dignitaries on the platform edged forward for a closer look.

A shot taken from East Beach of the launch of the lifeboats in 1901.
Littlehampton's *James Mercer & Elizabeth* is nearest the camera.

Close-up of the *Richard Coleman* at the point where it met the water at its naming ceremony in 1901.

Ladies on the Pier watching the 1901 lifeboat display, with *Warnes Hotel* in the background

There were three starters in the coastguard's four-oared service galley race, Shoreham, Newhaven and Worthing, the first-named crew winning the first prize of £3.

In addition to the races there were several features, including a rescue race and the usual walking the greasy pole contest, but the most spectacular was with a small craft, with two dummy occupants and moored to the west of the Pier, being blown up. The demolition of the craft was instantly accomplished by a 20 lb charge of explosive, fired by a connecting wire from a steam launch, a charge so powerful that it completely shattered a thick sheet of glass in the pay-box at the Pier entrance.

The day's events concluded with an illuminated carnival on the Pier with prizes for the best costumes.

Spectators on the Pier landing stage watching the same display, with the *Espanade Hotel* in the distance. [9]

September saw the first drill using the new lifeboat, the *Richard Coleman*. It lasted some 2½ hours and the boat performed remarkably well.

But the first serious trial of the *Richard Coleman* in a rough sea took place during the customary quarterly practice in November. There was an angry sky. The wind blew great guns, and wild 'white horses' roared on the tumultuous foam, as far as the eye could see.

The same excited crowd was there, full of enthusiasm, braving the rough weather and the stinging rain, as they streamed along the Parade, packed the beach and kept the Pier toll busy.

While they were waiting for the lifeboatmen, the sea got rougher and the wind blew more angrily until it became nigh impossible to keep one's footing.

The waves pitched and tossed and rolled before breaking on the beach, splashing the onlookers with spray and forcing them to stagger backwards and seek shelter.

The distinctive sound of the maroon could be heard and a description of what followed can best be summed-up in this poem, reproduced from a local contemporary newspaper.

The old Worthing lifeboat *Henry Harris* parked on the seafront road awaiting transportation to London. [10]

Harry Marshall with his boat the *Jolly Sailor* at his stand opposite the *Stanhoe Hotel*.

> Boom! Boom! The sound of the signal gun
>   Thrills the heart, as it startles the ear,
> And swift as their feet flying can run
>   The men rush out as the sound they hear;
> And swift as their strong hands can undo,
>   Tackle and fastenings are undone:
> And the coxswain and the lifeboat crew
>   Ready for duty which must be done.

Worthing lifeboat *Richard Coleman* prepared for launching. Note the haul-off warp from the Pier attached to the boat's forward port bollard.[11]

It seemed only a few minutes since the signal had been fired that the boat reached the usual launch point on the beach to the east side of the Pier. The great wooden craft was drawn heavily over the beach stones to the water's edge at high water mark and launched into the angry breakers.

What followed was a trial in real earnest, for the waves tossed her about with ease and pitched the brave crew from side to side.

By special arrangement with the Pier Company, a new method of launching was adopted. A stout hawser was passed through a block fastened to the N.E. pile of the landing stage, one end taken to the shore and tied to the bow of the lifeboat, and the other end brought onto the stage at the southern end of the pier where volunteers were employed to heave off the boat the moment she left her carriage. In the face of a south westerly wind of hurricane strength, and the heavy breakers, it would have been impossible to get the boat off by any other means. The plan was a complete success.

The sea frequently broke right over the *Richard Coleman,* filling her several times, even before the assistants had released the warp, but she soon cleared herself.

The crew found her heavier to row than the old lifeboat, but a splendid sailer, which was after all of greater importance. The lifeboatmen sailed well out to sea and had a thorough, though wet, hour and a half's practice.

On 10 October local fishermen and boatmen accumulated in one area of the beach, to bid for boats and fishing gear at Charles Paine's auction. A large crowd watched a 16ft lug sail boat knocked down at £5, a pleasure boat at 35s., 20 herring nets at 10s. each and two trawl nets at 10s. apiece.

In the spring of 1901 a local record was broken. Mr. F. Stubbs, a fishmonger of Montague Street made the largest haul of prawns that had ever been recorded in Worthing. No fewer than 5,000 were accounted for by his two boats, the *Britannia* and the *Skylark* on Thursday night, 2 May.

But in the herring season towards the end of the year, when fishermen on the east coast were breaking all records by bringing large quantities of good quality fish ashore, fishermen in the Worthing area had an unproductive season, the catches being extremely poor.

One Worthing fisherman, James Churcher of 48 Park Road had set off in his boat to try and find herring shoals on Tuesday afternoon 5 November, but failed to return.

Mr. John Roberts, honorary secretary of Worthing Branch RNLI, kindly bore the cost of sending out three search parties into the Channel, but they returned none the wiser.

Whilst on its passage down the Channel two days later, the steamer *Lestris* of Cork encountered a boat, bearing the name 'Churcher, Worthing', with a dead man in it. At the time the Antwerp bound steamer was eight miles out and 10 miles east of the Owers Lightship.

The captain buried the body at sea, lifted the boat aboard and continued the voyage to Belgium. On his return trip, he handed over Churcher's boat to the Receiver of Wrecks at Southampton, his first English port of call. The Receiver contacted Chief Officer Lester of the Worthing Coastguard, dramatically resolving this mystery of the disappearing fisherman.

Two months later, when his sister, Miss Jemima Churcher, who lived next door, proved his will, this hard-working fisherman was found to have left a modest fortune. Miss Churcher, surprised at the extent of his accumulated wealth, inherited his entire estate valued at £195 7s.

Fishermen were used to the freedom of the outdoor life and generally had no interest in formal stuffy meetings, not even for the local lifeboat A.G.M.

The Worthing Branch of the RNLI held its annual meeting in the Council Chamber at the Municipal Offices on Thursday 30 January 1902. Mr. H. Hargood J.P., the chairman, presided over those present: including Rev. W. B. Ferris, Rev. J. O. Parr, Alderman F. Parish J.P., Alderman E. C. Patching, Councillor G. Ewen Smith, Chief Coastguard Officer Lester, and Messrs E. G. Amphlett J.P., J. Andrews, L. W. Burnand, E. W. Bennett, J. G. Denton, M. Goodman, E. Meagre, G. Piggott, F. B. Tilt, and H. R. P. Wyatt J.P.

It was shown that owing to the falling off of annual subscriptions the local branch had been unable to support the parent Institution to such an extent in 1901 as it had done in previous years.

In submitting their report for the past year the committee stated that the annual subscriptions were down to £22 12s. This meant a decrease of £30 in the amount sent to Headquarters compared to the year before. That decrease was due mainly to the death of several old and valued subscribers, and by others having moved away from the area. At the same time the annual expenditure had increased because the *Richard Coleman*, being larger than its predecessor, required more horses and helpers.

The late collector, Mr. J. Long, had been unable through illness to collect the annual subscriptions at the usual time, and had finally been compelled to transfer his duties to Mr. J. Brown of 1 Barton Terrace, Westcourt Road, who had been appointed in his place. The past year's events were reported, including the double lifeboat service to the SS *Indiana*, officers were re-elected and the meeting closed.

Worthing had often gained distinction through the performance of its lifeboat. Once more the town was selected for this subject in the first of a series of articles, entitled 'British Lifeboats' published in the Navy and Army Illustrated.

About the pretty but unpretentious lifeboat house, the author wrote: 'In normal times there is an air of quietude and peace; everything is in order. All necessary appliances are placed in readiness for emergencies, and the general cleanliness and smartness prevalent suggest Naval jurisdiction.'

Members of the Worthing Branch RNLI committee, together with the District Inspector and Worthing's Chief Coastguard Officer, photographed in 1902. Seated from the left: Lieutenant Keppel H. Foote, R.N. (District Inspector), Harry Hargood (chairman), John Roberts (hon.sec.) and A.A. Ralli. Standing from the left: W.H.B. Fletcher, Dr. A.H. Collet, George Piggott, F. Parish, A.B. Dixon and Coastguard Chief Officer T. Lester

Information of interest was given: 'Since the station was formed the Worthing lifeboat has been the means of salving 12 wrecks and of saving 47 lives;' and, 'The *Richard Coleman*, one of the largest self-righting boats of the latest type, rows 10 oars double-banked, and represents the combined qualities of all that is best in modern lifeboat architecture.'

A word of praise was bestowed upon the Coxswain, Harry Marshall, who had been associated with the boat from the beginning, having served as volunteer, as second coxswain for six years, and as chief coxswain for the last four years.'

The writer also observed, 'that the Worthing men are immensely proud of their fine team of eight horses, which pull the carriage and boat to the place of launching. They are splendid animals, and have been so perfectly trained that they will face any sea in any weather without flinching, even though the waves break right over them.'

The article was illustrated by some interesting photographs showing views of the lifeboat on its carriage with the horses hitched-up, the lifeboat returning from the *Indiana*, and the local committee. In addition, Coxswain Harry Marshall and 2nd Coxswain Bill Blann were asked to pose in the *Richard Coleman* for a photograph. Harry held the yoke-lines over his shoulders to demonstrate the traditional way of operating the rudder. Whichever yoke-line the coxswain pulled on, the boat would steer in that direction. The foremast was normally stored flat down the centre of the boat – this too was apparent in the photograph. One could also see quite clearly that the bollards for securing ropes had a stained finish, as opposed to those on the *Henry Harris* which were painted white.

Coxswain Harry Marshall in the *Richard Coleman*, 1902

The *Richard Coleman* horsed and crewed on the seafront road, and ready for action. Taken by Fry of Brighton for publication in the Navy and Army Illustrated, this photograph clearly shows the little Victorian lifeboat house, with its turret window open, nestling between two attractive four storey 19th century terraced dwellings.

Bill Blann, along with other fishermen, took note of a new fishing bye-law which was adopted at a quarterly meeting of the Local Fisheries Committee of the Sussex Sea Fisheries District at Brighton, in January 1902. Mr. H. Hargood J.P., Worthing's representative on this committee reported the draft of the ruling discussed in Brighton a few months earlier:

'No person should use in fishing for sea fish any Seine or draft or tuck net having more than 30 rows of knots to the yard, measured when wet, except during the months of May, June and July in any year, when a net having not more than 36 rows of knots to the yard might be used. This bye-law should not apply to any person fishing for sprats during November, December or January with a net having not more than 90 rows of knots to the yard, nor to any person fishing for sand eels for the purpose of bait during May, June, July or August between sunrise and sunset, in any sub-district, within any area or areas approved for that purpose by the Local Fisheries Committee, such areas not to exceed in the aggregate in the case of each sub-district half a square mile.'

Any person who infringed the above law was liable to a maximum fine of £20 for the first offence, and in the case of a continuing offence a sum of £10 for each additional day on which the offence occurred. Any offender also had their fishing nets and the spoils of their misdemeanor confiscated.

This law was designed to stop small young fish being caught which would interrupt the breeding cycle and result in depleted fish stocks.

A closer shot of the Worthing lifeboat and only 12 instead of the usual 13 crewmen, taken just after the previous exposure. Standing in front of the wheel is Walter Butcher, supplier of the horses. One of the volunteers to assist with the horses, 'Soldier' Brown stands proudly on the chassis. From left to right the lifeboatmen are: George Benn, Steve Wingfield, F. Collier, George Belton, Jo Street(probably the youngest), Mark Marshall, William Curvin, Fred Marshall, Arthur Marshall (youngest of the four brothers), Tom 'Jumbo' Wingfield, Coxswain Harry Marshall and 2nd Coxswain Bill Blann.

At the other end of the size scale a rather large fish was caught and displayed in July by Mr. F. Stubbs, fishmonger of Montague Street. The remarkably fine specimen (Lampris luna), of the dolphin family, weighed nearly a hundredweight and was beautifully speckled with colourful silvery spots. The Opah, or Kingfish, as it was more commonly known, preferred deeper waters in the north temperate zone, but was occasionally found close to our shore. This type of fish was known by a variety of other names: sun-fish, sea-pert, carf and Jerusalem haddock.

At about the same time, two young lads celebrated their capture of an eel apiece by tying them together by the membrane-like mouths. To keep their proud catch fresh they dipped them in the sea, but the fishes revival was so phenomenally rapid that they wriggled out of the clutches of the surprised youngsters. Their ill-fortune allowed the local paper, which reported the incident, to state: 'We are now expectantly awaiting the tidings of the discovery of an extraordinary twin species of wriggling fish, which somebody will probably catch in open-mouthed wonder.'

Fishing was not the order of the day on one particular Saturday that summer. It was 9 August, the day on which the new monarch, King Edward V11, and his queen, Alexandra, were to be crowned in Westminster Abbey. In Worthing, local seafarers were about to enjoy the town's own planned festivities alongside other townsfolk.

West Parade at the very beginning of the century, showing watermen with their boats on the beach.[11]

West Parade photographed before 1905 from a point opposite Montague Place. The Bandstand can be seen in the centre of the picture; and the first building on the right hand side of the photograph is the Marlborough House Boarding Establishment on the corner of Paragon Street[12].

More than 18 months had passed since the death of Queen Victoria, and Worthing citizens, having been loyal subjects under their much-loved, late queen for more than 60 years, were adjusting to the fact that they now had a King.

It was 64 years since the last coronation, and it is interesting to recall that Worthing, loyal in its adherence to the throne, had celebrated that occasion with infinite credit. An excellent dinner had been provided for schoolchildren in a field which existed on the west side of South Street before that side of the road was developed. Tables had been put there but no seats had been supplied for the youngsters.

One of those children, Tom Blann, my great great grandfather, was just four years old at that time, but even so he had vivid memories of that day. He could remember what the dinner had consisted of for there had been a large piece of fat which he had been unable to eat. Tom laughed at the whimsical workings of his mind when he recalled that a decorated pole with a crown on top had been erected specially for the occasion in those pleasant fields bordering South Street.

That is how Worthingites celebrated the Coronation of Queen Victoria on 28 June 1838. This time people had been saddened by the king's serious illness and had been deeply disappointed at the subsequent postponement of his Coronation from its original date.

When the day arrived for Worthing citizens to honour their new king and welcome the beginning of their monarch's reign the town looked absolutely splendid. Indeed, it was claimed that no town of similar size in the kingdom could have lavished more on its artistic displays.

Booming 'guns' of the 'Howitzer Battery' at a very early hour of the morning, in a cloud of gunpowder smoke, announced the arrival of an eventful day. People were up early inspecting the gaily decorated streets.

Terraced cottages[13] on the north side of Richmond Road hung with insignia, motto and flags for King Edward VII's Coronation celebrations on 9 August 1902.

The most extensively decorated thoroughfare was South Street where private efforts were augmented by an official display. Ten year old Bill Blann junior, walking along the pavement with his mother, looked up at Venetian masts erected on either side of the street, puzzling over why some bore crossed flags entwined by a wreath of evergreens, while the crossed flags on others were surmounted by a shield. The masts were connected by strings of streamers; the Town Hall was crossed with festoons of artificial coloured paper flowers; and what mostly impressed young Bill's 40 year old mother, Elizabeth, was a banner inscribed 'Long Live Your Majesties' strung across the pier end of South Street.

In this part of Worthing, which was the commercial heart of the borough in those days, local businessmen were entitled to a good deal of credit for their celebratory efforts. Messrs. Jordan & Gray's large shop window in South Street was filled with a tastefully arranged artistic display of plants, the centre of which was occupied by a blue and white helichrysum, against a background of white curtains.

Nearby, Mr. C. J. Bentall's shop displayed two bold motifs: 'Peace and Prosperity to the Empire' and 'Long life to the King and Queen.'

Round the corner, the Victorian villa known as Highworth, had been prominently decorated by its owner/occupiers, the well-known partnership of solicitors Messrs. Melvil Green and Charles.

Sauntering along Chapel Road, Jesse Belville Blann together with his sister Mabel and her husband, Gus, were able to admire some very effective decorations. Mabel adored a pretty motto on the west side in Mr. W. J. Kettles window with the inscription 'May many years of happy days befall our King and Queen.' On the opposite side of the road the windows of four adjacent shops, belonging to Messrs. Davey, Watts, Ridley, and Vine were uniformly decorated to give a pretty effect. (Watts shoe shop is still there today.)

Worthing Town Hall colourfully decorated for Edward VII's coronation celebrations on
9 August 1902. Note the large letters E R erected on the clock tower.

Mr. T. Wilmer, a dyer, displayed the amusing but nevertheless sincere slogan 'God bless our King and Queen. We would *dye* for them!'

In Montague Street, over the premises of the Brighton, Hove, and Sussex Auxiliary Supply Association and Mr. W. Reynold's shop, this motto was displayed 'We wish King Edward a jolly good innings!', evidently the work of a cricketer.

Along the front of Walter Brothers' extensive premises ran the inscription:

> Our King and Queen, O Father bless,
>   Protect them by Thy loving care;
> Support and guide when duties press,
>   And each a fadeless crown prepare.

Town Councillors and borough officials gathered at the municipal offices near the Town Hall to march in procession to St. Paul's Church, a few hundred yards away up Chapel Road, where a special service had been arranged. The Mayor and mace-bearer were noticeable by their absence as they had been invited by royal command to attend the coronation ceremony in Westminster Abbey.

At St. Paul's a shortened form of the coronation service started at 10 a.m., a service which had been officially prepared for use throughout the Empire. The brief service, which included four hymns, was brought to a close by the singing of the National Anthem.

Services were held simultaneously at other churches in the borough, and then at noon came an act of united worship in front of the Town Hall. An area roped off to form an enclosure soon filled with councillors, local dignitaries and the Salvation Army Band.

Thousands of people were attracted, and even neighbouring windows and housetops were filled with spectators jostling for the best view. The service was impressive, although quite short and simple, and was one of the most notable features of the day's proceedings, with the huge public gathering joining together in harmoniously singing three hymns, which echoed loudly in the town centre. Once more the National Anthem was sung and South Street reverberated with three deafening cheers for the King and Queen.

Older members of the community were then entertained at a dinner for old folks given in a marquee in Steyne Gardens. This old Coronation Day tradition was considered essential for respectable people in the humbler section of the community.

Four hundred elderly folk had been invited but only 243 were fit enough to attend on the day. The 157 invalids did not lose out completely as they were sent gifts, tea, pipes and tobacco to the value of the meal they had missed. Each old person also received a new shilling.

A view looking south down Chapel Road from the junction with Richmond Road on the right, showing St. Paul's Church.[14]

At the 16 short tables in the marquee, the ageing guests chose from a menu of roast beef, boiled beef, roast mutton, boiled mutton, veal, ham, and vegetables, followed by plum pudding, fruit tarts, and cheese. After this generous selection they were offered a pint of ale or mineral waters and tea, according to their individual preferences.

Some of the guests were proper characters. One gentleman who was particularly noticeable wore a white old-fashioned smock frock that was immaculately clean and bright. This form of dress was more typical of a bygone age at the beginning of the previous queen's reign.

The Deputy Mayor joined the festive company at the tables, and shortly after the feast had begun, a telegram arrived from London with news that the king had been duly crowned.

Alderman Parish promptly sprang to his feet and mounted the platform to announce this vital communiqué.

On hearing those words, which were like magical music to these patriotic people, the elderly guests stopped eating immediately and passionately and strenuously cheered with a vigour that would have been far more typical of their sons and daughters.

After completing their meal, the aged guests enjoyed a musical programme performed by local entertainers.

By the time the various diversions were at an end, arrangements for the afternoon's procession were well in hand. Originally scheduled for 3 o'clock, it was found necessary to delay the start by half an hour to allow time for everyone to take up positions lining the route for a view of the royal pageant.

Moving off from Liverpool Gardens into Montague Street, a happy carnival atmosphere surrounded the long coronation procession, a procession which took place just 12 months after the massive parade which had welcomed the *Richard Coleman* in August 1901.

Leading the military as they marched along Rowlands Road was the local mounted squadron of the Sussex Regiment of the Imperial Yeomanry commanded by Sergeant Major H. Barnwell, who wore his South African War medal. Next in order came the H. Company of Volunteers under the charge of Lieut. W. H. Tribe and accompanied by their own band.

Beach House, built circa 1820, viewed from the south.[15]

The cadets, who had pitched camp in Beach House Park, were well-represented. This battallion had a cyclists' section which headed more than 400 cadets of varying ranks in this section of the parade. Lieut.-Colonel W. Watts was their adjutant.

Turning left into Heene Road there followed the Worthing Branch of the St. John's Ambulance Association, the Salvation Army Band, the Church Lads' Brigade, and the Amateur Boat Club with their new galley, the *Percy Burnand* (a name associated with the organising of the *Lalla Rookh* disaster dependants' appeal in 1850).

Although the various Friendly Societies each had a large membership at this time they were poorly represented in the next part of the procession, followed by Mr. G. F. Wright's Band and the Borough Fire Brigade with their appliances.

A prominent feature in the parade was the Worthing lifeboat, the *Richard Coleman*, drawn on its carriage by a sturdy team of horses – proud-looking beasts – and with a full crew aboard under the direction of Coxswain Marshall.

A gilded goat chaise used for pleasure rides on the promenade, and as an attraction in local parades. Pictured here at the top of the beach opposite Montague Place.

The new monarch's association with the RNLI was significantly described on the lifeboat, which had been prettily decorated by Miss Parish and Miss Kelly, and emblazened with the words 'God Save Our Patron!'

As the procession passed along the seafront to the Pier and up South Street, inquisitive people inspected the *Richard Coleman* and its gleaming carriage. The conveyance had had its annual spruce up using Head office's allowance of £1 15s. per year for revarnishing the wooden bed, runners and wheel spokes, and for protecting the cast iron parts, mainly the axles and cross members, from salt corrosion with galvanising paint.

Thousands of onlookers indicated their love and high regard for the lifeboat and crew by singling them out for extra applause and cheers.

Bringing up the rear of the procession, a gilded goat chaise, normally used for giving rides along the seafront, carried some exquisite dummies of the King and Queen. Liveried servants were in attendance.

Moving north up South Street the procession turned right into Warwick Street, right again at the Steyne and returned by way of Marine Parade and South Street once more towards the Town Hall and into a large, roped-off enclosure in front of the building.

Within the arena five local church choirs led the singing of the National Anthem with conspicous sincerity while the chairman of the procession committee, Mr. A. H. Collet, wielded the baton.

After calling for three cheers for the new King and Queen and the Army and Navy, the Deputy Mayor, amid other councillors on the Town Hall steps, listened intently to the cadets' band playing Rule Britannia.

A more impressive scene had never been witnessed in the broad length of South Street densely packed with people. For the Deputy Mayor, the spectacle of looking down upon the orderly assembly from the top of the Town Hall steps, was absolutely fantastic.

Thus the twentieth century had been welcomed with patriotic fervour by townsfolk who, not only hailed the crowning of a fresh successor to the throne, but who had wholeheartedly saluted the widow who had presented the town with a modern lifeboat.

The names of two men — Richard Coleman and King Edward V11 — were to be constantly in the minds of townspeople.

Footnotes

[1] The vacant site in the middle of the picture had been occupied by the *Royal Hotel* which burnt down in 1901.

[2] Photographed in the Excelsior Studio, 20 New Street, Worthing by E. Edwards.

[3] A series of three photographs taken by West & Son of Southsea.

[4] This shop building at 32 Montague Street is still there today, but radically altered.

[5] The garden sandwiched between Liverpool Terrace and Liverpool Gardens is now a public garden area. But gone are the perimeter iron railings, beautiful shrubbery and hedges.

[6] Looking at the photograph, where Liverpool Gardens merges with Liverpool Road, six young men can be seen standing on a garden wall. Within its mature gardens a doctor's house is concealed by trees and shrubbery. The first to occupy the premises was Dr. Collet, and the last was a Dr. Crabtree, before it was demolished in 1933. The Odeon Cinema arose from the debris, but even this picture house, a popular town centre landmark, was itself raised to the ground in 1988 to make way for the Montague Shopping Centre. In the same redevelopment scheme, Liverpool Road was pedestrianised and roofed.

[7] On the corner of Buckingham Road stood the *Buckingham Arms*. Closed as a public house in the 1980's, it is now the Body Shop with an extension built over part of Buckingham Road. Montague Street itself was paved into a pedestrian precinct some years before that.

[8] Second Coxswain Bill Blann is my great grand uncle, or put another way, he's the brother of my great grandfather, Harry Blann.

[9] Looking at the photograph, on the distant shoreline at East Worthing the spire of the *Esplanade Hotel* can be seen, and to its right is a windmill. The mill has long since gone, but the unmistakeable hotel was sacrificed comparatively recently in 1967, for a garage and a block of flats.

[10] Fred Marshall is standing far left and grasping a rope. Next to him, with hands in pockets and smoking a pipe, is 'Soldier' Brown, one of the launching assistants. Far right is a bewhiskered Bill Blann, with Harry Marshall standing next along.

[11] Photographed from the Pier by Worthing Portrait Company of 4 Railway Approach.

[12] The Marlborough House Boarding Establishment on the corner of Paragon Street. Now built over by a Marks and Spencer store.

[13] This site on the north side of Richmond Road is now occupied by the Public Library.

[14] Clothed, in the picture, with lovely mature trees the Greek-style St. Paul's Church assumes an air of majesty. On its far side is the junction with Ambrose Place, while in front of the church is one of the street lamp standards lit by gas. Electricity was introduced to the town in the Autumn of 1901, and the changeover from gas was a slow and gradual process.

[15] In more recent times, Beach House was saved by the late, battling conservationist, Mrs. Pat Baring, from wanton destruction by Worthing Borough Council, and still stands proudly by the eastern approach to the town centre.

Climbing the greasy pole at Worthing Regatta, 26 August 1902[1]

Chapter 2

On Film

1902-5

On Tuesday 26 August 1902, the Worthing Annual Regatta was held under more favourable conditions than those often experienced. It was a beautiful sunny day and yet was not oppressively hot, whilst the sea was so tranquil that the most delicate craft could have cruised about safely. The fine weather proved irresistible and people flocked to the seafront in their thousands.

Three of the races were specifically for boats belonging to Worthing fishermen and boatmen. The first, for sailing boats not exceeding 17 feet in length, with a dandy rig, was won by S. Bacon's *Adera*. George Wingfield's *Lancashire Lass* was second, and F. Collier's *Princess May*, third.

The next one, for first-class pair-oared boats outrigged, had five boats entered, three of them Wingfield-owned. Leading all the way Wm. Wells' *The Burma Ruby* rowed in first by a couple of lengths to win £2 5s.; Tom Wingfield's *Albert Edward* was second; and George Wingfield's *The Lily* was third. F. Collier's *Winnie* and Steve Wingfield's *Little Bessie* were unplaced.

The same three members of the Wingfield family entered a race using boats of the same type, but this time not outrigged. George Wingfield's *White Rose* won. The other four contestants were: Wm. Wells *Lady Annie*, Tom Wingfield's *Lord Roberts*, H. Wakeford's *Alfred*, and Steve Wingfield junior in *Primrose*.

Hove, Shoreham and Newhaven crews won prizes in the race for Coastguard four-oared galleys.

A greasy pole had been erected between the west side of the Pier and the first groyne for a contest between boys up to 15 years of age. The first prize of the traditional leg of mutton went to William Avis, and the second prize, six dozen bottles of lemonade presented by Messrs. P Fry & Co. Ltd., was awarded to Dick Tester. A special prize was given by the Bonbonniere Royal to any boy who pulled the string of the bell attached to the top of the pole.

At the end of the Regatta the orders for prizes were presented in the Pier Pavilion by Mrs. Campbell Fraser.

The Salvation Army Band playing in the bandstand in 1902.

One of the spectators, Tom Blann, cast his mind back to the early days of the Regatta when he had been a young man, when there was no Worthing Pier. In those days, Tom recalled, before the advent of rowing and sailing clubs, virtually all the contestants had been fellow fishermen and boatmen.

During the month after the 1902 Regatta, the Salvation Army Band, performing one Sunday evening in the Bandstand on the promenade west of the Pier, boosted RNLI funds by £3 10s. A similar amount, £3 12s. had been advanced as the result of a Sacred Concert held during another Sunday evening at the Pier Pavilion when members of 'Our Navy', an entertainment troupe or choir, performed for the benefit of the Institution.

Bill Blann junior, a mere stripling ten years of age, loved to watch 'Our Navy' perform and had sneaked out from home that evening to see his favourite act; but in doing so had invoked the wrath of his father who did not like his young son being out in the evening by himself, but young Bill felt it had been worthwhile.

Bill Blann senior was present at the Annual Meeting of the Worthing Branch RNLI on 29 January 1903. In a report for the year 1902, the secretary explained that while there was an increase of £14 7s. in annual subscriptions there was a decrease of £8 17 8d. in donations. The same amount as in the previous year, £70, had been sent to H.Q., whereas in 1900 a full £100 had been sent.

The balance sheet showed that receipts from subscriptions amounted to £118 8s, and from donations, £42 15s.

From the triennial Lifeboat Sunday, held in August, the sum of £67 6 5d. had been collected and remitted to London. On that day more places of worship had collected for the RNLI than ever before.

At this time the Institution boasted a fleet of 288 lifeboats. Unfortunately, the cost of maintaining them was becoming increasingly heavy, and as the amount of income was insufficient to meet expenditure the committee confidently appealed for the continued support of residents in Worthing and the surrounding neighbourhood.

The *Richard Coleman* and its heavy transporting carriage on the sands, preparing to launch at low tide.

The Chairman, Harry Hargood, commented on various features of the report, mentioning particularly the very generous gifts of half a sovereign by Mrs. Johnson of Grosvenor House to each of the lifeboat crew on Coronation Day. At the same time he gave assurance that none of the money donated to the RNLI was spent on bunting.

The re-appointment of John Roberts as honorary secretary was moved by Mr. E. G. Amphlett, J.P., who said they all knew that the success of their branch was due very much to the energy and valuable time which Mr. Roberts expended upon the work. The chairman said how he and the rest of the committee were indebted to Mr. Roberts. At any hour of the day or night, in any matter connected with the Station, Mr. Roberts was always ready and willing.

Coxswain Marshall reminded the committee of concern that, at low water, the new lifeboat, being heavier than its predecessor, might cause its carriage to sink in the sands. An exercise had been specially arranged and the meeting was informed that the *Richard Coleman* on its carriage went over the sands with the greatest of ease. The lifeboat and carriage together weighed 6 tons 17 cwt., 18cwt. more than the *Henry Harris* and carriage, at 5 tons 19 cwt.

At the end of the meeting in the Council Chamber, a Mr. Andrews amused everybody by acknowledging the chairman's vitality, "The very first time I came down here the chairman showed so much energy that he got a guinea out of me."

Mr. Hargood, replied, declaring that anything connected with lifeboat work was a labour of love to him. He could always cast his mind back to the days of his childhood, when he saw 11 of our gallant fishermen lost through the want of a lifeboat. Rapturous applause greeted his final statement: "I am very proud to say that since a boat had been supplied not a life had been lost here."

Steve Wingfield senior[2], bowman of the Worthing lifeboat, wearing oilskins and cork lifejacket, c.1903.

On Saturday 4 April 1903, the lifeboat crew were called out once more, when a barquentine loaded with granite ran aground about half a mile due south of the lifeboat house. The dilemma of the 500 ton *Lizette* became apparent at about 10.30 a.m. The maroon was immediately fired and the lifeboatmen, horses and their drivers all hurried to the Lifeboat Station, making it within 30 minutes.

The tide was half flood and, although the weather was fine, a strong WSW wind roughened the sea. The Lifeboatmen stood watching from the beach in readiness, but eventually, as the tide rose, she let go her anchors and floated off the sand bank.

Fortunately the Shoreham Harbour tug *Stella* arrived and towed her away from the coast and eastward to Newhaven, otherwise the Irish vessel would probably have become a total wreck on the next ebb tide.

As danger had passed, the services of the lifeboat crew were no longer required and, at half past three in the afternoon, the crew were stood down. Coxswain Harry Marshall, his brothers Fred and Mark, Second Coxswain Bill Blann, Steve and Tom Wingfield, Jo Street, Frank and Wm. Collier, J. Elliott, George Benn, Groves and Wells each received 5s. for standing-by for 4½ hours, ready to go to sea at a moment's notice.

The volunteers in attendance, ready to help launch the lifeboat, the signalman and the drivers, 11 persons in all, were each paid 3s. 6d.; while Mr. Butcher received £3 4s. for keeping eight of his horses hitched to the lifeboat carriage.

The total cost of just having everything ready to roll instantly on this occasion was £8 7s.6d.

There was a short epilogue to this story: a few days later, in the course of business, the Shoreham Harbour Trustees made a £200 claim against the owner of the *Lizette* for salvage services, thus ending this episode.

The human brain could also be wrecked: by illness; but salvage work on the central nervous system was still comparatively primitive. For any working class person struck down there weren't any advanced medical or neurological facilities available, just dependancy on herbal remedies and hand-me-down cures.

One such victim was Worthing lifeboatman, Steve Bacon, who died under very tragic circumstances on Friday 5 June. Forty year old Bacon, who had been separated from his wife for 10 years and had no children, lived with his niece, Georgina, and her husband, John Cager, a butcher, at 1, Anglesea Street. Sadly, Bacon, a boat owner and fisherman, had been suffering with severe headaches on and off for three months. When John Cager went home at 9.30 p.m. after work he found Bacon in his room, dead, with a five inch gash in his throat.

At the inquest the jury returned a verdict of suicide whilst temporarily insane.

A motor omnibus serving Worthing Railway Station, which is just a stones' throw east of South Farm Road level crossing.[3]

He was buried with full honours on Wednesday afternoon 10 June. The uniformed lifeboat crew in blue guernseys, white trousers and scarlet hats met at the mortuary at 2 p.m. Draped with the Union Jack, the coffin was borne by relays of four lifeboatmen as far as the level crossing at South Farm Road, where they were joined by relatives waiting in carriages. From there the crewmen continued to carry the coffin for the length of South Farm Road right up to the cemetery.

The scene at the graveside was impressive. As an indication of the respect in which the deceased was held, Mr. S. H. Day, the well-known barrister and Master in the High Court of Justice, who had engaged Bacon's services as a boatman during his frequent visits to the town, had telegraphed to Captain J. Haywood the previous day and had asked him to procure a wreath to be placed on the grave in his name.

A beautiful floral anchor was accordingly provided, whilst the lifeboat crew and the watermen from along the seafront jointly subscribed for their own large wreath.

Those who were acquainted with the traditionally unfavourable weather at the Annual Regatta again found threatening conditions on Friday 28 August 1903. But fortunately a postponement was avoided; the plucky competitors completed all but one of the events despite a heavy, frothy sea, which found its way into most of the boats to some degree.

The seafront was crowded as was usual on these occasions and a large number of people watched from the Pier, where the Blue Hungarian Band provided additional entertainment.

As well as the sculling races for south coast rowing clubs the programme included, as in previous years, three races specifically for Worthing boatmen and fishermen, a coastguard galley race, and a greasy pole contest.

George Wingfield entered a different boat in all three events for Worthing watermen. In the first, for dandy rig sailing boats not exceeding 17 feet, his boat was *Lancashire Lass* but his relative's boat, Tom Wingfield's *Baden-Powell* led at the start.

Watching from the beach to the west of the Pier, Tom Blann's eyes followed *Baden-Powell* westward in the direction of the lifeboat house. But when it turned at the marker buoy off West Buildings Tom's gaze continued on to where the old stone lifeboat house used to stand on the beach.

He was remembering another type of racing event, held on the seashore just beyond, that had filled him with excitement as a young man — horse-racing under the banner of Worthing Races.

So popular had this earlier, great event been that people had come from far and wide for the bristling, fervid spirit of the day. Even as far as Cornwall people had known of the Worthing Races, for one Cornishman had even telegraphed a betting entry from Bodmin.

Conditions on the sandy beach had been wet, and red-blooded fisherman Tom had drooled over the tantalising display of pretty feet and legs by numerous attractive women holding up their dresses.

Loud cheering brought Tom back to the present as F. Collier's *May* sped to the finish in front of J.G. Davis's *Adela*. Tom Wingfield's *Baden-Powell* which had been leading was relegated to third position. George's *Lancashire Lass* was unplaced as were J. Searle's *Shamrock* and Jo Street's *Gold Tip*.

Coastguards with their galley at Lancing.

In the race for first-class pair-oared boats with a coxswain, Harry Marshall's *Marie Elsie* won easily over Tom Wingfield's *Albert Edward*, J. Burgess's *Edith*, George Wingfield's *Lily* and F. Collier's *Winnie*.

George Wingfield's *White Rose* easily won his last race which was also for first-class pair-oared boats with a coxswain but this time not outrigged. A different set of boats was entered for this race: Harry Marshall's *Bertha*, F. Wakeford's *Alfred*, Wm. Collier's *Young Frank* and J. Burgess's *Grace Darling*.

The coastguard four-oared galley race was won by the Langley (Pevensey Bay) crew, with Blackrock second and the Lancing team third.

After the meeting, prizes were presented in the Pier Pavilion at the sea end of the pier by the Mayoress. An excellent promenade concert was followed by a firework display in Steyne Gardens to complete an eventful day.

A couple of weeks after the Annual Regatta, a novel craft built by Jack Belton's boatbuilding yard underwent its trials. He had built many boats in his time, but never one like this. The vessel, built for John Roberts junior, son of John Roberts, the honorary secretary of the Worthing RNLI, was a sailing boat on wheels, a land yacht intended for use on the sands. Apart from one or two hitches the demonstration proved that it was practical to sail on dry land, given the open space. Considerable interest was shown in the manoeuvres of the craft on its maiden trip; others were expected to emulate the idea after it had been made public, but my researches have failed to find any other references to a land yacht.

Another of the Belton family, a lifeboatman, was one of the full crew at the quarterly practice on Monday afternoon 24 August. The *Richard Coleman* was launched on the lee side of the Pier in a heavy sea that fully-tested the capabilities of the boat. While an extra large number of people watched from the Pier and the beach, as she got under sail, the second lifeboat crew went among them collecting contributions. They always took the collection boxes round the spectators during lifeboat practices, often resulting in large additions to local funds.

An extremely violent sea crashing explosively against the sea wall at Splash Point, and flooding the promenade.

The lifeboat was not called upon during a terrific gale on Thursday night 10 September, but, however, three boats were destroyed. Fishermen and boatmen pulled up most of the boats onto the Parade to protect them from the violent sea, but two small boats which had unwisely been left at anchor on the sands were torn away by the swirling sea and smashed on groynes.

A similar fate befell a trawler, *Shamrock*, belonging to 70 year old fisherman James Bacon, which also broke adrift and was driven to its destruction on Lancing beach. With his sole means of livelihood gone, for the *Shamrock* was not insured, Bacon and a member of his crew solicited aid from local residents. They went from house to house with an appeal, signed by a local councillor recommending the case to the benevolent, which brought in £44 19s. A further sum of £25 1s. donated by a Mr. H. Allen enabled the building of a new boat to commence immediately and help this old tar back to independence. James was a sailor who had served his country well in the Royal Navy: seeing active service in China, Burma, and Africa; winning three medals; and being wounded five times. On leaving the Navy he had served as Coxswain of the East London(South Africa) lifeboat.

The September storm was the worst for many years, wreaking havoc all over the town. The sea came over the asphalted walk in many places, including Splash Point, to the west side of the Pier, and by the Bandstand, its surrounding deck being covered with shingle.

The Bandstand itself was a venue used by the Salvation Army Band, 10 days later, when they played for the benefit of the RNLI. Their annual collection this year raised £3 for lifeboat funds.

The Parade was lined with spectators when a Sailing Regatta, supplementary to the Annual Rowing Regatta, was held three weeks later. The new attraction featured five events, the first of which was solely for our fishermen and boatmen. This race for sailing boats up to a maximum of 17 feet long with dandy rig, was won by F. Collier's *Princess May* which led the rest of the field by two minutes. George Wingfield's *Lancashire Lass* was second while Bill and Harry Blann's *Dandy Dick* came third. Four other boats sailed including Harry Marshall's *Ariadne*.

Chief Officer Lester of the coastguard acted as starter and John Roberts was the judge. A popular selection of band music entertained the crowds on the Pier, and the Pier Orchestra presented a pleasing programme inside the Pier Pavilion.

At the end of this week, on Saturday 26 September, Worthing watermen enjoyed a charitable outing to London. This customary treat, which had been dropped for a few years, was revived, and 26 of the poorer fishermen and boatmen left by the first train and had a good time aided by beautiful weather.

When the RNLI District Inspector arrived for his twice yearly inspection, Bill Blann senior was amazed how calm the sea was. But as the arrangements were always made well in advance, the boat always went out on the appointed day, no matter what the conditions might be. On this occasion, there was no need to seek the protection of the Pier, so the lifeboat was launched from a closer spot with a full crew under Coxswain Marshall opposite West Buildings.

During a visit to the town by 'Our Navy', portraits of the Coxswain and his predecessor Coxswain Lee were projected at a slide showing, where they received a cordial acknowledgement.

A fortnight before Christmas an invitation lecture on the work of the RNLI was given by Mr. H. Hargood J.P., chairman of the Worthing Branch. The audience at the Bedford Hall in Bedford Row comprised members of the coastguard, lifeboat crew, police, fire brigade, and friends. The speaker's remarks were illustrated with lantern slides, including several of local wrecks, shown by Major Lister J.P. In his lecture Mr. Hargood covered several topics: the history of the sea-going lifeboat since its inception; the state of our coasts during periods of lawlessness, when the inhabitants at some places lived mainly on plunder from wrecks; the various types of lifeboat and different ways of launching; and also the history of the Worthing lifeboats. At intervals during the evening, the audience was entertained by various singers accompanied by instrumental music; and the meeting drew to a close with a rousing rendition of Rule Britannia followed by God Save The King.

The new medium of moving pictures was employed to maintain and further people's interest in the work of the RNLI. Worthing was chosen for this purpose, and townsfolk felt deeply honoured that their lifeboat had been selected.

On Friday 15 January 1904, the *Richard Coleman* was launched and filmed in action by the eminent cinematograph specialists, Messrs. Gaumont & Co. On this bright, sunny morning they filmed the firing of the mortar by the coastguard, the arrival of the crew at the Lifeboat Station, the departure and progress of the boat along the Parade with Mr. W. J. Butcher's

Worthing lifeboat, the *Richard Coleman,* pulled by horses along the seafront road, circa 1904. Its crew are clad in cork lifejackets.

horses at the trot, the hauling of the boat over the beach, the launch and the picking-up and rescue of a 'drowning' man. Mr, Arthur Blunden, the assistant Pier Master, volunteered for this purpose. Filming continued of the boat under sail, both with and against the wind, and finally the return to shore.

Mr. A. C. Bromhead, the company manager, came down from London with his assistant to supervise the filming of these operations. In the film, the coastguard was supposed to have known of a ship in distress near the Whiting Rock and hoisted an answering flag signal. The loud boom of the mortar calling the lifeboatmen together at 10 a.m. quickly attracted many sightseers to the seafront. The crew were seen running to the boathouse, where the doors were flung wide open, and the splendid *Richard Coleman* was dragged out into the roadway.

Walter Butcher's fine team of sturdy horses, each ridden by a man in a sou'wester and oilskins, were quickly harnessed to the carriage. The crew in their lifebelts swarmed up the side of the boat as it moved off, together with the coastguard, willing helpers and a miscellaneous crowd of boys and men.

The launch was successfully accomplished under the protection of the Pier. Huge breakers rolled in as the gallant craft plunged forward. A big wave struck her and sent up a great column of spray high over the prow, soaking the oarsmen, but providing excellent film for the cameraman, who was positioned some way along the Pier.

Another exhibition launch of the *Richard Coleman* took place a fortnight later on Wednesday afternoon 3 February, watched by a large crowd. One of the observers on the Pier was Mrs. Coleman, the donor of the lifeboat. This time a boisterous wind made the sea even rougher, conditions which the lifeboatmen could tolerate better than the cameramen. This time the lifeboat was out for nearly two hours altogether.

A series of these films was to be shown throughout the country, in something like 150 to 200 theatres and other places of entertainment.

As one of their fund raising efforts, the Worthing lifeboat crew travelled to Kingston for its Annual Lifeboat Carnival on Saturday 25 June. The principal feature of the event was a lifeboat, with the inscription 'Chapel D8', being drawn through the streets, manned by the Worthing lifeboatmen, to the river at Kingston-upon-Thames, where it was launched and a mock rescue of a shipwrecked crew effected. The following day, when our men returned to Worthing, another crew took over and rowed the lifeboat up to Hampton Court, collecting more money on the way. This lifeboat was the *John Alexander Berrey* which had retired from service at Chapel in Lincolnshire and was now used as a demonstration lifeboat.

The Richard Coleman being launched in a heavy sea using the Pier for protection. Note the haul-off warp connected to the bow.

Worthing lifeboatmen at Kingston for the Annual Lifeboat Carnival wearing their cork lifejackets.[4]

41

Financial assistance was invited from the public for another Worthing boatman who sustained the loss of his ferry boat and therefore his livelihood. The craft, belonging to Mr. J. Riddles of 18 Prospect Place, broke away from her anchorage in the early hours of Monday 2 May and smashed onto groynes. It was the second time in six months that one of poor Riddles' boats had been destroyed, and the seventh since he started work as a boatman.

Not only did acts of God, as you might call storms, pose a threat to the well-being of watermen, but their health and safety came under threat from old rotting sea defences left sticking up in the sand. In fact these stumps of decayed wooden groynes posed a danger to life as well as property.

Fishermen and boatmen had been complaining about them for some time, and Harry Hargood had raised the issue at a meeting of the Sussex Sea Fisheries Committee the previous November, when he had told them: "It is our bounden duty to look after the interests of the fishermen." Consequently, the committee had agreed to send a copy of the report to the Board of Trade who were responsible for navigational safety.

At the committee's meeting on 10 November 1904, after discussing correspondence about the removal of these old groyne stumps, Mr. Hargood urged that the matter should be left with the Clerk to see whether the stumps, which were detrimental to fishermen, could be removed by the fishermen themselves with the permission of the owner; the wood to be used by the fishermen as they thought fit.

Alderman Patching thought it would be undesirable to make such a proposal at that time without all the necessary information and the matter remained unresolved.

A bountiful mackerel season in May provided many large catches for Worthing fishermen, so much so that supply outstripped demand: although the fish were of excellent quality, they only fetched moderate prices because of the large numbers for sale.

Two fishermen, Harry and Bill Blann, shared a stand together on the beach opposite New Street[5]. After being out fishing all one Saturday night, they started to walk home: Bill to a terraced house in Buckingham Road, just off the seafront; and Harry to a terraced flint cottage in Clifton Road[6].

As Harry was passing the Catholic Church at the top of Crescent Road, he discreetly glanced, like you do, at those entering the house of God for Sunday Mass. His face suddenly looked puzzled. Harry was a frequent passer-by and knew many of the faces, but he hadn't seen this one before. The man was rather short, and very smartly dressed.

He found out later it was Carl Adolf Seebold[7], who came and settled in Worthing this year (1904) after leaving Southend, which had been his family's base for the past few years. This Swiss-born professional musician and impresario was, over the coming years, going to change the face of Worthing's public entertainments.

The Catholic Church photographed from a house in Richmond Road, and looking down Crescent Road, before 1908.

On Friday afternoon 10 February 1905, Worthing RNLI, held its annual meeting in the Council Chamber. In a report for the past year, the secretary stated that in addition to the half-yearly inspections, a surprise visit had been made on 21 December when the following entry had been made in the visitors' book by the District Inspector:

'Paid surprise visit and found everything in most excellent order. I was glad to find the boathouse open on this fine day, which shows the Coxswain does his duty properly.'

It was further reported that during the last year, RNLI lifeboats around the country had been launched 294 times for service and had been successful in saving 519 lives, making a grand total of 44, 880 since the Institution had been founded in 1824.

The cost of maintaining the nationwide fleet of 285 lifeboats continued to increase heavily and the committee again appealed for further support from Worthing residents.

Net receipts for the year totalled £163 14s.2d., including £103 3s.6d. from annual subscribers, £2 3s.6d. from Mr. Hargood's lecture, £5 from Mr. T. Saunders' concert, £5 15s.10d. from a concert on the Pier, £3 10s. from the Salvation Army, £14 12s. steamboat collections, £9 0s.3d. collected in RNLI pillar boxes along the front, and £15 16s. collected during lifeboat exercises.

Looking from roughly the middle of South Street looking north towards the impressive Town Hall, circa 1905.[8]

The most expensive single service so far, for the Worthing Lifeboat Station, was soon to be effected on 15 March 1905.

It was shortly after 4 o'clock on this Wednesday afternoon when several people strolling along the promenade caught a glimpse of a small barque in the distance, several miles south east of Worthing Pier.

Rather scanty sails hanging from its masts aroused their curiosity, compelling them to inform the lifeboat coxswain, Harry Marshall, at his boatman's stand at the top of the beach.

At this time he was involved in discussing a boat trip with a potential customer, whom he quickly passed over to his brother Fred.

He rushed across the shingle to the neighbouring Blann's pitch, to consult with his deputy, Bill Blann. Together, they anxiously tracked the movements of the distant vessel which appeared to be in difficulties.

Apparently, the Swedish barque *Liburna*, bound from Gothenburg to Beira in East Africa, had encountered strong head winds in the Channel. Twice the 467 ton ship, loaded with timber, had got as far as the Eddystone Lighthouse off Plymouth, and both times she had been driven back by the west south westerly gale.

Off Worthing now the weather turned squally, and with the barque's steering gear evidently out of order, her master ordered a crewman to raise a distress flag.

Harry saw the signal through his telescope at 5.45 p.m. By now, Chairman Harry Hargood had joined them, and on seeing that the barque was now only about a mile south east of the Pier, they jointly agreed.

Launch the lifeboat immediately.

A coastguard officer fired the first maroon.

By the time he set it off a second time, indicating that this was not a practice, the ever-vigilant lifeboatmen, who had been on alert since the first sign of danger, had fully manned the *Richard Coleman*.

Eight horses, which had been standing by because it had been feared that the barque would be driven ashore at Lancing, drew the *Richard Coleman* on its carriage along the front to the east side of the Pier. Still mounted on the carriage it was backed down the sharply sloping shingle beach, with the horses taking the strain, and into the water bow first, where the eight extremely brave and efficient carters controlled their horses as the heaving breakers crashed into them with alarming ferocity; the repeated effect of which caused an almost deafening roar.

Twenty minutes later, at five minutes past six, no fewer than 45 volunteers hauled the *Richard Coleman* off its carriage, into the water, and as far as the Pier's protruding jetty, by means of a thick rope attached to its bow. With the warp over their shoulders the helpers strained as they made their way in a line along the boards of the Pier decking.

The lifeboat's crew used their oars to assist the launch, their hardy, weather-beaten faces taking the full brunt of driving rain and hail which inflicted pain like shot from a musket.

The *Richard Coleman* to the rescue, hauled by volunteers heaving the haul-off rope along the Pier, and propelled by oars.

Using the steering controls, which were a system of lines and pulleys attached to the rudder, Coxswain Marshall cleverly steered the lifeboat away from the lower deck jutting out at the pavilion end of the Pier.

By this means the Pier doubled not only as a jetty for pulling the lifeboat into the sea but the structure itself protected the heaving lifeboat to a certain extent from the prevailing swell. This method of launching worked admirably. The moment the boat passed the men on the Pier on its way out bowman Steve Wingfield released the warp.

For an instant the craft faltered, defenceless, alone in the face of the rough, boisterous sea as the line fell away!

Without hesitation the crew hoisted canvas and sailed off in an easterly direction with the wind behind them.

Whilst the *Richard Coleman* was being launched on this its first ever service, a telegram was received at the Worthing Lifeboat Station from the Lancing Coastguard Station stating that a barque was driving ashore west of Shoreham.

At 6.20 p.m., when the *Richard Coleman* was on its way to the distressed vessel, our Lifeboat Station received another telegram, this time from the Shoreham Lifeboat Station, saying that they had launched their lifeboat.

Almost an hour later, at a quarter past seven, the *Richard Coleman* reached the *Liburna* which had in fact run aground just off Shoreham, opposite the *Royal George Hotel*. Our lifeboat crew found that the barque's mainmast had been ripped away by the gale, and that the Shoreham lifeboat was already in attendance, taking off the crew one by one. But the Worthing crew were only a short time behind their Shoreham counterparts, in spite of the extra distance they had been required to cover.

While the *Richard Coleman* stood by to render assistance if necessary, Second Coxswain Bill Blann distributed among the lifeboatmen energy-giving rations, of brandy, biscuits and chocolate, to maintain stamina and keep their pecker up whilst exposed to this terrific storm.

The skipper of the unfortunate barque had a lucky escape. He fell into the heaving sea while trying to get into the Shoreham lifeboat. The two vessels were rising up and dropping down without synchrony. One minute they were together, the next they were apart.

The quick-thinking Shoreham crew managed to rescue the beleaguered skipper, but not without difficulty.

After the last of the ten Swedish sailors had been safely landed the Worthing lifeboat crew prepared for the homeward journey.

They had scarcely started their return trip when a giant wave struck the *Richard Coleman* and completely filled her with water. Coxswain Harry Marshall checked to see that all of his crew were safe while the automatic valve system readily drained the craft.

The horses had been despatched from Worthing to a hauling-up place on Lancing beach opposite the *Three Horseshoes Inn*, as it was thought that the *Richard Coleman* would return by road. But once the sails were set, Coxswain Marshall deemed it desirable to head straight for the Pier and they came ashore at 10.15 p.m. to Signalman Butcher's lights, after being at sea for more than four hours.

In the dark of night the return was witnessed by a considerably large crowd who raised a hearty cheer for the stalwart but weary lifeboatmen. The *Richard Coleman* itself had behaved splendidly throughout and sustained not the slightest damage. With the tide now low, Mr. Butcher's fine team of horses, assisted by able volunteers, quickly hauled her back to the lifeboat house, and half an hour later the lifeboat was ready again for active service.

The committee paid each of the 13 lifeboat crew, who all had previous experience as lifeboat service crew, 30s. They were: Harry and Fred Marshall, Bill Blann, Steve and George Wingfield, Fred, Frank and Bill Collier, Frank Burdon, George Benn, Wm. Cousins, Wm. Curvin, and George Belton.

Each of the extra helpers required on this occasion for the haul-off rope on the Pier received 5s.; but each of the eight carters was recommended extra pay of one shilling for the brevity and skill exhibited in taking their horses into the heavy sea. Councillor Butcher received £7 for the hire of eight of his horses and 7s.6d. allowance as Signalman.

The total costs of the *Richard Coleman's* service to the *Liburna* came to £38 2s.6d., a staggeringly high amount in those days, and the highest cost of any one service by the Worthing lifeboat up to this time.

If I added to this the cost of the Shoreham lifeboat's service and the coastguard expenses it would result in a figure that I am sure would have seemed formidable at the time but shows that no price is too high for human lives.

As a pleasant epilogue the Worthing lifeboat crew were generously entertained to dinner on the Friday at the *Spaniard Hotel* in Portland Road by a Mr. Walker, a naturalised American living in Monmouthshire but on holiday in Worthing, who had been so impressed by the prompt, smart lifeboatmen on the Wednesday night. Among the 30 guests was the former Coxswain Charlie Lee who, it transpired during the evening, had something particular in common with the host. They had both served in the Crimea in a nautical capacity in their younger days.

Sixty seven year old Mr. Walker installed Harry Marshall next to himself at the head of the table alongside Bill Blann and Walter Butcher. Behind them the Stars and Stripes and the Union Jack hung diplomatically on the end wall.

The host proved to be a humorous gent. After supper he indulged in a kind of roll call: first enquiring the name of the lifeboat, which was given as the *Richard Coleman*, and next ascertaining that all the crew members, except one, were present. Then he solemnly expressed his satisfaction that all of them were 'mustered'. This word association between the name of the boat and the table condiment amused his audience immensely, and was referred to on subsequent occasions.

Another great source of merriment was derived, this time at the pianist's expense. A large, white, blank card was seen hanging on the wall just above the piano. Then, when the accompanist, Mr. G. Stent took up his position at the instrument, a waiter received instructions from Mr. Walker to reverse the card, revealing the words written by a practised hand: 'Gentlemen! Please don't shoot the piano player, he is doing the best he can!'

Most of the time was occupied by popular instrumental selections given by a Mr. W. Smith on a cornet and a Charles Spinks with his clarionet. Songs were sung by Steve Wingfield jun., J. Groves, Charlie Lee, Jack Burgess and a Mr. Poland.

Mr. Walker paid a glowing tribute to the work of the lifeboatmen. We had, he said, the Victoria Cross which was given for killing people; let us have an Edward V11 Cross for saving people. Loud applause followed from the lifeboatmen who had turned out to rescue the crew from the distressed barque.

After a pleasant time the evening came to a close at 11 o'clock with cheers for Mr. Walker and for the hostess, Mrs. Tettersel.

Thousands of people went to see the stranded wreck, the busiest day being on Sunday when the afternoon trains from Worthing and Brighton were crammed with excited sightseers, as were trams to the east of Shoreham.

The stranded *Liburna* was sold to a Mr. Collard[9] of Newhaven. She was stranded for six days during which time several attempts were made to refloat her. After the last, successful, attempt, under the gaze of Worthing's watermen, she was towed off to Newhaven.

The Swedish barque *Liburna* stranded off Shoreham in March 1905, its mainmast ripped away.

Footnotes

[1] Reproduced from a photograph in the Penny Illustrated Paper, 6 September 1902 edition.

[2] Steve Wingfield senior was born in 1851.

[3] The early omnibus featured on this postcard (which was posted in 1905) belonged to the Worthing Motor Omnibus Company — a corporate body established in 1904 to compete with traditional horse-drawn transport.

[4] This postcard is incorrectly titled 'Worthing lifeboat at Kingston.' It is in fact one of the RNLI display boats, *Chapel D8*. Harry Marshall is in the stern. On the right of the man wearing a tie and straw boater stands Bert Marshall, and next to him is one of his brothers, Charlie. Both are sons of Harry Marshall. The next one wearing a lifejacket is probably Frank Cousins, then Fred Marshall and Jumbo Wingfield. One of the Beltons is standing far right.

[5] The Blann capstan is still on the beach today, opposite New Street. In 1989 it was restored at the instigation of the Worthing Society and painted blue.

[6] Clifton Road was formerly known as New Town Road, because when this particular area was developed it was on the outskirts of the existing town. Clifton Road Cottages were demolished in 1960.

[7] Carl Adolf Seebold was the son of a rope manufacturer from Zurich. The father fell on hard times and turned to entertainment, playing the guitar and singing, to support a large family of nine sons and four daughters. Ultimately, almost the entire family adopted a musical career. As a family act they toured Switzerland, under the name of Father Seebold and his Seven Sons. They performed well, and so great were their musical capabilities that they were invited to play before all of the individual royal households in Europe. An advantageous offer brought them to England, where they played at posh clubs, exhibitions and fashionable receptions in London; their stage name being the Swiss Band, then the Mountain Singers, and latterly as the Chamonix Orchestra. Seebold took out a lease on the Pier Pavilion at Southend, and that town became the family headquarters.

[8] This photograph illustrates the various modes of horse transport in early Edwardian times: firstly, the obvious sole rider in the centre of the picture; then there are the horse-drawn taxi-cabs behind him, lined up in front of the Town Hall; on the right is a two-wheeled cart; behind, looking through South Place into Ann Street, one of Mr. Stent's charabancs is parked in front of his booking office; moving now to the left of the picture, a four-wheeled carter's vehicle is clearly visible; while behind that, at the beginning of Chapel Road, is a horse-drawn omnibus.

[9] R.R. Collard, was a Hasting's potato merchant, who from 1887 had been owner and operator of several paddle steamers on the South Coast, as was his partner in the potato business, a Mr. Payne.

The Paddling Pebble

Chapter 3

One More Saved

1905-6

Boatmen Harry and Fred Marshall, who occupied a well-known stand on the front opposite the *Stanhoe Hotel*, added a new boat to their stock in 1905. They called it the *Jolly Sailor*, the same name as another of their boats. Launched for a trial run lasting two hours on Wednesday 22 March, the smart 20 foot sailing boat, built by John Belton's yard, performed excellently. The Marshall brothers were well-pleased with their new acquisition, which was to be used for taking out sailing and fishing parties. Belton's boatbuilding yard was particularly busy around this time, having a full order book.

Fred Marshall (wearing rolled-up white trousers) taking out a happy party for a cruise in the *Jolly Sailor*.

Another of the Belton family, George Belton junior, a boatman licensed under the recently passed regulation with Worthing Corporation and whose stand was opposite West Buildings, got into difficulties taking out a boating party.

On Sunday 21 May 1905, at about 8 o'clock in the morning, he put off from the beach in his sailing boat *Ina* on a pleasure cruise with a party of three: Mr. W. H. Pollard of West Buildings, Mr. Jesse Howell of the *Montague Hotel* and Mr. Worsfold of Felpham, Middlesex.

But it was not long before Mr. Howell, who couldn't find his sea legs, was sick and had to be put ashore. Belton with his remaining party of two went out again and continued to cruise about. Just before 11 a.m. they were near the wrecked *Indiana*[1]. From here they tacked westward until they were opposite Courtlands at Goring. Now and again a little wind was quite apparent.

The steamship *Indiana* wrecked off Worthing in March 1901, and now known as the Orange Wreck.

Suddenly a squall, probably from the north, took the boat and practically submerged it. Before they realised what had happened, they were also under the water.

Mr. Pollard found himself going. He grabbed a sail to keep himself afloat. Mr. Worsfold held himself up by the mast, and the boatman, Belton, was in the stern which remained submerged.

This accident happened about two miles off the uncompleted *Hotel Metropole*, on the corner of Grand Avenue.

The *Hotel Metropole*. The building stood like this for many years and was known as Worthing's White Elephant.[2]

Pollard, the only one who couldn't swim, was now on top of the sail, but hampered by a heavy overcoat and with little support, gradually felt himself going again.

Belton proved to be a great source of inspiration, continually repeating, "Keep up your pluck!" varied by such optimistic expressions as "Here they come - racing for their lives!"

As it happened, rescue was at hand, but from their positions neither Pollard nor Worsfold could see the approaching boats until they were close.

Five boats had put off from the beach when the accident had been spotted. The first to reach them was one manned by Percy Mills and a boatman named Grevatt, employed by Belton.

The latter shouted, "Save Mr. Pollard! He's the worst!"

The rescuers kept him afloat by positioning an oar under his arm.

Then another boatman, Jo Street, and his son, brought their craft alongside with Mr. Pollard between the two boats. He was lifted, in a state of collapse, out of the sea and laid in the Streets' boat which was hastily rowed ashore, while Belton and Worsfold were taken in the craft manned by Mills and Grevatt.

Pollard was landed by West Buildings, not far from his home, watched by hundreds of curious onlookers who had gathered in the excitement. He was lifted out of the boat in a half-drowned state, and was supported on the way home by Mr. J. Nye the Parade Inspector and Jo Street.

Pollard was put to bed for a time, but later rose, and fortunately did not require medical attention. The two others were none the worse for their ordeal, but Belton was somewhat poorly for a time.

Later in 1905, during the summer, the Belton family did not compete in either of two races exclusively for Worthing watermen in the August Annual Regatta.

In the sailing race, the four winning fancifully-named boats were Fred Collier's *Princess May*, Steve and George Wingfield's *Lancashire Lass*, W. J. Hutchinson's *The Kitty*, and Bill Blann's *Dandy Dick*.

Another Wingfield boat *The Lily* was among four finalists in the rowing race. The other three all bore women's Christian names: Fred and Arthur Marshall's *Marie Elsie*, F. Collier's *Winnie*, and Hutchinson's *Dorothy*.

The fixture was remembered for its sudden change in weather. For rain descended directly the day's proceedings finished, and the thousands of spectators rapidly fled.

A glimpse through the open doors of Worthing's lifeboat house, exposing the *Richard Coleman*.

Another competition, the Annual Sailing Regatta, only the second to be held, took place on Monday afternoon 4 September after two postponements due to bad weather. More than 50 entrants competed in five lengthy events. The course for one of the races was so long that the winner came in with a time of just over 3½ hours.

Only one of the races was solely for Worthing boatmen and fishermen. W. J. Hutchinson's *Kitty* was once more amongst the winners, this time taking the first prize of £2 10s. with a time of one hour and 19 minutes. Three other boats were placed: Collier's, George Wingfield's, and the one belonging to Harry and Bill Blann.

The traditional triennial Lifeboat Sunday, scheduled for 27 August, was advertised by Lifeboat Sunday bills posted on boatmen's and fishermen's boxes at the top of the beach.

On the day itself, the objectives of the RNLI were expounded upon at several churches in the town. Not only were collections made at churches, cash was donated at a sacred concert on the Pier; and on the front, collections were made by the lifeboat crew, who were characteristically attired, and carried lifeboat-shaped boxes.

To attract visitors the outside of the lifeboat house was decorated with flags and the doors left open to display the *Richard Coleman*. Passers by could stroll in and put a copper or two in the donation box after inspecting the magnificent boat and viewing the pictorial wall-mounted history of Worthing's lifeboats. A large frame on the right hand wall contained 11 photographs depicting the 1901 lifeboat parade.[3]

A total of £65 18s.1d. was collected on this day and subsequently forwarded to head office. As the weather had been poor, this amount was slightly down on that collected on the previous Lifeboat Sunday in 1902.

The Worthing Branch RNLI held its A.G.M. on Thursday evening 1st March 1906 in the usual venue, the Council Chamber.

The report for 1905, read by John Roberts, showed that the District Inspector at each of his half-yearly visits, expressed satisfaction with the excellent condition of the Station and the efficiency of the coxswains and crews, and also the able manner in which the drivers and horses performed their work under the superintendence of the signalman, Walter Butcher.

There was a slight increase in annual subscriptions to £116 12s., enabling the committee to forward £80 to H.Q., the same amount as in the previous year. As the Institution was greatly dependent upon remittances from its larger branches, such as this one, the committee confidently appealed for the continued support of Worthing residents. Donations amounting to £24 17s.1d. and £26 10s.11d. were emptied from collecting boxes. Including the balance of £107 1s.10d. brought forward from 1905 the total receipts for the year were £340 19s.11d.

Worthing's lifeboat house after electric lighting replaced its gas illumination in 1905.[4]

Worthing raised more in annual subscriptions and donations than any of the other 10 fund-raising branches in Sussex, even though some of the other towns were much larger.

Since being taken over by the RNLI in 1865, the Worthing Lifeboat Station had been responsible for saving four vessels from destruction, the highest number by any of the nine Sussex Lifeboat Stations.

During the past year, lifeboats of the National Institution had been launched 373 times for service, and had been successful in rescuing 550 people, making a total of 45,439 lives saved since 1824.

The chairman commented on the added convenience enjoyed by the coxswain and crew in having electric light wired to the lifeboat house and proposed a vote of thanks to the Town Council for installing it. Up until this time the building had been lit by gas. A new aid was the addition of an exterior light, affixed to the bottom of the lookout turret above the doors.

The Mayor, who was present at the meeting, remarked that they should not only do what they could to support the Lifeboat Institution but should always bear in mind the brave lifeboatmen who risk their lives to save others. The Institution themselves would help the families of any crewmen losing their lives whilst on service. Widows would receive at least £100 and £25 for each dependent child.

He mentioned that he had visited the Station, and praised the up-to-date and clean manner in which everything was kept, and the courtesy he received from the coxswain. He also made it quite clear that he was impressed with the marvellous adaptability and constant readiness of the *Richard Coleman*, especially when autumn storms could be so vicious.

For those lifeboatmen who depended upon fishing for their livelihood, the industry had not been at all satisfactory during the winter months, although there had been a good herring season. Owing to bad weather around Christmas time trawl fishing was not so good. As far as crustaceans were concerned, lobsters were scarce as well. But crabs bucked the trend: a fair supply was landed, although the income produced from this source was barely enough to feed a man let alone his whole family.

Boatman Harry Marshall recalled his earlier days when, as a young stripling, he had first gone to sea. Having joined the crew of the *Akbar*, a freight coaster from Shoreham, he had been surprised at being called a 'Porky' by his captain.

Later he had discovered the reason.

Apparently, in the latter half of the 19th century, when Worthing's deep sea fishermen left for fishing grounds, either in the North Sea or off the west of England, they were renowned for taking more pork rations with them than fishermen from other towns.

These other fishermen often felt that their Worthing counterparts were also greedy in another way in poaching on their fishing reserves.

Furthermore, a parallel had been drawn between the gluttonous way in which hardy Worthing fishermen ate their food to sustain their stamina, and the way in which a shark would bolt a bait of pork.

This is how the deep sea fishermen of Worthing had become known as Pork-Bolters, or Porkies for short.

Though the Worthing fishing industry had diminished in recent years it was still pursued to a modified degree and in May 1906 some excellent catches of mackerel were brought in. They had an unusually fine flavour this season, but they sold cheaply in the streets: five for as little as a shilling when there was a glut.

The decline in this means of securing a living, due particularly to the advent of large deep-sea trawlers that were best suited to a harbour which Worthing didn't have, led to a crisis meeting of the Worthing Fishermen's Mutual Insurance Association.

The organisation, formed in 1865 to insure local fishermen's boats and gear, had been excellent in compensating members' losses to the sum of £1,900 since it had been established.

But it now found itself with nothing to insure, there wasn't even one boat on its books. In these circumstances the trustees felt that the Association should be wound up or its horizons broadened, to enable the balance of £1,007 19s.5d. in hand to be used for the benefit of local fishermen and boatmen.

The Association's president and treasurer, Mr. Hargood, and its honorary secretary, George Piggott, held an exploratory meeting with its trustees, Messrs. Melvill Green, Golding Bird

Collett and John Roberts. Subsequent discussions between the fishermen who had contributed and the committee of management, did produce a solution.

The outcome was a decision to alter the rules, subject to receiving the sanction of the Registrar of Friendly Societies, so as to enable the funds to be used for the relief of boat-owners, fishermen and watermen of the town who may have suffered any loss or misfortune.

Harry Marshall[5] photographed in his boat, the Jolly Sailor, c. 1905.

When the alteration took place, Mr. Piggott and Mr. Hargood resigned their positions; the latter having taken considerable interest in the Association during the 30 years that he had held office. In reply to a vote of thanks for all he had done, he drew attention to the fact that during those 30 years the total management expenses had been only £19 13s.8d. or an average of 13s.1d. per annum, and that this included the annual rent of 10s. for use of the Workmen's Institute. This was considered a model of economical administration, worthy of emulation in other quarters of the town!

The title of the new organisation was the Worthing Fishermen's and Watermen's Benefit Association, and its new officers were: president and treasurer, Mr. James White; trustees, Messrs. Golding Bird Collett, John Roberts, and Robert William Charles; auditors, Messrs A. H. Collet, and W. Verrall; secretary, Mr. Frank Dean.

Under a new committee of management which, in addition to the elected officers, consisted of the following ageing fishermen – Tom Blann (my great great grandfather, then 73 years of age), E. Edwards, A. Beck, E. Haylor, W. Lucas and W. Benn. Worthing fishermen and boatmen were encouraged to join by applying to the office at no.1 Highworth (demolished in 1988 to build a C & A shopping store).

Boating for pleasure was a popular indulgence of ladies at this time, but at least two incidents in this year dampened the ardour of the sweeter sex.

In the first occurrence, during springtime, dresses of lady passengers were soaked when their hired rowing boat began to leak, half a mile out to sea. The seams of the boat were, apparently, not sealed properly and water was pouring in, so much so that, finding no bailer, the boatman had to pull hard for the beach on a scratch pair of oars that appeared to have the blades worn off.

When they had first got into the boat it was half full of water and the gentleman escort, who had hired the pretty little craft for 2s. an hour from the bronzed mariner, had apprehensively asked him why this had happened.

In reply the canny boatman had merely shrugged his shoulders saying: They do get like that on the shingle!

However, if the craft had been properly caulked after being high and dry on the beach all winter, this embarrassing situation would never have occurred.

Three young ladies being brought ashore alongside Worthing Pier after being rescued in 1906.

The other incident happened in the summer when a sailor visiting the town hired a small rowing boat from Mr. W. Wells to take out some young ladies, three good-looking females who had come down to Worthing for the day with an excursion party from the Presbyterian Church in City Road, London.

Rowing out with his glamourous girls to the yacht *Britannia* which was anchored some distance from the Pier-head, the sojourning seaman was overcome by egotism. In showing off to the women, he attempted to board the Worthing yacht, but while he was climbing into it the small rowing boat partly capsized, pitching the three young ladies fully clothed into the sea.

The sailor immediately jumped into the sea to help the screaming, panicking females.

But, fortunately, help from other fishermen was at hand and they were soon rescued, drenched and shivering, by Mr. Wells and his colleague Mr. Freeman in another boat. One of the women, suffering badly from shock, was taken by cab to the hospital. With the help of our local medical experts she recovered amazingly quickly and was able to rejoin her friends later the same day.

The *Britannia*, which had been the focus of attention, was owned by Charlie and Frank Stubbs, the fishmonger. Worked by Charlie Lee, the boat had two distinct uses: pleasure cruising for the well-to-do, and professional fishing. Bearing in mind what some may consider to be pungent odours associated with the latter you may well ask the question: how could these two interests be reconciled in the same craft?

These two quite different interests rarely clashed, for seasonal fishing did not normally coincide with the recognised holiday season; besides, a lot of fishing was done at night, leaving craft free for daytime pursuits. Imagine fashionable Edwardian ladies and gents in a boat that could never be completely free of fish smells, even if it had been cleaned up. I think that generally, natural aromas were more accepted by people in those times.

A pre 1906 photograph of the double-masted gaff-rigged ketch *Britannia*.[6]

Worthing watermen displayed their dexterity as oarsmen in the Annual Regatta in August. The sculling race for Worthing boatmen was won by Harry and Fred Marshall's *Marie Elsie*, followed by F. Collier's *Winnie* and George Wingfield's *Lily*.

Thousands of residents and visitors participated in the delights of this traditional festival on the seafront. People in the crowds cheered for their particular favourite competitor in each race, while, between races, the Borough Band played on the Pier, which was gaily adorned with flags and bunting.

Fishmonger Stubb's *Britannia* won a sailing race, which was specifically for local trawlers, followed by Hutchinson's *Lion*, Blann's *Eclat* and J. Bacon's *Albatross*.

A view of the north end of Steyne Gardens showing a canvas-covered bandstand and grass tennis courts.[7]

There was also a race for licensed Worthing watermen, in dandy or lug-rigged boats up to 17 feet long. In this event both first and third prizes were won by two old favourites, George Wingfield's *Lancashire Lass* and F. Collier's *Princess May* respectively, but second place was taken by a young man named Jack Burgess in *Spare Moments*..

The happy and relaxed carnival atmosphere continued into the evening with an extravaganza that was familiar on these eventful occasions, the illuminated concert and firework display in Steyne Gardens. Watched by thousands of people, the arena was full to capacity, and joyful crowds thronged the surrounding streets, thus bringing to an end this regatta day. A day which was always considered to be the big day of the year, a holiday, and a time to be remembered.

The well-known Worthing boat-builder, John Belton, who had turned his attention to pleasure craft when the fishing industry began to decline, passed away on 27 November.

Fifty nine year old Belton had started learning the trade at the early age of 10, and had developed a thriving business. His yard had been responsible for constructing two particularly well-known sailing yachts, the *Maud* and Alderman E. T. Cooksey's *Edna*.

In his latter years, since the advent of the motor-boat, he had moved with the times and adapted his men to making that type of craft.

But, although his health had been failing him for some time, he did not take to his bed until the day before he died. His characteristic perseverance kept him active right up to the end.

Such was his popularity that his loss was felt throughout the town and beyond. His widow, four sons – Henry, Herbert, Albert and Edward – and four daughters, mourned the untimely departure of a good husband and father.

One of the Marshall brothers' boats, the *Jolly Sailor,* on the beach west of the Bandstand.

John Belton was buried in Broadwater Cemetery on the following Saturday afternoon, after a service conducted by the Rev. C. Douglas Crouch, Pastor of the Tabernacle. At the graveside the hymn, Rock of Ages, was solemnly sung by Belton's relatives: including his daughters, Miss Mabel and Miss Alice Belton; his daughter and son-in-law, Mr.and Mrs. Dudney; brother George and his wife; brother Tom; brother-in-law, Mr. Farrow; cousin, Mrs. Field; and niece, Miss L. Belton.

The Sailing Club, of which the deceased had been a founder member, was represented by its commodore, John Roberts, a well-known figure; the treasurer, H.S. Johnson; the honorary secretary A.J. Newington; the sailing secretary J.K. Hubbard; and members: T. Butler, C. Barnwell, E.H. Cooksey, R.R. Wentworth Hyde, J. Newman and J. Stoddart.

Throughout his career, many of the boats built by John Belton had been to fulfil orders from along the coast, particularly Brighton. This was self evident when a delegation from the Brighton Naval Volunteer Cruising Club attended the funeral as a mark of respect and to offer their sympathy to the bereaved family. The party from this Brighton club comprised their commodore, James S. Smith, and three members, W. and T. Ashdown and V. Ball.

The widely acclaimed Brighton yachtsman, Capt. Fred Collins, for whom John Belton had built a succession of yachts, attended to pay his last respects. So popular was Belton that even local coastguards attended as a final tribute. Two well-known Worthingites, Charles Paine and Mr. C.H. Aldridge were also present.

A contingent of boatmen and fishermen associated with the lifeboat: Harry Marshall, Bill and Harry Blann, Brown, Charlie Lee, George Newman, John and James Tester, Tom Wingfield and Wakeford, completed the large, sorrowful gathering.

Fisherman and former lifeboat crewman, Charlie Wells, died this same year, having lived all of his 60 years in the town. At this funeral, lifeboat crew members, Harry Marshall, F. Collier, George Wingfield and Fred Marshall acted as bearers. A wreath, paid for and sent by a large number of Worthing fishermen, was laid on the grave.

An exciting, but sad, incident occurred one Sunday evening during this year, involving local fishermen who were associated with the lifeboat. One of their boats, the *Lion*, a fishing boat belonging to W.J. Hutchinson, was damaged beyond repair in a storm.

The drama began one morning. When riding at anchor among other boats off the town, a gale suddenly sprang up.

Launching the *Richard Coleman*.

The *Lion* started dragging its anchor.

By 4 o'clock in the afternoon the boat was dangerously close to the beach groynes. Two fishermen, James Curvin and James Groves, went off with the intention of bringing it ashore.

But in the ferocious conditions it was some three hours before a suitable opportunity presented itself to bring the boat in.

Suddenly, just as they were about to succeed in their task, the wind dropped, leaving the boat entirely at the mercy of the waves!

The next moment the craft was hurled onto one of the groyne piles!

Curvin and Groves were instantly thrown out and buffeted about in the surf.

They succeeded in wading ashore, fortunately not much the worse for their exhilarating experience. But when the tide receded leaving the boat high and dry on the sands it soon became apparent that the sadly battered craft was completely wrecked.

It was, however, not the first loss of its kind for Hutchinson. He had lost three earlier boats in similar circumstances during the previous few years.

Acting on the suggestion of several friends, who had seen the disaster that Sunday evening, a Mr. W. A. Hewer of 15 Rowlands Road very kindly set up an appeal to reimburse the boat's owner for his latest loss.

As the amount raised fell somewhat short of the cost of a new boat, Hutchinson was unable to replace it for some time.

The *Richard Coleman* and crew returning from exercise c. 1905, and about to descend the ramp in front of the Pier to the seafront road.

Boatmen and fishermen who were members of the Worthing lifeboat crew travelled to Kingston-on-Thames to take part in the Annual Lifeboat Demonstration on Saturday 23 June 1906. During the event they gave the King a naval salute, and His Majesty responded by raising his hat and smiling at the stalwart sons of the sea.

Two days later, back at Worthing, the lifeboat maroon was fired. Its sharp explosion prompted a large number of residents and visitors to rush onto the Pier, while others assembled on the beach to the east.

Before long, the enormous-looking lifeboat carriage came rushing over the promenade, chains clanging and harnesses jangling, as the stout hauling steeds were brought to a halt by experienced horsemen.

As the carriage was backed down the sharply-falling, stony gradient of the beach, with the boat's bow foremost in anticipation of the menacing water ahead, the crowds instantly separated to allow the rescue vehicle through.

It was 2.30 p.m. when the *Richard Coleman* was pulled through the rough sea by a body of men heaving a towline as they advanced along the deck of the Pier. Once past the pierhead the lifeboat was under its own power, using oars and sail, as it manoeuvred eastward in the very high wind.

The spectators waited for some time to watch the boat come in, from what had been a quarterly practice.

After running ashore on the leeward side of the Pier, the weighty lifeboat was winched back onto the carriage. As the burly horses dragged the mighty, cumbersome load up the steeply sloping stony beach, the heavy, spoked wheels sank rim-deep in the finer shingle close to the water's edge.

Once on to the asphalted promenade, the going was easy. A gently sloping ramp led down to the road.

One may be tempted to think: oh yes, well that was only an exercise, the lifeboatmen weren't truly at risk. Believe me, when you talk with the old lifeboat families, you begin to understand that each time the crew went out in the lifeboat, danger lurked. Whether it was on service or for an all-important quarterly practice these guys got in there to do the job. It was for real.

This is the year in which representatives of the Worthing lifeboat crew had the honour of being chosen to appear in the Lord Mayor's Show in London once more. Members of the crew selected for duty were Coxswain Harry Marshall, 2nd Coxswain Bill Blann, Bowman Steve Wingfield, Fred Marshall, George Newman, George Wingfield, F. Collier, W. Collier, Jack Burgess, George Benn, Charlie Wingfield, F. Burton and W. Cousens.

As they progressed along the selected route in the *Jane Caroline*, the old Weston-super-Mare lifeboat, they were loudly cheered by the huge concourse of spectators.

A lifeboat was re-introduced as a feature of the show after an interval of four years, but the last time our Worthing lifeboatmen took part was in the Jubilee Year, 1887, although our old lifeboat, the *Henry Harris*, was used in 1901 when it was manned by the Deal crew. Eastbourne was the only other Sussex RNLI Station to have been previously honoured in such a way.

The Worthing lifeboatmen returned home that evening and, fortunately, slept well. For the very next day the excitement of their involvement in the Lord Mayor's Show came to an abrupt halt.

The sound of the maroon being fired was heard. It was half past eleven in the morning. Within a few minutes the crew hastily assembled at the lifeboat house.

Being low tide with relatively calm inshore waters, it was not necessary to seek the protection of the Pier or the assistance of a haul-off warp.

Aided by a multitude of volunteers the *Richard Coleman* was brought out of the boathouse, horsed, dragged over the beach and quickly launched off the sands opposite West Street at precisely 11.45 a.m.

Their target was a small rowing boat more than three miles out, whose sole occupant was one Thomas Anderson, a London visitor staying at York House Boarding Establishment on the seafront.

He had gone out before breakfast, about 8.30, for a row in the 14 foot craft belonging to the boarding-house. The sea had

A Worthing coastguardsman scanning the Channel with his telescope steadied on a capstan.

been quite calm close in shore, but it was not until the young fellow had tried to return that he had found it impossible to make any headway against the strong north-easterly wind blowing off-shore.

Instead of throwing out his anchor and waiting either until someone noticed his difficulty or the tide turned in his favour, he had continued to pull towards the shore, hoping to beach at Goring. When that had failed, due to the boat rolling almost broadside in the waves, he had started rowing eastward again, with the result that his frail craft had gradually drifted out to sea.

Around 10 a.m. the boat had been noticed about three miles off the beach and, as the wind was gusting to moderate gale force, the Worthing Coastguard had kept it under observation.

When a small schooner had passed down the Channel, Anderson had endeavoured to attract attention by holding up one of his oars, but his signals had passed unheeded.

The tiny craft had been driven further out to sea by the off-shore wind until it had been diminished to a mere speck on the horizon.

Its position by then had been considered perilous. Shortly after 11 o'clock the lifeboat chairman, secretary and coxswain had held a crisis consultation on whether to launch the lifeboat. Chief Officer Lester of the Worthing Coastguard had agreed with them that the sea was too rough for the coastguard galley or a shore boat to travel that distance from land.

"Launch the lifeboat!"

Once away, it was speedily sailed before the wind by its skilful crewmen in a south westerly direction to where the uncontrollable craft had last been seen.

After being at sea for an hour the lifeboat crew found the small vessel nearly six miles from land, still drifting further out at the rate of about three knots, and only visible as it rose on the crest of each wave. Young Anderson himself was lying in the bottom of the boat, drenched with spray and completely exhausted.

The *Richard Coleman* was quickly alongside. Assisting him over into the lifeboat, three of the crew administered brandy and rubbed his almost lifeless, numb limbs to increase his blood circulation, and put on his shoes and socks.

Meanwhile the remainder of the crew had turned the lifeboat around and were heading back to Worthing with the tiny rowing boat in tow. The north east wind, which had worked in their favour on the outward bound voyage, now slowed them considerably. To sustain their stamina during the long return journey the crew consumed biscuits, which they shared with the rescued young fellow. Tacking against the wind it was nearly two hours before they made landfall at 2.30 p.m. As the lifeboatmen approached the beach they could see the familiar, large, welcoming crowds on the promenade and on the pier.

With the help of the volunteers and uniformed coastguards the *Richard Coleman* and the tiny rescued craft, which looked a little worse for its adventure, were brought in.

By now, Anderson had recovered sufficiently for him to return to his lodgings in a cab. He stated later that out in the Channel he had given up all hope of reaching Worthing that night, and had been on the look-out for tramp steamers or a schooner plying the coast when he had seen the fawn-coloured sail of a vessel heading in his direction.

With fresh inspiration he had picked up the oars to row towards it, but on dipping one in the sea, it had very nearly been wrenched from his weakened grasp, and for a second had thought he would lose it under the boat.

He had only just managed to ship it when, on looking round, had seen the vessel was taking in sail. At first, the thought had struck him that the boat was out to fish.

Suddenly five white oars shot out from one side of the vessel, five blue oars from the other.

The lifeboat was here to rescue him, halleluyah!

Members of the 13 crew on this mission were Coxswain Harry Marshall, 2nd Coxswain Bill Blann, Steve Wingfield (bowman), two of the coxswain's brothers – Fred and Mark, Bill's brother Harry Blann, Frank Collier, Wm. Curvin, George Newman, Tom Wingfield, George Belton, George Benn and Jo Street. They were each paid 15s., the basic winter rate.

Thirty four men, who assisted the launch and haul-up of the lifeboat, received 4/6d. each from branch funds, half as much again as the summer rate; and six horses were hired for 10s. each. In all, the costs of this service totalled £20 12s.6d.

One more life had been saved by a Worthing lifeboat, but this was the very first by the *Richard Coleman*. Subsequently this entry was painted on the Station's service board – '10 November 1906, saved one life and pleasure boat'.

Thomas Anderson and rowing boat. Both rescued from the clutches of the English Channel in 1906.

Footnotes

[1] See pages 167 - 171 about the *Indiana* in the book 'A Town's Pride'.

[2] The *Hotel Metropole* was the first stage of a magnificent development project at Grand Avenue, started in 1893. According to published plans, the scheme was to culminate in an elegant pier to be constructed as an extension of Grand Avenue over the sea. But it was never to be. Funds ran out, and the hotel building remained unfinished until 1923, when it was put to use as a block of flats known as The Towers. In 1971 it was renamed Dolphin Lodge. A modern block of a completely different character now overpowers the southern end, where the original intention had been to match the northern end of the building.

[3] The large pictorial frame containing 11 photographs depicting the 1901 lifeboat parade is now stored away in Worthing Museum.

[4] Worthing's lifeboathouse, a fine brick and flint building at 107 Marine Parade, survives today but very much altered, now a dwelling.

[5] Harry Marshall's grandson Derrick Marshall Churcher lives in Worthing. Derrick is the eldest of four brothers: Brian-Harry also resides in Worthing, and Colin at Rustington. The youngest, the late David Clifford Churcher started a business in a shop at West Buildings in the 1950's, before it moved to Montague Street. That business is still there today, now called Churcher Audio & Video.

[6] At one time, the backboard from the yacht *Britannia* hung in the Guildbourne Shopping Centre. It is now in Worthing Museum.

[7] Between the trees on this picture postcard, part of Colonnade Buildings, the Broadway can be seen. Situated on the corner of Brighton Road and High Street, they were built in 1901 in what was the grounds of Warwick House.

Looking down South Street towards the sea

Looking east into Warwick Street – today a pedestrian precinct

A Few Plums from Worthing.

Chapter 4

The Watermen's Day

1907-8

January, 1907 was very cold. Extremely low temperatures beset Worthing and caused even the hardiest of 'old salts' to shiver. Youngsters who dared to venture down to the beach on the 24th of that month, thought to be one of the coldest days on record, were confronted by a strange spectacle, sea foam, frozen into wave sculptures and left behind on the beach by the receding tide.

Frozen sea foam on Worthing beach, 24 January 1907[1]

The following month, on Thursday afternoon 28 February, a successful fund-raising year was disclosed at the annual meeting of the Worthing Branch RNLI, held in the Council Chamber. Those present were Mr. H. Hargood J.P.(chairman), Mr. John Roberts (honorary secretary), Alderman J. White J.P.(Deputy Mayor), Alderman G. Ewen Smith, Rev. C. J. Hollis, Rev. J. O. Parr, Admiral Leicester Keppel, and Messrs J. Andrews, E. G. Amphlett J.P., R. Selway Chard, A. Buckland Dixon, F. C. Gates, G. H. P. Livesay, T. Lester (Chief Coastguard Officer), Harry Marshall (lifeboat coxswain), F. W. Patching, W. G. Patching and F. J. Timms.

With regard to the financial position the committee had been able to forward £75 to head office, compared with £80 in the previous year. This decrease might have been caused by the loss of several annual donations from supporters who had passed away; and the hope was expressed that there would be an increase in the number of new subscribers.

Worthing lifeboat crew pictured in front of the lifeboat house in March 1907. In front of the *Richard Coleman* are (left to right):-
Frank Burden, George Benn, William Cousins, Harry Marshall, Walter Butcher (signalman),
Fred Marshall, Bill Blann and Arthur Marshall.[2]

The financial statement showed that there had been a balance at the beginning of the year of £115 14s.4d.; that subscriptions, donations and collections amounted to £160 4s.; and that after expenses had been deducted, the sum of £99 7s.5d. remained.

It was mentioned in the course of proceedings that the sum of £6 18s.9d. had been received from Mr. T. Anderson, who, some three months earlier in November, had been plucked from certain death by Worthing's lifeboat crew. He had made a collection among his fellow clerks in the General Post Office in London and added some money of his own, as a token of gratitude and appreciation for his timely rescue.

Also in November, the Worthing lifeboat crew had been selected out of 285 crews nationally to represent the RNLI at the Lord Mayor's Show. Coxswain Harry Marshall made it clear to the meeting how deeply honoured they had felt to have been chosen.

A report, prepared by the secretary, stated that the District Inspector had once again expressed his satisfaction with the condition of everything connected with the Station.

Concluding the meeting with a vote of thanks to the chairman, Alderman Smith remarked that for as long as he could remember, either Harry Hargood or his honoured father had been associated with lifeboat work.

An occasion in November 1908, which would have particularly appealed to the late Mr. Hargood, had been a special commemoration service at St. Paul's, Worthing, on the 56th anniversary of the *Lalla Rookh* disaster – a time when Worthingites had been plunged into the throes of misery and distress. In remembrance, the vicar had preached an appropriate and impressive sermon: 'He saved others; he cannot save himself.' (St. Matthew ch.27 v.42)

A former Worthing lifeboat crewman, Mark William Benn of 31 Surrey Street died on Wednesday 13 February 1907 after suffering from an attack of influenza lasting seven days. He was the son of Mr. and Mrs. William Benn of 19 Graham Road, both of whom survived him, the father being 81 years of age and the mother 76 when Mark died.

Mark Benn, who had been a seaman by occupation and a highly respected man, had suffered ill health for many years. On one occasion, some 26 years earlier, he had caught a cold while serving on the lifeboat. This had developed into asthma, from which he had never since been free; and his condition was such that he had been unable to lie down in bed for the past 25 years.

Mark left a widow and three grown-up children. One son, a chief petty officer in the Royal Navy, was away at sea when his father died. The other son was a carpenter, and the daughter's husband was a chief stoker in the Navy.

During the funeral, at Broadwater Cemetery on the Saturday afternoon, respect shown by the deceased's friends and companions was quite apparent. For there was an unusually large attendance of seafaring men accompanied by their wives and relatives at the graveside.

An impressive service was conducted by the vicar of Holy Trinity, Rev. C. J. Hollis, and mourners were emotionally affected by the intense grief shown by the stricken widow, who found it impossible to contain her sorrow.

Floral tributes displayed the large measure of respect that Mark Benn had commanded, particularly from the sea-going community.

Ten weeks later, on Thursday morning 2 May, a fierce storm blew up unleashing its terrible might on trawlers anchored off Worthing. One of them, belonging to George Newman, a fisherman and lifeboatman, was driven ashore onto one of the long groynes east of Splash Point smashing one side of the boat in several places.

It seemed to be a total wreck, until a local boat builder examined it and cut away some planking for a closer examination. He estimated that £27 would cover the cost of the repairs necessary to make the craft seaworthy once more.

Newman, like other fishermen, did not have this kind of money. On his behalf a public appeal was instigated by the commodore and vice-commodore of the Sailing Club, Alderman E. T. Cooksey and John Roberts respectively. It resulted in the sum of £20 0s.6d. being contributed by sympathisers.

At a meeting of the Fishermen's and Watermen's Benefit Association on Thursday evening 9 May, secretary Frank Dean was instructed to pay the balance of £7 from their funds. Repairs were then carried out on George Newman's boat, enabling him to continue fishing for a living.

The Marshalls pushing off their *Jolly Sailor* with pleasure trippers aboard.

Worthing fishermen were governed by regulations set by the Sussex Sea Fisheries Committee who continued to hold regular meetings at Brighton. At one of these quarterly meetings it was reported that the clerk had received a letter of resignation from one of the fishery officers for Worthing, George Belton, in which he wrote that he would be leaving the town shortly. It was decided to take no steps to fill the vacancy for the time being.

Local fisherman and boatman Harry Marshall discovered a body on the beach early one May Saturday morning. He found the corpse at 5.30 a.m. lying about 25 feet below high water mark, in line with his stand opposite Augusta Place, having evidently been left there by the receding tide.

The deceased was identified as a domestic servant by the name of Alice Stock, who had been lodging with Mrs. Elizabeth Jane Bush of 42 Orme Road. She had been in service in Worthing for little more than a year, having come from Woolwich originally, or so it was thought. Drowned just eight days after arriving at Mrs. Bush's house, the news came as a great shock to her landlady.

Orme Road looking west from its junction with South Farm Road.³

A lovelorn tale came to light at the ensuing inquest, where it transpired that the landlady's son, William Charles Bush, who lived with his parents, had known Alice for about six months. The 23 year-old told the coroner that he had been out with her occasionally but had not been courting her.

He confessed to the foreman of the jury that he believed that this 30 year old woman had fancied him!

Since she had been living in the same house as the young man she loved, her health had deteriorated rapidly. She had complained of being unable to sleep and of pains in her head, and on three days in the last week of her life she had not got up until after dinner as she felt so bad.

A feeling brought on, no doubt, by depression as a result of her being unable to satisfy her cravings for this younger man whom she had come to love so much.

On examining the evidence I would say that she had made a decision to end her life on the Friday. She had got up after dinner, seeming quite bright when she went downstairs, and had even washed-up her landlady's dinner things for her.

At four o'clock in the afternoon she had left the house, never to return!

She would have been determined to succeed with the suicide, because had she been found alive, she would have been charged with attempted suicide. The penalty could have been horrendous - a long term prison sentence.

Such a heart-wrenching story and an unnecessary waste of life.

We now move from a seaside suicide to a matter of a more positive nature: raising funds to maintain the RNLI's round-the-clock life saving service.

In much a similar way as they they did in the previous year, Worthing lifeboatmen travelled by train to the inland market town of Kingston for the borough's Lifeboat Saturday. Here, they boarded a demonstration lifeboat, which was pulled through the town on a carriage. It proved to be a great attraction to the carnival crowds, and many people were tempted to part with a few coppers. The pennies mounted up into numerous pounds, satisfying the erstwhile efforts of the crew and organisers.

A demonstration lifeboat manned by Worthing lifeboatmen at Kingston on Lifeboat Saturday, 6 July 1907.

The *Richard Coleman* putting to sea, east of the Pier.

At Worthing, the lifeboat was involved in a demonstration of lifesaving lifebuoys. The rings, intended to support people who had fallen into the sea, were tested during the quarterly lifeboat practice on Thursday afternoon 15 August.

A very large gathering of visitors witnessed the launch of the *Richard Coleman* from the beach to the east of the pier.

Soon after the boat had gone out, three members of the Swimming Club - Mr. E. A. Paine (captain), Mr. F. P. Twine (honorary secretary) and Mr. J. M. Head - all dived from the Pier into the sea clinging onto one lifebuoy between them.

It kept all three of them afloat adequately proving its buoyancy.

To complete the practice, the lifeboat moved in, picked all three swimmers up and landed them at the Pier head in such a precise manoeuvre that the *Richard Coleman* never touched the piles.

In Library Place, not far from the Pier, a change in the constitution of the boat-building firm Belton & Sons took place. A new partnership was formed in 1907, embracing E. H. Cooksey, eldest of Alderman E. T. Cooksey's three sons, with Messrs H. J. and H. G. Belton[4].

The new firm was to be known as Belton & Co.

Adapting themselves to the changing demands of the times their business included an increasing amount of motor launch construction. But they continued to build the traditional type of craft; in fact one of their most important commissions at this time was the building of a new pleasure yacht for that Brighton celebrity, Captain Fred Collins, who had been a regular customer over the years.

The boat, which was 28 feet on the keel with an overall length of 35 feet, was a great credit to the yard, and particularly to Jack Dowds, the foreman responsible for getting the hand-crafted boats finished to a high standard, and out on time.

The boatbuilding premises of Belton & Co. in Library Place. Second from left is bowler-hatted Jack Dowds.

The late John Belton had commenced business on his own account about 30 years earlier at a yard in Alfred Place. Prior to that he had served his apprenticeship in James Hutchinson's yard, near the present lifeboat house on the seafront.

It was from Hutchinson's yard that, among other craft, a succession of yachts had been built for a Captain Thulleson of Brighton. The fourth vessel crafted for him, a beautiful yacht 32 feet on the keel and with a 10 foot beam, had been launched in 1858. Said to have been the largest on Brighton beach, she had been much admired by all who had seen her.

In 1888 the yard had been sold by auction for development; this being the only available spot for building operations between the Pier and Heene Terrace in the late 19th century. Such was the irresistable advance of the enterprising builder that it deprived the seafront of one of its most interesting places, where the curious in such matters would linger awhile to see the busy workmen deftly fashioning the craft that were to sail upon the sea.

Belton-built boats were frequently used at the various Town Regattas along the Sussex coast.

The beach east of Worthing Pier, busy with Edwardian holidaymakers and pleasure craft.

The 1907 regatta season in Worthing was dominated by animosity between the Worthing watermen and the Town Regatta Committee. Bad feelings between the Worthing boatmen and the Regatta promoters were deep-rooted, for as long ago as 1859 Worthing boatmen had been at logger-heads with regatta organisers.

At that time, some 48 years earlier, Worthing boatmen had refused to enter their boats for two reasons. Firstly, in their exclusive race, Worthing watermen had been offered prizes of less than half the value of those offered to competitors in other races. Secondly, they had known that the Worthing boats, built principally for pleasure trips and made flat to haul up on the beach, would have been up against unfair competition from lighter boats, built purposely for sailing and rowing matches, from Shoreham, Newhaven, Littlehampton and Brighton.

The regatta committee, however, determined that the sport should not be sacrificed, had then thrown open all of the prizes to entrants from the other Sussex towns. Having then found entries pouring in, the Worthingites had decided to swallow their pride and join in, even though they would have been up against superior craft. That was in 1859.

Back to 1907 now, the watermen expressed a preference to hold their own separate regatta this year, but the Town Regatta Committee tried to persuade them not to and to make do with the usual watermen's races in the principal fixture.

Only a few weeks before the Watermen's Regatta was scheduled to take place, the secretary of the Town Regatta wrote to his counterpart on the Watermen's Regatta committee:

'At a meeting of the committee of the Town Regatta held last evening, it was suggested that I should write and ask you to kindly call a meeting of your committee, to appoint two of your members, with power to act, to meet in friendly conference my committee, with the view of adjusting any little differences that may exist, and to enable both committees to work amicably and cordially together.

'As soon as I hear from you that you have appointed your delegates I will arrange for an early meeting between us.'

The honorary secretary of the Watermen's Regatta, Steve Wingfield, junior, pertly replied thus:

'At a meeting of the committee held last evening it was decided to carry out the Regatta themselves. Thanking your committee for kind offer.'

Having declined the offer of association the Worthing fishermen and boatmen were determined to proceed with their projected regatta.

This is how the editor of the Worthing Gazette published his opinion on the matter:

'We shall thus get a supplementary season for the entertainment of our visitors, though it is greatly to be regretted that the present situation has arisen. It would probably have been possible to obviate the trouble if the subscribers to the Town Regatta had been called together at an earlier date, so that time would have been given for friendly negotiations between the persons more immediately concerned.'

Acting in the interest of unity, Councillor G. H. Warne made a special offer of five guineas to the prize fund; but it was all too little and too late, for by then the watermen had announced a date, 14 August. They were determined to go ahead with their projected regatta two weeks prior to the Town Regatta even though the date clashed with that which had been set a long time ago for another event in the town, the Horticultural Society Summer Show.

Waterman Fred Marshall 'oiling the tarpaulin' at his stand on the beach.

Tom Wingfield acted as Collector raising a grand total of £51 15s. 6d. in subscriptions from local businesses and townsfolk to enable the additional event to be staged. The sturdy team of fishermen cum lifeboatmen who had organised themselves into a committee included George Belton (chairman), Jack Burgess, Tom Belton, Harry Blann, T. Clark, F. Collier, J. Hutchinson, Harry and Fred Marshall, Charlie Stubbs, Jo Street, Steve Wingfield senior, George Wingfield, Wm. Wells, and Fred Wakeford.

On the day arranged for this Watermen's Regatta, a strong south westerly wind and a choppy sea prevented the fixture from being held, and it had to be postponed to the following day. The next morning the outlook was far more promising but in the afternoon the weather deteriorated again, becoming particularly unfavourable for the rowing boats, many of which shipped a good deal of water while negotiating the course.

Many hundreds of people had gathered on the Pier and the adjacent beach to watch an attractive programme of nearly a dozen events, including a sailing race, a water polo match, and the inevitable competition of walking the greasy pole.

First-class pair-oared boats lined up for the start of the first race under the authority of the two starters, Messrs H. Pocock and H. Allen. They were away. It was a good race despite the choppy sea causing intakes of water. Harry and Fred Wingfield's *Marie Elsie* won by about four lengths to gain the first prize of £2 10s. The Wingfield family did well in this race: George Wingfield's *Lily* came second to win £1 10s., while Tom Wingfield's *Albert Edward* was third, winning 15s. In fourth place came Wm. Wells' *Burma Ruby* for 5s. prize money; and George Belton's *Ivy* was unplaced.

A north east view of the Bandstand and the shelter on its seaward side.[5]

A sailing race, which was open to members of the sailing club, was won by F. Dean's *Peggy*, completing the course in 45 minutes, two minutes ahead of J. Newman and J. Hubbard's *Lily*. An easy decision for the two judges, Messrs. H. Allen and J. Howell.

Several local dignitaries graced the afternoon's proceedings with their presence. One of these upper crust spectators, Sir Henry Aubrey Fletcher, took a particular interest in the race for first class three-oared boats. I am not sure why he singled out this event; but it may have been that one of the boat's names printed in the programme caught his eye, being as the sporty boats were named after various females, and Sir Henry tended to live up to his reputation of being a ladies' man. With avid intent, he watched this most exciting race which culminated in a dramatic finish with Jack Burgess's *Ethel Mary* first past the marker buoys. By barely a quarter of a length it beat William Wells' *Nellie*. In turn, she only just beat Fred Wakeford's *Kathleen* by a similar margin. They won £3, £2 and £1 respectively. Two boats were unplaced: Tom Belton's *Fanny* and George Wingfield's *Blue Eyed Maid*.

For the old-timers exclusively, that was fishermen and boatmen over the age of 60, there was a double sculling race. Tom Clarke in *Dorothy* was the first to finish, winning goods to the value of £1. George Wingfield, a hoary old fisherman in *Water Lily*, came second for a prize worth 10s., followed by Charlie Lee, ex-coxswain of the Worthing lifeboat, in *Maid of the Mist*, who qualified for the third prize valued at 5s. The venerable George Belton finished unplaced in *Florry*.

An interval during the afternoon's events was occupied by a water polo match played between two local teams, one headed by Mr. A Hudson and the other by Mr. E. A. Paine. In an exciting game four goals were scored. Each captain netted the ball once as did Nicholls and F. Cogar, to finish at a draw, two all.

Boat racing events in the latter part of the programme continued with one for 2nd Class three-oared boats. Harry Hargood, observing the race from a prominent position on the Pier, shouted words of encouragement to each of the competitors in turn. Although he was a well-to-do and hard-working businessman, he had always enjoyed a special comradeship with the watermen: not only did he represent them when dealing with various authorities, but he also liked to see them enjoying themselves. His inspiring cries led to to F. Collier in *Mizpah* winning easily by almost 12 lengths to net a prize worth a magnificent £3. Second and third positions were both taken by two Wingfields, George and Steve, in *Master Donald* and *Olive Branch*. Again one of George Belton's boats *Elsie* was unplaced as was Jo Street's *Pansy*.

There followed a pair-oared race for mature licensed watermen over 45 years of age to be rowed in second class pair-oared boats. Steve Wingfield in *Primrose* won by two lengths to qualify for a prize of £2, closely followed by his relative George Wingfield in *White Rose*. Two lengths behind George came Harry and Fred Marshall's *Bertha* and in fourth place was S. Wingfield's *General White* leaving Fred Wakeford's *Alfred* unplaced.

Swimming Club members walked the greasy pole for a total of five prizes. A. Street won the first prize of 10s. which had been donated by Mr. J. Cove, a draper from Montague Street. Legs of mutton, generously given by several companies, the Canterbury Mutton Company, Messrs W. and R. Fletcher Ltd., Messrs Ainslie Bros. and Messrs Nelson Ltd, were awarded to four runners-up – E. A. Paine, S. A. Cragg, W. Boyse and A. Parsons.

A relative of Parsons had competed in the greasy pole event at the 1863 Worthing Regatta 44 years before. Another contestant on that earlier historic day, a young man named James Burtenshaw (related to my great, great, great grandmother whose maiden name was Mary Burtenshaw) had been disqualified for cheating – he had got astride of the pole instead of walking on its slippery surface. Apparently he had been under the influence of alcohol, a practice not uncommon, but, some young men could not hold their drink.

The disgrace that had been attached to scenes such as this at early regattas had been felt more by their relatives and friends than by the perpetrators themselves.

We return now to the 1907 Watermen's Regatta. Here the penultimate race involved sculling in skiffs. Under the scrutiny of the Mayor, watching from the beach, Fred Searle in *Francis* beat Steve Wingfield in *Hilda* by one length to take first place. Four lengths separated Steve from George Grevatt in *Lily* and Fred Marshall came fourth in *Annie*. The two unlucky contestants who did not qualify for a prize were C. Collier in *Lilian* and Wm. Wells in *I'm a-Coming*.

The final event, the double-sculling race in first-class pair-oared boats, was again won by Steve Wingfield, this time in *Water Lily*, easily beating F. Collier in *Winnie* by three lengths. But it was a close finish for second place between Collier and J. Hutchinson in *Dorothy*. About 12 yards before the finishing line the *Dorothy* started to overtake F. Stubbs' boat, and only just secured third place by a touch.

At the close of the afternoon's events the winners were presented with their prizes in the Pier Pavilion at the southern end of the Pier by the Mayoress, Mrs. F. C. Linfield.

Towards the end of the afternoon the weather had worsened to such an extent that one of the sailing races had to be postponed for two weeks until Thursday afternoon 29 August, the day after the Annual Regatta.

On the newly appointed day there were 13 competitors in all. The winner was Bill Blann in *Never Can Tell*, followed by F. Collier in *Princess May*, a boat named after Princess Alice Mary,

A smartly-dressed lady customer[6] assisting boatman Fred Marshall
in rotating his capstan to haul up his boats, c.1907.

A goat chaise on West Parade. In the background is the Pier Pavilion, and in the foreground a capstan,
on which a poster is displayed, reading: Watermens' Regatta Sailing Race Thursday August 29th.

the wife of the Prince of Wales, and who was to become Queen Mary in the fullness of time. Jack Riddles secured third place in *Breadwinner* while Fred Wakeford came in fourth in *Petrel*. George Wingfield was fifth in *Lancashire Lass* and Jack Burgess sixth *in Spare Moments*.

Over the course of the afternoon, a goat chaise, which was by now a familiar sight on Worthing seafront, gave rides for children on the promenade.

This Watermen's Regatta proved to be financially viable. Subscriptions collected amounted to £51 15s.6d. Out of this, £34 15s. had gone on prizes; £3 10s.10d. had been spent on items such as printing; a swimming club permit cost 5s.; collector's commissions came to £2 4s.6d., and £10 had been disbursed on the open sailing race on August 29th; making the total expenditure £50 15s.4d.

The surplus of £1 0s.2d. encouraged the watermen, who hoped to make their Regatta an annual fixture of equal success.

The traditional Annual Regatta itself was more fortunate weatherwise and was not subjected to postponement. It took place on a brilliant afternoon, so bright that the blue sea appeared to smile in the glowing light of the late summer sun.

Beauty's fairest daughters among gaily-clad throngs of holiday makers teasingly flaunted their attributes to catch the attention of muscular, tanned oarsmen.

Quite slack, gleaming sails of countless boats studded the sea. It had never happened that absolutely perfect weather prevailed for this fixture. For although conditions were magnificent for the rowing contests and for the large crowds of spectators who watched the proceedings, there was not enough wind to speed the sailing boats over the course, with the result that one of the events did not conclude until 20 minutes past seven in the evening.

Edwardian ladies on cast iron seating at the sea end of the Pier.
This panoramic view of seafront buildings also shows the Pier's gas lamps and flagpoles.

More than 2,000 people were said to have paid for admission to the Pier during the day but this number could not be claimed as a record.

The occasion was organised by a committee of more than 20, under the chairmanship of Alderman E. T. Cooksey, and comprised representatives of the several local sporting clubs whose co-operation enabled an extensive programme to be framed.

A fairly new and popular feature was a handicap for beach motor boats which produced 17 entries, to be judged by Mr. E. G. Pope. But instead of all competing together several heats were raced and the handicaps worked out afterwards. More than half an hour elapsed while they were doing all this and the event proved to be the most boring part of the afternoon for the spectators.

The first race on the programme was a race for dandy or lug-rigged boats not exceeding 17 feet, belonging to licensed watermen. Ten contestants were despatched by the official starter, John Roberts. Bang went the gun. They were off, but their progress was sluggish. Riddles in *Breadwinner* later recalled that he had never known such a slow race. He had all the sail exposed to what little breeze there was, and he just managed to ease ahead of Collier's *Princess May*.

"I managed to maintain my lead until the last leg", explained Riddles, "but then the *Princess May*'s superior canvas edged her into the lead to win." The first prize was £2, and the second, £1 10s. Steve Wingfield's *Kitty* came in third, and was awarded £1 in prize money. Fourth position was attained by *Dandy Dick*, a boat belonging to the Blann brothers, Harry and Bill. They were not totally disappointed, for they won 10s.

In a pair-oared race for local amateurs the second prize to the value of £1 was awarded to F. Stubbs and H. E. Snewin.

Coastguards' four-oared galleys competed for a first prize of £2, which was won by the Kingston-on-Sea crew. As Lancing and Worthing rowed a dead heat, the official judge, Mr. C.H. Aldridge, declared that the second and third prizes of £1 10s. and £1 were divided between them.

A Coastguards tug-of-war in boats resulted in the defeat of Lancing by Kingston.

In a greasy pole contest, three of the competitors were successful, Feest, Parsons, and the favourite, Jo Street.

Jo Street junior[7] proudly displaying a prized catch of a large conger eel at his stand opposite Prospect Place.

A display by members of the Amateur Boat Club from a raft moored close to the Pier head provided some additional amusement.

Prizes were distributed by the Mayoress in Steyne Gardens before the usual and very popular firework display finale.

The turning of the sea, from being a relatively placid medium providing pleasure, into a powerfully monstrous element could affect the comparative stability of family life. I can understand this for whereas the Blann's have derived much enjoyment from Regattas since they first started they have also suffered the loss's of several loved ones at the hands of the wickedly cruel sea – John Belville, my great great great grandfather, drowned in the attempt to render assistance to the distressed barque *Lalla Rookh* in 1850, and Edwin and Ellen Blann, my great great grand uncle and aunt, drowned when a freak storm blew up in 1858 whilst they were taking a party out for a pleasure cruise. The boat sank.[8]

In a wider concern for imperilled sailors local interest in the Shipwrecked Mariners' Society was promoted by their two Worthing representatives: Rear-Admiral Leicester C. Keppel of Strafford House, Downview Road, and Councillor W. Walter of Marden House, Grafton Road.

Regular subscribers to the charity were interested to learn that the collection box attached to the Coastguard's flagstaff on the Parade near the lifeboat house yielded the sum of £2 4s. for 1907, compared with £2 15s.9d. for the year before that. The sum of 5s.6d. was also collected in the box in one of the refreshment rooms at the railway station.

In earlier days when Worthing possessed a large number of fishing luggers, the Fishermen's Mutual Insurance Society had been of considerable use. Locally-built luggers had been made to a high degree of strength to withstand the tempestuous conditions of the North Sea herring fishery. One such craft had been the *The Daring*, constructed by a Mr. W. Richardson of Worthing, and registered at 31 tons. This heavy lugger had been able to venture forth in rougher seas than many of its lighter counterparts.

With the decay of the fishing industry the need for such an institution as the Fishermen's Insurance Society had now virtually disappeared, yet the excellent work was continued on a somewhat different basis.

Chapel Road looking north c. 1907. Worthing's General Post Office is on the facing corner of Market Street.[9]

The newer rules, which had now received the sanction of the Registrar of Friendly Societies, permitted the application of funds to boat owners, fishermen and watermen of the town who may have suffered a loss or misfortune which in the opinion of the committee of management entitled them to relief.

The Society's fund at this time, the major part of which was on deposit at the Post Office Savings Bank, stood at nearly £1,000. It provided some useful financial assistance to needy boatmen during 1907. A total of £62 16s.6d. was disbursed in allowances of half-a-crown (2s.6d.) and three and six (3s.6d.) per week to a dozen old fishermen who were about 70 years of age. Out of these 12, three passed away before the end of the year.

The management committee: Messrs F. Beck, W. Benn, G. Benn, T. Davis, E. Edwards and W. Lucas also instructed that £7 be given towards the cost of repairing a damaged fishing boat.

Business meetings never commanded large audiences unless the occasion was of an exceptional character. One such gathering with an unusually high attendance was the annual meeting of the Worthing RNLI – the largest so far in the history of the branch.

Held in its usual place, the Council Chamber, on Wednesday afternoon 11 March 1908, the meeting was presided over by the Chairman, Mr. H. Hargood J.P. It is interesting to note that there were a number of ladies present, including Mrs. Hargood, Mrs. Livesay, Mrs. Latham Brown, Miss Parry and Miss Wigham.

Others in attendance included the Mayor, Deputy Mayor, an alderman, a councillor, a captain, a vicar, John Roberts (honorary secretary), Mr. R. J. Fry (Collector) and Coxswain Harry Marshall. It was recorded that the District Inspector had at each visit expressed his satisfaction with the excellent order of the Station and the efficiency of all the staff.

Fortunately the services of the *Richard Coleman* had not been required during the past year, but during the severe autumn gales, when so many casualties had occurred around the British coast, everything had been ready for a launch at a moment's notice.

The coxswain, second coxswain, bowman, signalman and indeed all the crew were always ready at any hour of the day or night. They had never failed the committee yet, and the service board outside the Station showed a record of 48 lives saved[10], which could bear comparison with any other Station on the Sussex coast.

With regard to the financial position the committee regretted a further decrease of £5 in the annual remittance to head office. The amount being £70 compared with £75 the previous year. And whilst they were sorry to lose, through death, an unusually large number of old and generous subscribers, they earnestly trusted that their places might be filled by some of the new residents moving into the town and its neighbourhood.

A view from Steyne Gardens looking northward up High Street. On the left is Colonnade House.

The seafront *Stanhoe Hotel*[11] at the junction of Augusta Place.

The Mayor pointed out that the Branch had raised an average of about £5 per week throughout the year, and to him that appeared satisfactory.

Reviewing the operations of the past year, the chairman pointed out that the smaller grant to the parent institution might be accounted for by the fact that there had been no collection last year by the Salvation Army, as they had been unable to secure the Bandstand for the Sunday they thought it had been promised. They hadn't made their usual collection at the Sacred Concert on the Pier in August either.

Winding up the annual meeting, the Deputy Mayor moved a vote of thanks for Harry Hargood in recognition of his untiring energy and perseverance.

The good work of the lifeboat service was illustrated later that evening by an interesting lantern lecture entitled 'Our Brave Lifeboatmen.' It was shown at the Primitive Methodist Mission Chapel in Lyndhurst Road by a Mr. W. T. Streader, who it was said possessed an intimate acquaintance with the noble work of life-saving.

At this time the RNLI had 285 lifeboats stationed around the British Isles, and expenses were increasing every year, especially with the introduction of motor and steam lifeboats.

During the past year the Institution had been instrumental in saving 932 lives, compared with 561 in the preceding 12 months, making a total of 47,345 lives saved since its inception.

Our own vigilant coxswain, Harry Marshall, spotted a vessel in difficulties in this same month of March. It subsequently grounded off Worthing and this lead to a spot of nautical unrest. When the barque *Truro* stranded, the crew became insubordinate, claiming that the vessel ought to be surveyed for damage before proceeding on her voyage. But when the British sailing ship did manage to continue her journey without such an inspection her Russian crew mutinied.

When the *Truro* neared Spithead her Captain requested help by flying distress signals. The captain of a vessel in the vicinity, the cruiser H.M.S. *Berwick*, responded by sending a naval party of 12 armed Royal Marine Light Infantrymen aboard, who took charge of the barque and sailed her into Portsmouth. Here, two members of the crew, considered to be the ringleaders, were removed from the ship and taken to the Russian Consul, while the rest were pacified.

Another maritime incident, one of quite an alarming nature, created a sensation at Worthing during Easter. Two gentlemen, named Porter and Renton, accompanied by a lady friend, had set off in a small sailing boat from one of the bungalows on Shoreham Beach in the direction of Worthing on the Sunday morning.

They passed Worthing Pier about 10 a.m. and when they were a short distance west of the structure they decided it was time to head back for Shoreham.

Whilst in the act of turning the boat about, disaster struck!

A sudden wind capsized it, throwing all three occupants into the sea!

Promenaders on the seafront were alarmed when they saw the accident happen some three to four hundred yards out from the shore. But fortunately for the Shoreham joytrippers their plight had been noticed by several watermen on the beach who, in a very short space of time, sped in their boats to the rescue.

A boat belonging to a Mr. Tuff of High Street was the first to reach the spot, quickly followed by Harry Marshall and his brother, who brought the immersed passengers ashore. All three were absolutely exhausted and received every attention, including restoratives and a change of garments from the proprietor of the *Stanhoe Hotel*.

The feeling among the large crowd of excited onlookers, who had gathered on the seafront, was that, but for the promptness of the rescuers, the accident would have resulted in a fatality.

Yet another mishap occurred during that springtime. Two fishermen suffered from a serious misfortune when they lost some valuable equipment in April. Nearly new trammel nets worth about £25 went adrift while my great grandfather, Harry Blann, and his brother Bill were out fishing with them.

As it happened at the beginning of the season 50 year old Harry and Bill, 47, were likely to experience considerable hardship. It was hoped that some assistance may have been forthcoming from the Fishermen's and Watermen's Benefit Association, but as this would only represent a portion of the loss the case was laid before the public in anticipation that some would be disposed to assist the worthy cause. The brothers Blann, both members of the lifeboat crew, were considered 'Men of the very highest character for industry and respectability.'

Donations included 3s. from a Mr. G. Pilgrim and a cheque for £1 from their member of Parliament, Sir Henry Aubrey-Fletcher, Bart. About £25 in all was received, and the two Blann brothers expressed their sincere and heart-felt thanks, through the Worthing Gazette, to all who so generously assisted them.

Facing Steyne Gardens is the Broadway in Brighton Road, photographed between 1902 and 1906. Worthing was well-known for its mature trees, but like so many others the fine shade-providing specimens pictured here have since been removed to ease 20th century traffic congestion.

Footnotes

[1] Photographed by Edwards & Son.

[2] The young lad peeping out from the boathouse, and just seen between Bill Blann and Arthur Marshall, was told to keep out of the way while filming was in progress. He is Harry Marshall's 3rd son, Harry. The Station's service board can be seen in its normal position, affixed to the wall adjoining the left hand side of the boathouse.

[3] Orme Road runs parallel with the railway, just south of the South Farm Road level crossing. Little has changed since this photograph was taken: the rows of terraced houses are still there today; and even the corner shop, then occupied by Patching & Co., is now stocked with antiques behind the same shopfront.

[4] Herbert George Belton's grandaughter, Janet Belton, lives in Worthing.

[5] The shelter to the seaward side of the bandstand was put up in 1907.

[6] On the back of this photograph, the woman is identified only by the initials J.G.

[7] Joseph Thomas William Street was born at Plymouth in 1876, and moved to Worthing with his father.

[8] The full story of the 1858 boating disaster can be found in 'A Town's Pride' on pages 17-19

[9] Market Street, which went from Chapel Road through to High Street was almost completely obliterated in a town centre restructuring scheme which destroyed the character and the heart of Worthing. Now all that remains of Market Street is a truncated stub at the west end.

[10] The figures on the Worthing Lifeboat Station's service board, now in Worthing Museum, total 43 lives saved up until 1907. There is a blank space opposite '1899 *Prince Llewellyn*' where there should be a figure 5.

[11] A picture postcard published by G.H. Austin of 77 Montague Street. Originally Augusta House, the *Stanhoe Hotel* was demolished in 1948. The levelled site was used for car parking until the 1960's when a monstrously ugly, concrete multi-storey car park was thrust upon Worthing's coastline. This abscess interrupts a hitherto unspoilt view of Worthing's grand Victorian seafront. I see no reason why the multi-storey should not have a period facade to blend with its neighbouring buildings. What an asset to the town that would be!

Henry Hayden, Worthing Piermaster 1869-1886.

Chapter 5

Loyal Servants, Supporters & Subjects

1908

Salty ex-mariner Tom Belton retired from his post as Piermaster in March after nearly 21 years in the service of the Pier Company since taking over from Henry Hayden[1], who had died in 1886. Seventy two year old Belton[2], who in his colourful life had sailed many parts of the world, was now suffering from asthma, and sought to lighten his daily labours in his advancing years. On Saturday 7 March, this ex-fisherman appeared at the toll-house for the last time as the Pier's recognised custodian. His successor was a Mr. C. Irvine Bacon from Brentford, the first non-seaman to be appointed. His official title was Piermaster and Sub-Manager.

Not far from the Pier, another branch of the Belton family continued to produce high quality craft. Craftsmen at industrious boatbuilders Belton & Co., in Library Place, turned out another new boat for Captain Fred Collins of Brighton.

The new yacht was christened by Worthing's Mayor, Alderman F. C. Linfield, J.P., during the afternoon of Wednesday 8 April 1908, and was named *Skylark* after its predecessors. On its inaugural trip, that afternoon, Captain Collins raised funds for one of his favourite local charities, the Brighton and Sussex Eye Hospital, by charging a considerable number of passengers a fee for the pleasure of being the first to sail in his new craft. Entertained by music on board they throughly enjoyed the novel experience.

Supplementary to the boatbuilding operations Belton & Co. ran a chandlery stores from a shop not far from their yard. They advertised all types of motor launch and boat fittings, fishing tackle, varnish and paints for sale. They supplied ropes, lines and twines wholesale as well as retail; and carried out all kinds of canvas work on sails.

The *Richard Coleman* being led by horses eastward along Marine Parade, passing its junction with Paragon Street.

The shop is still there today, Ken Dunman's, 2, Marine Place, just off the seafront east of the the Pier, now specialising in providing fishing tackle.

When the quarterly lifeboat drill fell due at the end of May, it was coupled with the RNLI inspector's half-yearly visit. Lieutenant Keppel Foote, R.N., the Inspector of lifeboats for the southern district, which extended from Harwich to Devonshire, viewed the boathouse before going out in the *Richard Coleman*. Having got off in a calm sea the lifeboatmen practised for an hour and a half under sail in the gentle south westerly wind, observed intently by branch chairman Harry Hargood, and honorary secretary John Roberts, beside a throng of attentive spectators. As a result the inspector was very pleased with the ready state of the station and the efficiency of the lifeboat and its crew.

Boatmen on the beach to the west of the pier, concerned that a proposed extension of breastwork on the beach would interfere with their occupations of fishing and boating, consequently complained to the authorities in London. In a petition, written to the Board of Trade in May, five Worthing boatmen urged that the scheme, which concerned the beach to the west of the bandstand, would be dangerous for boats, and that the proposition had been resolved without regard for the boatmen or their right to use the foreshore.

The board subsequently wrote to Worthing Borough Council, who attempted to settle the matter by recommending that it would not contemplate any works below high-water mark of ordinary spring tides, and that for the time being the breastwork would only be continued for 25 feet. However, before proceeding with the remainder of the work the council were to endeavour to reach agreement with two of the boatmen who were to be particularly affected, by re-siting them elsewhere on the beach.

Individuals wanting to become professional licensed boatmen had to apply to Worthing Borough Council in writing. But applications were considered only once a year, traditionally 24 June.

Names of applicants were posted on the beach at the beginning of June, several weeks prior to the committee meeting, during which time objections could be lodged by existing watermen if they felt that any of the aspirants were not proficient, whereupon proper enquiries would be made by the committee.

Youngsters watching a white-trousered boatman on the beach west of the Bandstand.

At its sitting, on 24 June 1908, the Mayor mentioned that he had received an invitation for the Council to attend St. Paul's Church in Chapel Road, Worthing, on 19 July for Lifeboat Sunday. Although many councillors would be taking their holidays at that time, the Mayor welcomed the opportunity of attending the established Church for the first time during his term of office. But Alderman Patching questioned the wisdom of this suggestion stating that they attended divine worship officially with the Mayor, regardless of denomination, but if they did in this case they would have to conform on every Lifeboat Sunday.

Councillor Morecraft was quick to point out that Lifeboat Day occurred only once in three years. But the matter was left in abeyance until the July meeting to enable His Worship to ascertain how many members would be likely to accompany him.

The question of whether circumstances would permit the municipal authorities to attend the triennial Lifeboat Sunday was ultimately determined. Townsfolk were gratified to learn that the local authority took an interest in this worthwhile fund-raising day: they were duly represented at the morning service alongside Harry Hargood J.P.

Wearing his scarlet robes and chain of office, and preceded by the mace-bearer, the Mayor, Alderman F. C. Linfield, J.P., was accompanied by the Deputy Mayor, the Town Clerk, the Medical Officer of Health, the Borough Surveyor, the Rate Collector, the Sanitary Inspector, the Corporation Cashier, the Assistant Clerk to the Education Committee, the Chief Officer of the Borough Fire Brigade, and a number of aldermen and councillors.

The Public Library and Museum[3], opened in December 1908.

On their way in to the church, many of them faltered to glance right at a building site on the opposite corner of Richmond Road, previously adorned by Richmond House. The new building was to be the town's Public Library and Museum.

Once inside the church, the noblemen were shown to pews reserved for them at the front before the service began, then the whole congregation sang the National Anthem.

The vicar, the Rev. E. J. Cunningham prefaced his sermon by a few words of welcome for the Mayor and Corporation, and said that this visit was another illustration of the great truth that where the public good was concerned they were able to lay aside the differences that divided them.

They were more than welcome because their presence marked the importance of a great institution for saving life. The RNLI had a grand history and now controlled nearly 300 equipped boats, whose crews were prepared to go forth in the fiercest storms to rescue human beings.

This noble work depended, in the first instance, upon the courage and devotion of our sailors and fisherman in pulling together, but courage and devotion, the vicar reminded his attentive audience, would be useless without organisation and the boats which the Institution provided, and he accordingly appealed for their generous monetary support.

The service concluded with the fellowship fervently singing two appropriate hymns: Eternal Father Strong to Save; and Fierce Raged the Tempest; to the accompaniment of Mr. C. Robinson at the organ.

The lifeboat crew themselves attended evening service at St. Paul's when more cash was collected for the philanthropic cause. Funds were further boosted by collections made at most of the 14 churches in the town, as well as at those in the immediate locality.

To the same end, the Salvation Army Band performed in Steyne Gardens, and the Ladies' Orchestra and Male Voice Choir gave a Sacred Concert on the Pier in aid of lifeboat funds. Altogether, amounts totalling £166 were collected as a result of this triennial appeal.

A year ago, in 1907, Worthing had been favoured with two regattas – the town's Annual Regatta as well as the Watermen's Regatta – both held in the same month, putting a strain on local resources.

But this year the prospects of the town's Annual Regatta appeared to be hanging in the balance. In July still nothing had been arranged. As a result a strong feeling existed among regular supporters of the Town Regatta that a carnival should be held instead, thereby promoting various local sporting clubs. The profits arising from such an event could be passed, it was thought, to Worthing Hospital.

The interior of St. Paul's Church, looking towards the high altar, c.1908

A view of the east elevation of St. Paul's Church, Chapel Road.

The last regatta had proved successful with the assistance of the Worthing Amateur Boat Club, when the race for motor beach boats had attracted a large number of competitors from Brighton and Littlehampton as well as Arundel.

However, the Regatta committee's chairman did not want to be re-elected this year, even though he had been associated with organising the event for over 20 years. As his reasons for stepping down he cited the lack of unity and the friction of the previous year.

Following an announcement in June that the Watermen's Regatta would take place in August, some of those collecting subscriptions for the event stated that theirs was to be the only regatta this year. But one of these collectors, Mr. Wingfield, who was also associated with the Town Regatta had kept an open mind on this point when dealing with subscribers.

August soon arrived and, despite Worthing recording more bright sunshine than any other U.K. town during 1908, showery weather prevailed during the Watermen's Regatta on 5 August. But that Wednesday afternoon the sea was fairly calm and an attractive programme of 10 events including a swimming race and diving was held. In addition all the traditional rowing races for the licensed boatmen and fishermen, as well as the traditional Walking the Greasy Pole were run.

It had all been arranged by a committee of local watermen-cum-lifeboatmen under the chairmanship of Fred Marshall with his brother Harry as treasurer. Four members of the Wingfield family were on the committee: Steve junior (secretary), his father, Steve, Tom (collector) and George. The other four committee members were well-known: Jo Street, F. Collier, Wm. Wells and Fred Wakeford.

In the evening the Mayoress, Mrs. F. C. Linfield, presented the prizes during the interval at an illuminated promenade concert in Steyne Gardens. Then she herself received a bouquet from Lifeboat Coxswain Harry Marshall's little daughter.

Speaking on behalf of the watermen, the Mayor thanked the townspeople for the generous support that they had given to the Regatta that afternoon. In expressing that the boatmen fully deserved this recognition he assured visitors that they would be perfectly safe in entrusting their lives to the Worthing watermen whenever they went for a row on the sea, and he even ventured to think that they would not find a better class of man, or a more civil and obliging set of boatmen, at any seaside place.

Three steamers[4] at Worthing Pier, c. 1908. The one seen leaving on the right is the *Worthing Belle* of the Brighton, Worthing & South Coast Steamboat Company.

At the end of his speech the Mayor was enthusiastically applauded by the large crowd.

During the following week the Watermen's Regatta committee tendered their special thanks to Sir Henry Aubrey-Fletcher, the Mayor, Councillor Denton and the directors of the Pier Company, Mr. Hargood and Mr. Shanley; and showed their appreciation to subscribers generally for their kind patronage and support. The Regatta was a financial success as the balance sheet reveals:

Receipts

Balance from 1907	£1 0s 2d
Entrance fees	1 1 0
Subscriptions	45 10 0
	£47 11 2

Payments

Prizes	£34 15 6
Committee boat	10 0
Laying buoys, anchors and lines	1 18 0
Hire of gun	2 6
Printing, stationary and postage	1 11 9
Collector's commission, etc.	4 16 9
Balance in hand	3 16 8
	£47 11 2

Sir Henry Aubrey-Fletcher photographed in a cab outside domestic ironmongers Wm. Woodroffe at 5, Chapel Road.

In July, a fisherman's boat as well as one belonging to the coastguard were used to search for a man who disappeared whilst swimming in the sea at Goring. James Greenfield, a carpenter living at 39, Marine Parade, was with his son fishing from a groyne opposite Sea Place, when they saw a young fellow swimming just off the end of the groyne, about 100 yards from the beach. He appeared to be a strong swimmer. Greenfield even remarked to his son on the apparent professionalism of the man's strokes. He seemed to be playing about in the water and frequently changed his position, sometimes swimming with just his right hand and at other times with his left. The man also practised floating on his back.

The attention of two ladies walking along the beach some distance away was diverted from the swimmer to the fisherman, but when they turned round again they could not see the swimmer.

Holidaymakers on the beach at West Worthing. Note the wheeled bathing tents, and also the familiar seaweed.[5]

Excursionists enjoying a paddle on Worthing beach, and local lads shrimping with purpose-made nets.

Greenfield's son mounted the groyne to look whilst Greenfield himself ran up the beach but the young man was nowhere to be seen.

They signalled to some motor boats but they took no notice!

The two ladies went to inform the coastguard while Greenfield and his son continued to try and attract the attention of boatmen on the sea.

Eventually, Mr. Davis's boat came up in response to their signals and rowed about for some time looking for the man.

Worthing Coastguardsman George Crew received information at the flagstaff near Worthing Lifeboat Station, a mile away, that a man was drowned or drowning out to the west. Together with Chief Officer Prowse they immediately took some grappling irons and launched a boat in the direction of Goring.

On arrival at the spot indicated they dragged the grappling irons behind the boat over an area 100 yards either way of the place where the swimmer was last seen. Their efforts, however, were to no avail and at length the chief officer returned to the coastguard station, leaving Crew to wait until the tide receded.

About half an hour later Crew noticed a body lying in some three feet of water, about 100 yards west of the spot where the bather had been seen. Assisted by a police constable by the name of Walder he then brought the body ashore.

Meanwhile, Greenfield's son had found the 'mystery' man's clothing under a groyne and had handed it over to the policeman. It consisted of a dark grey tweed suit, a blue striped flannelette shirt, a lambswool vest, merino pants, elastic braces, a green cap, white knitted tie, a white 'polo' collar, a white handkerchief, black merino socks and a pair of nearly-new boots.

But there was no name on any of the clothing!

There was also a silver Geneva watch, latch key, a second-class return ticket for the Worthing Belle steamer, and £1 9s. 1¼d in cash.

It was estimated that the man was between 25 and 28 years old and from the appearance of his hands it was thought that he might have been a mechanic. Two or three bites on the lip suggested that the man may have had an epileptic fit while in the water.

In an attempt to identify the body the police photographed the drowned man's face and distributed copies to other towns along the coast, as well as to London, and to various other police stations.

This sad bathing fatality occurred so rapidly that even though the incident was seen, it was not possible to save the man, despite it happening in inshore waters.

The pleasure steamer *Worthing Belle* coming in to berth at Worthing Pier.[6]

At the same time as this tragic occurrence, Worthing lifeboatmen were away at Teddington Reach raising money for the RNLI. As part of the local annual carnival and water sports they effected a mock rescue of a number of 'shipwrecked mariners in distress.' Under Coxswain Harry Marshall and his assistant, Second Coxswain Bill Blann, the crewmen launched a lifeboat on the River Thames, with Steve Wingfield as bowman.

At Worthing, the dithering committee set up to discuss the plight of the town's Annual Regatta at last reached a decision – to hold the event on 1 September – and further planned to turn the occasion into an extravaganza by following it up with a Motor and Cycle Carnival the very next day.

Just three weeks before the acquatic event, entries were invited from the public for two sailing races and eight rowing races. There were to be two other races, one from each of the two sections, exclusively for licensed watermen. To enter, a fee of 6d. each was charged.

Townsfolk entered into the carnival spirit and flags began to appear in the town centre.

On the day allotted for the Regatta the weather was awful. Having enjoyed such brilliant summer weather it was most disappointing to find this special day imperilled by unfavourable conditions.

As a consequence the Regatta had to be postponed for three days until the Friday, even though crews had taken the trouble to come from along the south coast, some from as far as Dover and Folkstone.

Wednesday 2 September, the second of the three allotted carnival days, featured the Motor and Cycle Carnival, the only event which was able to be carried out on the appointed day.

People walked into the town from the villages and surrounding area. For those who could afford it, omnibuses provided an important service.

Motor & Cycle Carnival, 1908. Decorated cars in procession along Marine Parade, east of the lifeboathouse.

Motor & Cycle Carnival, 1908. Floral-clad bicycles parading past *Stanhoe Hotel*, Marine Parade.

Motor & Cycle Carnival, 1908. Baby-on-Swan and other bicycle entrants lined up to be judged.

The Arundel omnibus from the Sussex Motor Road Car Co. Ltd. collecting passengers.

Visitors to the promenade on Friday would have soon concluded that something was astir. Gaudy flags were fluttering in the breeze from almost every available point: along the entire length of the Pier, the sea walk, and in front of and on top of many hotels and houses on the seafront.

The state of the weather was still far from desirable but surprisingly a large crowd congregated in defiance of the depressing climate for the deferred Regatta.

Fortunately, however, the sea was fairly smooth and served competing rowing clubs from along the south coast well.

Childrens Carnival on Worthing Pier, 1908

Childrens Carnival on Worthing Pier, 1908

In the coastguard service boats race a team from the Worthing Station pulled into second place, winning a prize worth 25s. The same crew beat the Kingston Coastguards at the tug-of-war by two pulls to one to capture an award worth £1 10s.

Two of the Marshall brothers, Harry and Fred, won the licensed Worthing watermen's race for three-oared 2nd class boats in *Shamrock* to receive £2 prize money.

First place in the sailing race for licensed Worthing watermen was gained by Bill Blann and his brother Harry crewing their craft *Never Can Tell*. They received £2 10s. in cash for this honour.

Amongst allcomers, Messrs Belton & Co. achieved third place at the finish of the handicap motor boat race, which was run under the rules of the Sussex Motor Yacht Club. The performance of their boat *Grass Widow* won goods to the value of 25s., the boatbuilders themselves having donated the 1st prize of a dinghy to be built by their yard.

During the evening, prizes were presented in the Pier Pavilion by Sir Henry Aubrey-Fletcher, Bart., M.P., the carnival's patron.

The children's fete was to have taken place on the Thursday, but as this turned out to be the most wet and discouraging day of the week, the fete was postponed until Saturday. With no fewer than 331 entries in the various classes, including a baby show and dressed dolls as well as races, and the main body of spectators numbering more than 3,000, it was clearly the most successful feature of the carnival.

The Amateur Boat Club played a comic cricket match to lightheartedly conclude an eventful time.

In the summer of 1908, in fact just one week before the big Carnival, a Worthing fisherman had suffered a severe financial loss as the result of a storm. James Bacon's *Albatross* had broken its chain when anchored off the town, had driven ashore and was smashed to pieces.

The total extent of the damage together with the loss of nets and fishing gear was estimated at £50, a calculation supported by a George Bashford who was familiar with the 20 foot long boat which measured 8 feet across the beam.

Bacon, who resided at 32 Stanley Road, successfully appealed to the public for monetary assistance to repair his boat and was eventually able to resume his prawn-fishing livelihood.

One day in December 1908, something was afoot in Marine Parade. Looking through the window of his kiosk, the Piermaster could see a crowd of people following a shiny black car. A local waterman, Tom Wingfield, who was about to pass through the turnstile confided in the Pierkeeper: "I did hear some gossip that the King might come to Worthing."

And, apparently he did, in search of a suitable residence so it seems. It was on 12 December and the King came by motor car. His Majesty's car was mobbed by excited crowds seeking a glimpse of their Monarch. Rumours spread like wildfire about his brief stop, for he showed more than a passing interest in Beach House, a regal-looking residence with grounds that stretched to the beach. But he never did live there.

King Edward VII in his royal car, photographed by Edwards & Son outside the *Marine Hotel*.

To ensure that lifeboats were kept in high order and ready for emergencies the RNLI inspected stations regularly. One such arrangement was made for the Inspector to visit Worthing on Friday 9 October.

On the appointed morning a large crowd of local residents as well as visitors to the town turned out waiting to see the *Richard Coleman* ride the waves. But, unfortunately, the Inspector was delayed at another station and was unable to keep the engagement. However, so as not to disappoint the public, the Worthing lifeboat was still launched as arranged to the east of the Pier in front of a delighted, large gathering of spectators.

One of the most difficult launches of the Worthing lifeboat was arduously undertaken on 10 December 1908. At 5.30 p.m. on that Thursday evening Coxswain Harry Marshall was informed by several people that they had seen flares and flashlights out in the offing to the south east of the town.

Naturally regarding these as signals of distress from some vessel in need of assistance Harry immediately ordered the signal for assembly of the lifeboat crew. The mortar boomed loudly!

Hundreds of townspeople rushed to the seafront where the air was tense with apprehension.

Lifeboatmen and other willing helpers busily engaged themselves in pulling the craft out of the lifeboat house while arrangements for horsing its carriage were personally superintended, in the usual manner, by Walter Butcher.

Less than ten minutes sufficed to get the boat out and along to the east of the pier, but when it came to launching, considerable difficulty was experienced. It was almost low water of a spring tide which meant that the sea was a quarter of a mile from the beach.

A rough marl prevented the horses from getting a good foothold and a downpour of rain, driven by a strong south westerly breeze, only added to the difficulties as the lifeboat on its carriage was at length dragged across the long stretch of sands, seaweed and slippery boulders to the water's edge, helped by dozens of volunteers.

At about quarter past six a loud cheer went up from the assembled crowd of onlookers, conveying the welcome information that the *Richard Coleman* was off on its errand of mercy in the rough sea.

Viewed from the pier and the Parade, the lights carried by the numerous assistants created a weird scene as they moved about on the sands. Loth to leave the vicinity of the seafront, even after the lifeboat oarsmen, all pulling together, had disappeared into the darkness, the loyal spectators moved back only as far as the top of the beach.

After rowing the *Richard Coleman* through the breakers the lifeboatmen hoisted the sails and cruised about for some time, burning two white lights and making a thorough search as far east as Shoreham and extending some five or six miles out into the Channel.

As the evening wore on the uncertainty amongst the waiting crowd on the shore increased.

After more than three hours, at 9.30 p.m., their prevailing anxiety was set to rest when the lifeboatmen returned, having failed to find any trace of a vessel. The origin of the lights which led to the boat being called out remained a mystery, the only logical conclusion being that some vessel had gone ashore on the outer banks and had immediately fired distress signals, but when the tide had risen, the captain had been able to float his craft and make off, possibly covering-up his lights to escape detection. For it was well known that a captain would be ashamed of being found in difficulties with his ship.

The chairman of the local committee of management, Harry Hargood, had been returning from a meeting of the RNLI in London that day when the launch had taken place. On arriving at the railway station and hearing the news he went down to the seafront at once and, together with other members of the committee, remained there to see the lifeboat safely re-housed.

A large crowd of people watched the return of the *Richard Coleman* and the hauling of the craft onto its carriage and back over the sands. Just before 10 o'clock the lifeboat was returned to its station and ready for service once more. The lifeboat house remained open, and Coxswain Harry Marshall made all preparations for an immediate launch in case of further news being received, but it was not necessary to call the crew out again that night.

This service had been exceptionally severe on helpers as well as horses so in addition to paying each of the high number of volunteers the normal 6s. for help during the hours of darkness every one of these 48 men received a bonus of 3s. Mr. Butcher himself was paid 9s. for his services as signalman and also £6 for the hire of eight of his horses. The cost of two messengers was 3s. each.

The Richard Coleman *returning from daytime rescue work.*

The Richard Coleman *being hauled back to the lifeboat house.*

The crew of 13, including two 'novice' lifeboatmen, were each paid 30s. For George Finnis and Steve Wingfield junior it was their first experience on actual service.

In terms of the length of time served as crew members, the most accomplished were Coxswain Harry Marshall, his brother Fred, Second Coxswain Bill Blann and bowman Steve Wingfield senior.

Strong family connections linked the crew: two other Wingfields, George and Tom, completed a total of four from that family; Mark Marshall made three brothers in all from the Marshall stable, Bill's brother Harry Blann was present; Frank and Fred Collier; and last but not least, George Benn.

The direct costs of this fruitless mission were £47 17s. But it wasn't a waste of time because at least the crew were satisfied that no-one was in danger.

Nothing more was heard of the curious lights in the Channel which had been taken for signals of distress.

Footnotes

[1] Henry Hayden, born at Newport on the Isle of Wight in 1810, was the son of a shipmaster who owned his own trading brigantine. After completing 12 years service in the Royal Navy he married Ann Gerard, the daughter of a baker from Kemp Town, Brighton. Her family were of Huguenot stock. Hayden entered the coastguard service, and after being employed at various Stations along the Sussex coast over a period of 17 years, he came to Worthing Coastguard Station in 1857, where he remained until he became Piermaster in 1869. Henry's great grandson, Philip Hayden lives in Worthing, and has retained the wooden chair that Henry used to sit on by the Pier's toll-house.

Parkes was Pierkeeper 1862 - 1869
Hayden was Piermaster 1869 - 1886
Belton was Piermaster 1887 - 1908

[2] Tom Belton was born in Marine Place in 1835, into an established Worthing family. Tom joined his father in the fishing industry. (A picture showing Tom Belton with his father is reproduced in 'A Town's Pride' on page 31.) On that fateful day in 1850 when 11 fishermen drowned, young Belton was only on his second voyage. When he was 30, Tom married. He quit fishing and signed on as a merchant seaman, sailing between British ports at first, and then on longer voyages to various parts of the world. His world-wide escapades were numerous, but that's another story. When Tom eventually returned to Worthing, he couldn't turn his back on the sea, salt ran in his veins so to speak, and he resumed deep sea fishing with his ageing father. For about 11 years Tom skippered the *Good Hope*, until the fishing industry went into decline. Then he turned to crewing yachts, firstly for Mr. F.J. Aldridge, and then for a Mr. Rowden, the brother-in-law of Harry Hargood. By 1887, at the age of 52, Tom was yearning to settle down, and successfully applied for the position of Piermaster. One of Tom's former skippers, Captain Wade, was living in Worthing in 1908.

[3] The Museum, entered by the door on the far right of the photograph, is today still there. The door to the left, which was the Library entrance, is currently a tourist information centre. The Library was rehoused in a concrete monstrosity built next door in Richmond Road in 1975.

[4] The steamer on the east side of the Pier could be the *Majestic* owned by Cosens of Weymouth. The one berthed on the west side is most likely P & A Campbell's *Cambria*, which only came to this part of the south coast once, and that was in 1908.

[5] Even though the beach is strewn with seaweed in this photograph taken before August 1908, daytrippers were not put off by the smell – the aroma was more natural at this time, unlike the obnoxious acridity that emanates from today's polluted weed. A young boy standing to the left of the first bathing tent is reading a magazine entitled 'Captain'. In the background is the uncompleted *Hotel Metropole*.

[6] This postcard was posted at Brighton to a Streatham Address on 28 July 1908.

"Don't mind me, Girls, I'm only a Baby.

Chapter 6

Rejoicings & Laments

1909

During the early part of the 20th century there were feelings in many quarters that no charity work done locally was more worthy of support than that of the RNLI. This humane cause had saved no fewer than 638 people from the seas around the British Isles in the year 1908.

Thus it was gratifying for the chairman of the Worthing Branch to see that the annual meeting, in the council chamber in February of 1909, was so well-attended, even more so as it coincided with a royal visit. King Edward again paid an impromptu visit to Beach House on Worthing's coastline that same afternoon.

Branch Chairman Harry Hargood welcomed the Mayor, Councillor J.G. Denton, J.P. Among those present at the meeting were two aldermen, a doctor and two vicars.

The balance sheet showed that £110 4s. had been received in subscriptions over the past year; donations amounted to £29 14s.; and static collecting boxes in various parts of the town brought in £20 1s.1d. Out of this income £70 had been forwarded to the parent Institution, as had been the triennial church collections of £88 17s.10d.

Mr. Hargood, who had also been elected to the RNLI General Committee of Management in London, had been surprised to find just how meticulous that national committee was, and how the funds placed before them were so carefully budgeted. If it had not been for large legacies bequeathed to them each year they would have had a running deficit, as the amounts received from all the various branches around the country were insufficient to pay all the expenses of the Institution.

The chairman, however, was glad to report to the gathering that, here in Worthing, the RNLI was generously supported, and that the town had always stood high in the estimation of the General Committee. By pulling together, they had in fact managed to send up a larger remittance than any other place on the Sussex coast.

The hard-working committee was re-elected, and it was considered that as long as their interest continued, Worthing would retain its proud distinction of being one of the best-equipped and most satisfactory lifeboat stations on the south coast.

According to a Board of Trade return for the year ended June 1909, the number of shipping casualties off U.K. coasts amounted to 3,660 with 248 persons losing their lives, 232 of them having been officers or seamen from shipwrecks. Only 16 had been passengers.

On our storm-beaten shores, between 1861 and 30 June 1909, there had been a total of 117,326 human casualties to British, Colonial and foreign shipping accompanied by the terrible loss of 29,000 lives – a figure that was equal to the entire population of the Borough of Worthing at this time. During the same period, the Lifeboat Service was proud to have been involved in saving more than 36,000 lives.

The father of lifeboatman George Benn passed away in the month of March. He was one of the oldest fishermen in the local community and died at his home in Ferring Cottage, Graham Road (betwixt Montague Street and Shelley Road.) William Benn had named his residence after the village of Ferring where he and his brother had been born.

His brother, Sergeant Mark Benn, although younger, had died during the previous summer at the age of 79 years.

Eighty two year old William's funeral at the cemetery was attended by Worthing fishermen wishing to pay their last respects.

Fishermen as well as coastguards anxiously searched for a boating party that had gone missing one morning during that same month of March.

A family of holidaymakers pose for a photographer from Edwards & Son on Worthing beach before putting off in a hired boat.

Three gentlemen and a lady had put off earlier that day opposite a boarding house on the Parade to go fishing. A Mr. Pusey of York House, Marine Parade, together with three visitors from London – Mr. & Mrs. Cobby and Mr. Rawlinson – left the beach in a small open boat at about 10 o'clock in the morning, announcing their intention to return in time for lunch.

At 11.30 a.m. they were seen in the vicinity of the spot where the *Indiana* had foundered eight years earlier, a good fishing ground, but a passing shower of rain subsequently obscured them from view.

When the haze cleared the boat had disappeared!

Worthing Coastguard, informed of the situation, immediately put off in their galley. At the same time, three or four fishermen launched their boats to assist in the quest.

An extensive search of the place where the boat was last seen failed to find any trace of either the craft or its occupants. Telephone enquiries westward along the coast to Littlehampton were also unsuccessful in producing any information as to the whereabouts of the overdue party.

Later that day at about half past six in the evening, all anxiety was set at rest when, quite out of the blue, the fishing party returned in the boat, quite oblivious of the worry they had caused during their fishing trip.

Three days later the Worthing lifeboat itself put to sea in the midst of tempestuous weather. Happily the lifeboat gun sounded only once, signifying that the launch was for the regular drill and not in answer to any distress call.

Exceptionally unfavourable conditions prevented anything like the large customary assembly of spectators, and the *Richard Coleman* braved buffeting breakers under the gaze of only a few watching eyes.

Notwithstanding the severity of the weather the exercise proved to be satisfactory and worthwhile, as usual. For the first time, our lifeboat crew wore kapok lifejackets: the latest thing in body buoyancy, and replacing the cork ones which had been in service here in Worthing since 1862. Lifejackets provided essential protection for our lifeboatmen, should they be washed overboard or in case the lifeboat capsized.

Surprisingly, few of them could swim.

Worthing lifeboatmen[1], wearing kapok lifejackets first issued in 1909, going out for practice in the *Richard Coleman*

One month after the lifeboat exercise, when the sea happened to be calm, two local fishermen prevented a woman from committing suicide. Albert Bashford, of 6, Field Row, and John Riddles had been standing at the top of the beach at about seven o'clock in the evening when they noticed a woman walking into the sea.

The tide was just on the flow at the time, and they ran down to the water's edge and struggled to pull her out.

At one time she was completely submerged. When they attempted to rescue her she cried: "Only let me die! I want to die!"

They eventually managed to pull her out and as they were walking back over the sands she retorted: "You were unkind to take me out of the water!"

At this point P.C. Charles Hills arrived at the scene to take her to the police station on a charge of attempting to commit suicide. The woman who, in spite of smelling of drink, was still sober declared: "I wish those men had left me alone and let me drown! I want to die! I ought to have gone in when the water was up high!"

At the police station the accused told Superintendent Bridger that she had come from Victoria on the previous day and had stayed at Brighton before walking through Shoreham the next morning. When she had got to Worthing she didn't know where she was.

Later she said: "Having no home, friends or employment, I purchased sixpennyworth of brandy to help me to do the job." She refused to see a doctor or give the name of any relative or friend.

Before the Bench, Martha Mary was charged with 'Casting herself into the sea with intent to kill and murder herself. She appeared in the dock wearing sombre clothes, was a woman of very respectable appearance, seeming about 45 years of age, though she was said to be a little older.

After hearing the evidence, a remand to the Petty Sessions was called for, and Mr. H. Hargood on the Bench advised the prisoner to co-operate with the police and reveal the names of her friends so that they might get in touch with them. She was given to understand that if she declined to do so it would be greatly to her disadvantage and could possibly result in her detention at Lewes to await trial.

Martha Mary firmly replied that she did not wish to involve her people and requested that she might be sent to a convent.

Thereupon she was removed in custody.

The sea was calm when the *Richard Coleman* was launched as part of the District Inspector's regular visit on Friday 18 June. The Worthing lifeboat looked particularly smart in a fresh coat of navy blue and white paint when it was trundled along to the east of the Pier for a short instructional cruise.

Afterwards, Lieut. Keppell Foote expressed his thorough satisfaction both with the station and the efficiency of the crew.

The Parade east of the Pier.[2]

Four days later, on Tuesday 22 June, rough sea prevented a new boat being launched during a naming ceremony. Yet another *Skylark* had been completed for Captain Fred Collins, one of Brighton's best known townsmen. It was a compliment to Worthing that for some years past Captain Collins had been in the habit of having his pleasure boats built in the town, the contracts being successfully carried out by the boatbuilding firm now called Messrs Belton & Co.

The latest craft to bear the familiar name of *Skylark* was a motor boat of between 18 and 20 horsepower, and was licensed to carry 10 passengers, although in practical terms it was capable of accommodating more.

Some years earlier, the vessels that Captain Collins had commissioned were sailing craft, but with the advance of the times he had found it necessary to go in for the latest innovations.

After a luncheon at the *Steyne Hotel* for a few friends with the Mayor at the head of the table, Collins stated that the building of yachts in this town had always proved satisfactory to him. He had been reponsible for introducing many people to Worthing, daytrippers he had personally entertained by song or recitation on the cruise, some of whom ultimately settled here.

After lunch, the company adjourned to the beach shingle opposite Beltons' yard where the new yacht lay. Breaking a bottle of wine across its bows the Mayor christened the craft, naming it *Skylark Motor No. 2* and wished everyone who sailed in it a safe return.

The National Anthem was sung followed by Rule Britannia, after which the bright and cheery-faced Captain Collins called for three cheers for the Mayor and Mayoress.

The magnificent *Steyne Hotel* on the seafront, with its robust porchway over the main entrance[3].

For many years proposals to provide a properly constructed fish market a little to the east of the Pier had been the subject of lively debate at council meetings. Now at last the sanitary reformers demonstrated their sincerity by putting the plan into effect.

It consisted of paving slabs laid on a good thickness of tarred clinker, which could flex on those occasions that the sea flooded the market. The area measured 60 feet by 35 feet, and from the sides it sloped slightly to a grid in the centre which was linked to the town's sewage drains. This principal merit of the scheme, which was designed and carried out by the borough surveyor, surpassed all former methods of treatment, even in the case of an earlier market where the allotted space was duly flagged, railed round, and made to look very ornamental.

Although it was recognised that the fishing industry had lost much of the magnitude and importance it once possessed it was deemed essential that the highest degree of sanitation should be effected with the provision of a standpipe and hose to clean the surface regularly.

For the past few years Worthing watermen had been in the habit of organising a Regatta on their own account, but this had upset the Town Regatta committee who consequently called a meeting at the Town Hall on Monday evening 14 June in the presence of the Mayor. It proved to be quite lively.

As the watermen intended to hold their own fixture once more the Mayor enquired as to whether there was any prospect of combining the two Regattas.

The chairman, Walter C. Patching, said he was glad the Mayor raised this question, especially as he saw they had two representatives of the watermen present that evening. Turning to Tom and Steve Wingfield he asked if there could be a merger.

Tom exclaimed, "I don't think so! Whereas the Town Regatta is run for the benefit of clubs, in our regatta about 30 of us, all different individuals, take part."

Steve insisted, "Certainly not as it stands now! You only give us one or two races out of 14 or 15."

Needless to say, the tenacious watermen, who could not be persuaded to combine their fixture with the Town Regatta, cheekily announced the date for their own Regatta – 6 August – to be held 18 days before the Town Regatta.

Again Worthing was the sunniest spot in the United Kingdom; and when Friday afternoon 6 August arrived it was no exception, it could hardly have been more suitable as regards the weather. Numerous spectators thronged the Pier and the adjacent esplanade, able to follow the races in very pleasant conditions.

A Regatta Day between 1909 and 1912.[4]

An omnibus from Worthing Motor Services on the seafront.

Visitors from outlying villages were brought into the town by omnibus, courtesy of Worthing Motor Services Ltd., a company formed in 1909 taking over the remaining vehicles of the Sussex Motor Road Company. The new offices were at 23 Marine Parade[5].

One of the directors, Alfred Douglas Mackenzie, a man well-known in Worthing, particularly for his cycling activities, was the friend and associate of another canny Scotsman in the area, William Reid[6]. Both men had been ships' engineers. Like Mackenzie, Reid too was an entrepreneur, and in 1909 purchased the paddle steamer *Worthing Belle* from Mr. J. Lee of Shoreham. Under its new ownership, the pleasure steamer continued to make short coastal excursions. Sailings from Hastings, Eastbourne, Brighton, Littlehampton and Worthing proved to be both popular and profitable, especially in bringing hundreds of people to Worthing for the Regatta.

Edwardian ladies watching the paddler dock at the landing stage remarked at the pretty tricolour flag fluttering from its mast together with a blue pennant emblazoned with the words *Worthing Belle*.

This year's Regatta was organised by a committee of watermen, which seems to have been dominated by the Wingfield family, – George Wingfield (chairman), Tom Wingfield, Steve Wingfield sen., Steve Wingfield jun. (hon. sec.), Fred Wakeford, Wm. Wells, Jack Burgess, F. Collier, Harry and Fred Marshall – the fixture lasted for three to four enjoyable hours.

Only seven boat races, all of them rowing, were programmed and the extended intervals between them were filled with displays of swimming and diving by the swimming club as well as walking the greasy pole.

The watermen themselves were to be congratulated on their typical enthusiasm displayed when competing in the various events. Worthing's ancient mariners, sturdy specimens of their class, certainly proved their capacity in two of the afternoon's events which were for men over the age of 50 years. It is interesting to note that in both of these races, using pair-oared boats, the fourth prize of 15s. in each contest was taken by the same team, Harry Smith and Charlie Wingfield, whose combined ages totalled 129 years.

Street entertainers amusing a young audience at Christmastime
in Sugden Road, East Worthing, c.1909.

Charlie, a wise ageing man with a well-worn gnarled face, possessed a remarkable memory. Youngsters mobbed his boat as it came ashore, begging to be spun a yarn of the old days. Kids love to be entertained.

"Come and sit 'ere in the boat wi' me," he said, beckoning to them, "and I'll tell y'ers about a duck hunt."

"What's a duck hunt?" asked an inquisitive toddler by the name of Harry Blann (my uncle).

"Well, young Harry me lad, listen carefully and I'll tell 'ee." replied Charlie as he picked him up and sat him upon his knee.

"More'an four decades since, we had a duck hunt at the end of a Regatta. More often than not though, it was a goose."

Charlie revealed that it had been a grand day for young lads. Erected on a quieter part of the beach a tent had contained a performing animal, an extraordinarily clever monkey that drew crowds of admirers with its show of tricks. Juveniles had tried their luck at the coco-nut shy and numerous firing stalls whilst eating gingerbread made by a travelling vendor.

"But what about the duck hunt?" insisted Harry in a high-pitched voice.

"I'm just coming to that," gleamed Charlie. "I remember it well. I was standing next to Pier-keeper Parkes for a time."

Charlie recalled that three tubs had been provided, each crewed by a lone oarsman to paddle the unstable craft by rotary motion and to chase the poor goose.

However, the tubs had been averse to the chase and no sooner had each man got comfortably seated than the strange craft had begun to twist and turn, until one after another the contestants had been pitched headlong into the sea and hence had been compelled to resort to swimming after the goose.

Taking advantage of its watery surroundings the goose would have been difficult to trap had it not been for the surrounding boats which had confined the poor creature. He who caught the wretched bird claimed it.

The man whose indefatigable exertions had been responsible for organising the early Regattas and was still associated with the fixtures in the 20th century, Harry Hargood, J.P., chairman of Worthing RNLI, presented the prizes in the Pier Pavilion after the 1909 Watermen's Regatta.

Relaxing in a shelter outside the Pier Pavilion.

Lifeboat funds benefitted by several pounds as the result of a special concert at the theatre on Sunday evening 15 August. With a desire to assist such a good cause Mr. C. Adolf Seebold lent the building free of charge to a friendly association known as the Grand 23 Order, who submitted an attractive programme at popular prices.

A fortnight on, another Sunday concert was held for the RNLI. In reporting the show a local newspaper described the beneficiary thus: 'There is one institution which deservedly appeals to the public for funds, and it must be recognised that it does not appeal in vain. That is the Royal National Lifeboat Institution, which does splendid work around the coast when the occasion demands it. A very large sum of money is needed by the executive to carry on the operations, and we have been told that Worthing is not slow in the matter of contributions.'

This event in the pavilion had been arranged by the committee of the Male Voice Choir, who had enlisted the services of the Ladies' Orchestra for the evening.

Mr. W. Binstead[7], the regular conductor of the choir, was unable to lead on this occasion, and so the duty was undertaken by George Long, one of the bass section of the choir.

The choir, who sang several items to a packed audience, was honoured with recalls. In addition, two hymns were sung accompanied by the orchestra. Miss Edith Bartlett warmly recited the poem, 'Remember the Lifeboat,' and Miss Nancy Packham received a splendid ovation for the final item on the programme when she sang Land of Hope and Glory, joined by the choir for the chorus.

Unlike the magnificence that had prevailed for the watermen, conditions for the Annual Town Regatta turned out to be somewhat erratic. Tuesday 24 August, which was to have been the Town Regatta day, was beset by inclement weather and was postponed until 6 September. A substituted attraction was provided during the afternoon by the Worthing lifeboat crew, who held their quarterly exercise. Despite the driving rain, a large number of people gathered on the seafront and on the Pier to witness the launch of the *Richard Coleman*, and while this was being effected collections were taken on behalf of the RNLI.

The *Richard Coleman* and crew returning from practice, photographed from the Pier landing stage.

The occasion was reported, two days later, in a national newpaper, the Daily Sketch, with an illustration showing the lifeboat being launched to the east of the Pier and accompanied by a photograph of Coxswain Harry Marshall.

On Monday 6 September conditions were again unsuitable for the Regatta and because of the lateness of the season and the uncertainty of the weather the illuminated promenade concert and the fireworks display were cancelled for the year.

It was decided to make one more attempt to hold the aquatic programme two days later on the Wednesday afternoon. It was a typically glorious September morning, but it was less radiant as the day advanced, and there was a positive coolness in the air towards the close of the afternoon.

Owing to the state of the tide the first of 12 contests, which was a watermen's sailing race, could not start until three o'clock. The licensed watermen were allotted only one more event, a race for first-class pair-oared boats. It was followed by a double sculling race for ladies and gentlemen, using watermen's boats.

There was no formal prize-giving ceremony, the chairman and honorary secretary simply attended to hand over the awards at the sailing club headquarters on the seafront.

Tom Blann who had witnessed the day's events reminisced with his associates. At the time of what he believed to be the first ever Worthing Regatta, which took place the year before the *Lalla Rookh* disaster, Tom was just 16 years old.

As the able fisherman grew a little older and possessed his own boats he had competed in the Worthing Regattas. In 1864 his boat *Charlie* had won first prize of £2 in a race using one pair of sculls, but his *Lady Victoria* had come in unplaced in a match for first class pair-oared boats.

During September 1909, three Worthing families with maritime connections each mourned the loss of a loved one.

Alfred (Fred) Beck, of a large, old Worthing family, died, aged 71 years, at his home in Graham Road. Fred, who had been an active man and looked much younger than his age, was a descendant of the late Sydney Beck, who for many years had been the landlord of what used to be the *Wellington Inn* on the seafront, and was now the *Pier Hotel*.

Looking eastward along the promenade and Marine Parade, this view shows the *Pier hotel*.[8]

Sydney Beck had been the owner of the doomed open ferry boat known as the *Lady Lump*, which had been launched from the beach on the occasion of the great disaster in November 1850[9], when 11 Worthing fishermen heroically sacrificed their lives.

Fred Beck himself was connected with the fishing industry, and, on the death of old Tom Burtenshaw at the age of 82 years, Fred had become the recognised salesman at the fish market on the beach, conducting Dutch Auctions there.

Consequently two of the wreaths sent to the funeral bore the following messages: 'In token of sincere sympathy from fish hawkers,' and 'With the deepest sympathy from friends and patrons of the fish market.' Other floral tributes were sent by his widow, the Edwards', the Bakers, the Whittingtons, the Worleys, the Benns, the Osbornes, the Martins, and also from some friends as far away as Folkestone.

The second person in the sea-going community to pass away that month was the widow of a well-known local waterman, Walter Burden. Eighty seven year old Mrs. Hannah Elizabeth Burden had lived here in Worthing from the age of 21.

Sixteen months earlier, on 6 May 1908, the Worthing Gazette had published her portrait as the oldest guest at the May Day Dinner given by Alderman and Mrs. F. C. Linfield for the old folks of the Borough at the Winter Hall.

Mrs. Burden was buried at Broadwater cemetery in South Farm Road after a service conducted by Rev. Lovell, pastor of the Shelley Road Congregational Church, her regular place of worship. In addition to all the Burden family, the chief mourners included Mrs. F. Jupp, Mrs. Charles West and Walter Budd.

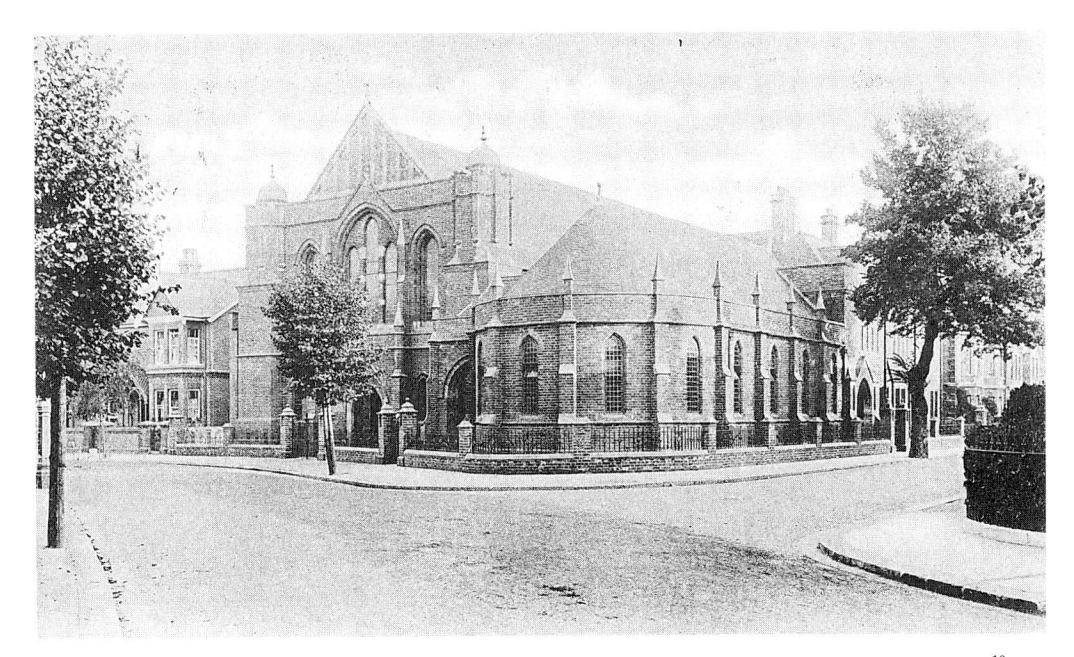

The Congregational Church built in 1903 at the junction of Shelley Road and Buckingham Road.[10]

Walter Burden had set his will some 28 years earlier on 7 February 1881, bequeathing his property to his wife. It had been further directed that income from his houses in Chapel Street (now Portland Road) and Chapel Fields was to maintain his son, also named Walter. These rents were at present being collected by Mr. Patching for the benefit of Walter junior. It was further provided that after the mother's death the property should be equally divided among his children then living.

But all was not well in the Burden camp. A dispute erupted as to whether certain monies were part of the widow's estate. Her two sons insisted that this cash belonged to their father's estate, thereby making them the beneficiaries.

The argument persisted and became public knowledge at a hearing at the Town Hall, brought to determine the outcome of the will. Held before Judge Scully, the case of Burden versus Burden received a thorough airing during an examination of witnesses. A Mr. Du Parcq, who had been instructed by Messrs. G. H. King and Frankus of London, contended that a sum of money, more than £160, which was in the hands of the Receiver, was the separate estate of Hannah Burden.

Frank Burden of Paragon Street, a 56 year old boatman, told the County Court that he had had a conversation with his father on the morning of his death, and that he had told him then about some money, £200, he kept in the house.

After her husband's death, Mrs. Burden had kept house for her brother, Mr. Feest, for which she had received 18 pence per week. Frank insisted that the only other money she had had to live on was that left by her husband.

On the day that his mother died, Frank's elder brother, William Henry, read the will, but as Frank was not satisfied he obtained a copy from Somerset House in London, and found that there was something in it that his brother had concealed from him.

Whilst being cross-examined by Mr. Du Parcq, Frank stated that an agreement had been made in 1883 whereby he was to buy from his mother his father's boats for £70. An integral part of this agreement was that a share of the boats' earnings would be paid to his mother. In spite of this arrangement Mrs. Burden had sold some of the boats. Incensed by her attitude, Frank had told his mother that he wanted to wipe his hands of the whole sordid business.

Mrs. Emily Beatrice Jupp, a daughter of the late Burdens, who claimed to be 38 years old but was in fact 47, and who at this time lived in Horsham, when questioned by Mr. Du Parcq, admitted that she knew of the £200 which had been hidden under the stairs.

In a dramatic scene Counsel accused her of stealing most of that money, which she emphatically denied. "Five pounds is what I took, sir!" she cried.

Mr. Du Parcq then called her brother, William Henry Burden, 65, who was a masseur and had lived in London since 1862. In 1886 he had seen his sister, Mrs. Jupp, spending money lavishly on presents and riding about in cabs while holidaying in London. He had thought this strange because, at that time, she had been earning only 9s.6d. per week at Mr. Smith's Emporium. She had even taken William's son Henry John, who had been about 18 years old at the time, to theatres in expensive cabs.

William's mother, who supplemented her income from garden rents and by dealing in furniture, had later gone to visit him in London to discuss the problem of his sister; and, as a result, arrangements had been made to send her out of the country.

In summing up, His Honour upheld that Burden had not intended to give his wife more than a life interest, and that the off-spring were entitled to participate in the estate. Subsequently, an order to this effect was made by the registrar.

A south east view of Worthing's Christ Church[11] taken from Portland Road.

The third relevant death in September was that of Samuel John Sayers, whose wife was the Pier toll-keeper at that time, and whose late son-in-law, Tom Belton, had been the Piermaster. Fifty six year old Samuel's sudden death shocked the community, and a memorial service was held at Christ Church, where he had been a chorister for many years.

In December, one of the best known fishermen and boatmen, Frank Collier, passed away. At his funeral, a large crowd, which included most of the watermen from the seafront, attended to pay their last respects.

Until a few days before his sudden death, hard-working Frank had been helping out with some alterations to the theatre.

Frank, who was 51, had been a member of the lifeboat crew for more than 20 years. His father before him had also served as a lifeboatman. The Collier family were devoted to lifeboat service: Frank's two brothers were still associated with the Worthing Station.

Full lifeboating honours were bestowed on the late, lamented lifeboatman. Draped with the Union Jack, the coffin was conveyed from Frank's home on the seafront to the cemetery in South Farm Road by his fellow crewmen, wearing blue jerseys and blue cloth caps. After he had been laid to rest Coxswain Harry Marshall laid a wreath on the grave, from the lifeboat crew, who had all clubbed together for this last tribute to one of their number.

Footnotes

[1] Coxswain Harry Marshall is hidden from view behind bearded 2nd Cox Bill Blann standing in the stern.

[2] This postcard was sent by a Londoner called Max, on holiday at 6 Buckingham Road, Worthing, to his girlfriend, Miss Batten, in service at a house in Delaware Road, Maidahill, West London. In his message he remarked that there were plenty of people here in Worthing, especially for the time of year (21 September).

[3] Today, the porchway is much reduced; the *Steyne Hotel* has been renamed the *Chatsworth Hotel;* and the south-facing part of the ground floor is a public house called *The Prom.*

[4] The omnibus in this picture is a Milnes Daimler, registration number CD 408, with a 'slipper'-type body. The bus company – Worthing Motor Services Ltd. – existed as a corporate body from 1909 to 1915. This Daimler bus was not acquired by Southdown Motor Services Ltd. when they were formed in 1915.

[5] Present-day offices of Southdown.

[6] William Reid — the maternal grandfather of Philip Hayden. Born in Aberdeenshire in 1858, Reid left school at the age of 12, became apprenticed to a blacksmith, and later studied engineering. After marrying Beatrice Melvin, also from Aberdeenshire, in 1884, they went to live in Liverpool, where he had secured a job as a ship's engineer. But after only one voyage to the west coast of South America, the couple returned to Aberdeenshire, where he took up farming, firstly as a tenant before buying his own farm. Eventually, he owned a dairy in Aberdeen as well. He came south to Brighton in 1905, possibly at the instigation of a fellow Scot, former ship's engineer Alfred Mackenzie, who was by then, with his partner Alfred Cannon, involved in running several local bus companies, then operating pioneer motor omnibus services in Sussex and Hampshire. William, an opportunist like Mackenzie, also started the Cliftonville Press Printing Works in Hove.

[7] I mentioned the surname Binstead on pages 84, 85, 93, 126 and 137 of 'A Town's Pride'. I am now able to trace a present day link in the town. Bandleader Edwin Binstead sired 15 offspring. Most survived childhood to produce a further generation. Mr. P.C. Wicking, is one of 10 of Edwin's grandchildren living in Worthing today.

[8] On the far left of the photograph, a lady walks past the hoarding around the vacant site left by the *Royal Hotel* at the bottom of South Street, while passengers alight from an omnibus. Behind the bus is the *Marine Hotel* on the opposite corner of South Street, and next to it stands the smaller *Pier Hotel.*

[9] Full details of the 1850 disaster can be found in the 1st chapter of 'A Town's Pride'.

[10] This Congregational Church replaced one at the corner of Montague Street and Portland Road. The illustration was reproduced from a postcard that was posted in 1907.

[11] This photograph clearly shows the choir vestry, added in 1893 to the main church which had been built in 1843. The right hand door in the picture opens into the choir vestry.

"Just as you are for ninepence!"

Chapter 7

Six Cheers for the King

1910-11

Just after Christmas 1909, Harry Hargood and his wife were invited to the New Theatre Royal[1] in Bath Place. Closed for the past two months while being extensively altered, the refurbished theatre boasted a packed house. Impresario Carl Seebold, who instigated the dramatic transformation of the interior, costing approximately £3,000 (a lot of money in those days), was applauded for his enterprising investment.

Looking around the theatre, Mrs. Hargood noticed that the seating had been greatly improved by extending the dress circle and the gallery, and by tiering these seats. On the north side of the dress circle, it became apparent that Seebold had arranged for a corridor to be converted into a most comfortable lounge, exclusively for the ladies. To encourage members of the fair sex into this special room, tea and coffee were served there in the intervals, thus stimulating conversation.

Another marked feature which Harry noticed was the disappearance of a succession of perilous steps from various parts of the auditorium, that had previously constituted a considerable inconvenience.

The building works had provided much employment for locals at an otherwise lean time. Between 600 and 700 cart loads of earth had been removed, and the floor was now inclined with a rake of about five feet. To improve even further the audience's view of the stage, the orchestra pit had been lowered.

While waiting for the performance to start, Hargood's eyes glanced around the stage curtain at some more changes. The proscenium had been altered. During the course of the evening he found out why: scenery changes were quicker, thus reducing the length of the intervals. Scenery could now be raised bodily, instead of having to be rolled up gradually. These stage alterations brought the theatre more into line with metropolitan playhouses. Mrs. Hargood discreetly pointed out some ornate plasterwork around the proscenium: replicas of air, water, earth and fire signs, from original designs by John Flaxman, R.A. This noted sculptor was a designer for the firm of Wedgewood, and the models at the theatre were of a similar style.

A new and handsome domed ceiling had been created, with a sliding roof, which was to be opened during summer months to keep the theatre cool. For winter comfort, new heating radiators had been installed, and new electric lamps had been fitted for better lighting.

The magistrate's wife approved of the interior design with its new predominately green colour scheme. She found the new seating and expensive-looking carpet very comfortable.

On the subject of tobacco-smoking patrons, the question of whether this vice should continue to be allowed had led to some discussion. Now it was severely curtailed, being permitted in only two places, and then only during intervals. As the lady sitting next to Mrs. Hargood affirmed: "These restrictions are enforced so that no annoyance need be feared by the general body of playgoers who may not be devotees of the weed."

Seebold's commercial courage in carrying out this bold venture had meant the employment of about 80 men on site, tiding them over a season of considerable depression. The men had worked conscientiously from six in the morning, sometimes not finishing until midnight. A couple of figures may be quoted to illustrate the magnitude of operations: in the course of construction work, 15 tons of steelwork were deployed, and even the astonishing quantity of nails used weighed a ton.

Carl Seebold lived up to his description of impresario, for he set about fulfilling another entertainment need in Worthing – an up-to-date roller skating rink and public hall.

He fixed his sights on a seafront property between Bedford Row and Library Place – Bedford House and its extensive garden, owned by the Hall and Winter Gardens Company. At a special meeting of its shareholders in December 1909, Seebold put forward his proposals to those present, who included: Aldermen E.T. Cooksey, E.C. Patching and R. Piper; as well as Colin Moore, H.E. Snewin, W.E. Wenban Smith; together with the secretary, Mr. A. Stubbs.

Seebold explained that he proposed to erect a large building, approximately 150 feet long by 60 feet wide. Inside would be a big public hall at the north end, doubling as a skating rink, with an entrance from Bedford Row. At the seafront end, he wanted an open-air theatre with a tea balcony on the first floor, with two or three shops underneath. The total cost of this project he estimated would be £6,000.

Apparently, the company were only too willing to allow this well-known gentleman to take the property off their hands, and agreed to lease it to the entrepreneur at a starting rent of £275 a year with an option to purchase for £6,150. Seebold hoped to have the new hall ready by June the following year.

At times, parts of the south coast suffer from seaweed being washed ashore by the ton. None more so than Worthing, which has suffered greatly from this persistent problem.

The town's seaweed harvest featured in a daily newspaper in 1910. The article was illustrated by a photograph showing a traction engine and lorries on the beach to the west of the Pier. Its caption read: 'At Worthing the council authorities cope with the matter in a businesslike manner by carting it inland, for fertilizing purposes, for the farmers' and fruit-growers' benefit.' (What a shame this practice has been discontinued.)

Seaweed was never a rare sight on our beach; but a rare species of fish, known as the tunny fish, most certainly was. A specimen of the tunny, a Mediterranean variety virtually unknown here, was discovered off Splash Point one evening in February 1910. Put on display at the fish market the next morning, this sizeable fish, weighing all of 2 cwt., attracted a large number of inquisitive strollers from the promenade who were fascinated by what they saw.

A photograph taken from Splash Point looking towards Beach Parade.[2]

A month later, on a Thursday afternoon, the annual lifeboat meeting was held in the Council Chamber. The chairman, Harry Hargood, reported that Walter Butcher had resigned on 30 June last, after 22 years as horse contractor to the Worthing Lifeboat Station and also as a competent signalman.

A Mr. B. Haslett had since undertaken to provide horses for the boat carriage; while Fred Wakeford, an experienced, mature crew member, had been appointed signalman.

Mr. Hargood was delighted that during the past year the crew had been supplied with the latest type of lifebelts, kapok, which were far superior in buoyancy to the old cork life jackets. Harry Marshall and Bill Blann donned the new belts, which were inspected in detail by those present, and the consensus of opinion favoured them being much lighter to handle and more convenient to use.

Also displayed before the committee was an improved lifebuoy, which also had greater buoyancy than its predecessor.

Referring to the national work of the Institution over the past year, their 281 lifeboats were launched 429 times on active service and 1,075 times for practice; and it was gratifying for members to know that not one lifeboatman died whilst on duty.

The total number of lives saved from the murky depths, since the beginning of the Institution, now stood at 48,267.

The financial position of the branch was such that annual subscriptions had increased slightly from the previous year to £112 9s.6d., while donations actually fell to £24 14s., partly attributed to heavy rain spoiling a collection when the *Richard Coleman* had been launched in August.

During 1909 just over £16 had been deposited in static collection boxes. Quarterly practice expenses had totalled £41 7s.; and the usual remittance of £70 had been forwarded to H.Q.

At the end of the meeting the Mayor declared that the chamber could not be put to a better use than for the Lifeboat Institution, which he hoped the townspeople would continue to support.

A few weeks later one April evening, a strange thing happened to a Worthing boat. After a busy day's trawling, the crew of the lugger *Lucky George* anchored her on the west side of the Pier, while they went to get their tea.

But, unbeknown to them, she had sprung a leak and began listing to one side. Still heavily laden with nets and the successful day's catch, the boat keeled over, and most of the haul of fish was washed into the sea.

On seeing the catastrophe, some watermen on the beach took to their boats in a bid to rescue the ailing craft, which, at length, they succeeded in doing and towed it ashore.

A brief inspection revealed some major damage. What with the disappearance of the huge catch of fish the *Lucky George* was far from lucky for her owner, Robert Williams. This occurrence set him back several pounds: a considerable amount of money at this time.

Now from a local fisherman's loss to a national bereavement. King Edward VII's comparatively short reign ended abruptly in May 1910.

His 44 year old son, George, who as a young man had been trained for the sea, and had risen to the rank of commander in the British Navy, was quickly appointed as his successor. On 9 May, the proclamation of King George V was read out by the Mayor from the steps of Worthing Town Hall to an eagerly listening crowd.

The townspeople paid tribute to their late Monarch some 11 days later on 20 May. A large concourse of mourners formed in Worthing town centre, then marched slowly up Chapel Road. Most of the local public bodies, including the lifeboat crew, the coastguard, the fire brigade and the military, were represented in this procession which solemnly wound its way up to Broadwater Church for a memorial service.

A month later boatman Harry Marshall was elected to a newly-formed committee, appointed to organise the Worthing Town and Watermen's Annual Regatta.

At the annual meeting of Regatta subscribers at the Town Hall only 20 people turned up. Half of the previous year's committee failed to appear, although they were re-elected en bloc in their absence. This year the watermen had decided to amalgamate their Regatta with that of the Town, and were present in force at the meeting.

Among officers elected were: Mr. H. Hargood, J.P., who became patron in place of the late Sir Henry Aubrey-Fletcher; Mr. W. C. Patching, who was elected chairman; and Mr. C. Wingfield, who was voted vice-chairman. A date for the fixture was not set at this meeting, which concluded with Harry Marshall proposing a vote of thanks to the chairman.

The Mayor on Worthing Town Hall steps, reading the proclamation of King George V, 9 May 1910.[3]

Councillors leaving the Town Hall to join the King Edward V11 memorial procession, 20 May 1910.

King Edward V11 memorial procession[4] passing the Town Hall at the southern end of Chapel Road.

King Edward V11 memorial procession moving up Chapel Road past the junction with Chatsworth Road.[5]

King Edward V11 memorial procession in the northern part of Chapel Road, passing Worthing Lodge[6] on the left of the photograph.

Not long after the Regatta meeting had been held, one of Harry's sons, Albert, an Able Seaman in the Royal Navy, was killed in an accident whilst on duty. News of the tragedy stunned Harry. He received an official telegram at the Lifeboat Station on Saturday evening 2 July.

After working for a Mr. W.H. Clarke in South Street, Albert had joined the Navy nearly four years before and was making excellent progress in his maritime career.

On that fateful Saturday afternoon, when he had been standing in a cutter next to his vessel, HMS *Bellerephon*, in Portland Bay, a rope hoisting a copper punt, used for painting the side of the ship, had snapped and the heavy punt had crashed down onto the unsuspecting Albert. It had inflicted horrific injuries from which he died only 15 minutes later.

Both his captain and the chaplain, of the *Bellerephon*[7], wrote to his grief-stricken parents, speaking of the highest regard they had had for Albert. His unexpected death had come as a great shock to Harry, who, together with his brother Fred, was among the most respected watermen on the seafront.

At Harry's request, his son's body was brought from Portland to Worthing for internment in his home town.

The first part of the burial service was conducted at Holy Trinity Church, where members of the Holy Trinity Naval Brigade formed a guard-of-honour as the coffin was carried into the church on the shoulders of four members of the lifeboat crew – Bill Blann, George Wingfield, George Benn and Steve Wingfield junior. Accompanying Harry Marshall and his wife were their two sons, Charlie and Harry junior, and their daughters, Annie and Alice.

Albert was buried at Broadwater Cemetery, which was crowded with sympathisers, including virtually all the local boatmen, fishermen and lifeboat crew. Uniformed coastguards attended under the command of Chief Officer T. Prowse.

From the cemetery gates, eight fellow sailors from his ship carried the coffin which was covered in a Union Jack, brought from the *Bellerephon*, and laid young Albert to rest in the grave.

A large number of wreaths testified to the high respect in which he had been held: nine from crewmen on differing sections of his ship and three from officers. Others were sent by the Worthing Coastguard, his old schoolmates, the Navy League, Mr. and Mrs. Hargood, and from his many friends and family.

Albert Marshall (far right) when he was serving in HMS *Barfleur*.

The Marshall brothers and other licensed boatmen who had stands on the beach experienced problems with people interfering with their boats and equipment.

Personal responsibility was accepted by the owners but they felt that the authorities should take a lead in reducing this form of nuisance.

Accordingly, in the summer of 1910, one Willy Kiernander[8], a local seaman who in his younger day had rounded the Horn, took a prominent part in the protection of watermen's gear by collecting a petition of 60 signatures which he presented to the Town Council.

In October, flags at watermen's stands on the seafront were lowered to half-mast, indicating that a member of their calling had passed away. Charlie Lee[9] died at home in Gloucester Place where he had lived for many years.

His wife had died suddenly some 14 years earlier in the same month of October.

Seventy seven year old Charlie had been second coxswain on the lifeboat for eight years until being made up to full coxswain, a position he had held for 18 years until his retirement in 1898.

He had been the proud bearer of the RNLI Silver Medal, awarded to him in December 1891 for his courageous conduct whilst rescuing sailors from two shipwrecks – the *Capella* and the *Kong Karl* – on the same day.

At a presentation ceremony in August 1895 he had received a framed portrait, presented by Captain Yves Rivvel as a mark of gratitude to the lifeboat crew for service to his vessel, the *Halycon*, during the previous month.

Soon after lunch on Thursday 13 October 1910, Worthing lifeboatmen were at the lifeboat house, ready to leave for their former coxswain's funeral when an urgent summons reached them.

A telegram dispatched from Shoreham read: 'Upturned boat drifting your way. People hanging to keel!'

There was no time to lose!

Coxswain Marshall ordered the *Richard Coleman* to be launched, compelling those mourners who were members of the first lifeboat crew to abandon the funeral. The second crew remained and followed the cortege on foot to the cemetery, where there were numerous floral tributes from lifeboatmen and branch officers.

At the Lifeboat Station the first crew quickly donned their kapok life-jackets.

Without waiting for the horses, the lifeboat was pulled manually by many willing helpers over the beach a little to the east of the boathouse.

At 1.50 p.m., just 15 minutes after the telegram had been received, the *Richard Coleman* was launched into a rough sea at low tide, the horses arriving as the boat left its carriage.

All pulling together the crewmen rowed out of view into a north-north easterly gale of moderate force which drove cold rain into their weather-beaten faces. About three miles windward they met a beach boat from Shoreham containing four men who informed the coxswain that a man had been rescued.

Later in the afternoon the lifeboat was seen returning, this time under sail and with a small boat in tow. When it beached at 4 o'clock a crowd of excited spectators mobbed the lifeboatmen, eager to find out the nature of their mission.

Worthing lifeboat *Richard Coleman* returning from service under sail.[10]

It transpired that a Shoreham resident, Gordon Hobden, of Alexandra Terrace, had gone out fishing in a small boat whilst the sea was comparatively calm; but when the storm had arisen, his craft had been blown out to sea. At one stage he had been thrown overboard by the powerful force of the waves but, being a strong swimmer, he had managed to regain his boat, which had fortunately not capsized, and had clung to it for a while before mustering the strength to heave himself aboard.

His attempts to row ashore had been confounded by the forceful head wind and so he had hoisted a distress flag. Meanwhile, after a most severe struggle and a rare buffeting from the elements, he managed to reach the beach close to Lancing village. He had been nearly spent with his mighty struggle against the odds when two Shoreham men, Tom Hughes and George Ledward, who happened to be near at hand at the time, helped Hobden in his moment of need.

The distress signal, however, had been seen from the beach at Bungalow Town (between Shoreham and Lancing) at around 2 o'clock, and a Shoreham boat, the *Mauretania*, manned by four sturdy Shoreham mariners, Charlie Oram, Edward Page, Henry Smith and Bob Young, had been quickly launched on an errand of mercy. They had gone off westwards in the direction of Lancing, after the boat, but by this time Hobden had safely landed. When the Shoreham four, who were lifeboatmen themselves, had found it impossible to row homeward in the teeth of the gale the *Mauretania* had been taken in tow, to Worthing, by the *Richard Coleman*.

By 4.15 p.m. the Worthing lifeboat was safely housed, and Coxswain Harry Marshall was able to reflect on the afternoon's events. The quest had not quite been in vain, and he was convinced that circumstances had fully justified the launch. The crew, who had been anxious to join the funeral cortege and pay their last respects to their old comrade, but for whom duty had come first, were: Second Coxswain Bill Blann, Bowman Fred Collier, Fred Marshall, Wm. Cousins, George Benn, Tom and George Wingfield, Steve Wingfield junior, Frank Burden, George Finnis, and two 'novices', Jas. Groves and Jack Burgess, who experienced their first emergency call-out.

Each lifeboatman was paid the standard winter rate of 15s. for his services, and 50 volunteers, employed to launch the lifeboat by hand and haul it up on its return, received 4s.6d. per man.

During 1910, the RNLI was responsible for saving 767 lives – an exceptionally good achievement - by 280 Lifeboats around the United Kingdom's coastline. Since its formation in 1824, a grand total of 49,394 people had been saved. Pensions and gratuities had been awarded, in addition to compensation for injuries sustained in the service.

Some of the lifeboat helpers at Worthing were boatmen from along the beach, who were glad to supplement their income by assisting with the *Richard Coleman*. Their usual charges for taking people out on fishing and pleasure trips, were 2s.6d. per hour for two persons and 3s. per hour for three. Unable to charge whatever they fancied, the boatmen's hire prices were fixed at pre-set limits, supported by bye-laws.

Boatmen with their craft left behind on a Worthing rock bed by the receding tide.

Professional fishermen had to adhere to a law governing the size of fish to be caught. But in November, Chief Inspector E. Page of the Sussex Sea Fisheries District caught a young Worthing man in the possession of a lobster 7¼ inches long, less than the size prescribed by the Act.

At a meeting of the local committee of the Sussex Sea Fisheries District, held at Brighton Town Hall in the presence of Worthing member E. B. Edwards, it was reported that the offender had only recently taken up fishing. He was let off with a caution.

Old fishermen and fishermen's widows received an allowance of half a crown (2s.6d.) per week from the Fishermen's and Watermen's Benefit Association. During the year 1910, £132 was disbursed to 22 recipients, leaving a balance of £726 2s.5d.

At their annual meeting at Highworth the committee, which consisted of mature fishermen, was re-elected, namely secretary Frank Dean, George Benn, J. Searle, T. Clark, T. Davis, J. Tester, and Ed Edwards.

The association had been formed a few years back to administer a sum of almost £1,000 from the defunct Fishermen's Insurance Society.

Old Ed Edwards brought back memories when he reflected on the original rules of that Society, made in 1865, that had required boat-owning members to pay a premium of just £2 per vessel in advance of each season's voyage, to cover loss or damage to their gear or the boat itself.

At one time during the course of 1911, a record catch of fish was brought in by some Worthing fishermen. The sizeable haul, which was the largest amount of bream and bass that had been seen in this neighbourhood, amply rewarded the patience of five fishermen, for it was not infrequent for fishermen to return from a voyage disappointed.

The lucky fishermen, F. Bashford, R. Bashford, F. Searle, W. Searle, and D. Laker had been out Seine net fishing when they had unexpectedly found themselves among huge shoals of these two species of fish. Laker was reported to have said that there were so many fish, acres upon acres of them, that they had had to cut their way through them.

They emptied the huge quantity of trappings from their Seine nets into what was known as a tuck boat, which became so heavily laden that its gunwhales were forced dangerously low in the sea. The larger boat, which carried the nets, was thus compelled to tow it ashore, for without such assistance the tuck boat would have undoubtedly sunk.

On a beautiful June Sunday morning the bountiful cargo was unloaded. The unaccustomed sight of sun shining brightly on the silvery scales of such a vast heap of fish soon attracted many people.

But the mountain of slippery sea food decreased as some was packed with ice in boxes and barrels and sent to Brighton by Mr. F. Worley, one of the recognised local fish salesmen. The remainder was kept for local use.

Fish hawkers and fishmongers at an auction of freshly-landed fish.

A man was seen to be in difficulties one Thursday afternoon at the beginning of July in the sea to the east of the fish market. A boatman on the beach, by the name of Stubbs, saw his predicament.

With no time to lose, he dived into the sea and rescued him!

How the man, who was still fully dressed, came to be in the water in the first place was never discovered. But, fortunately, beyond getting a soaking, the rescued man was none the worse for his traumatic experience.

The following afternoon, just after lunchtime, another beach incident occurred, off the west end of the Parade. When a lad was swimming across a groyne his leg struck it, disabling him.

"Help! help!" shrieked the young bather.

Hearing his cries for assistance, two men named Hollands and Shorten, who had also been swimming, promptly ran into the water to assist him without troubling to remove any of their clothes.

With much difficulty they eventually brought the injured lad ashore, where, after some first aid, he recovered sufficiently to go home.

The beach to the east of the Pier c. 1910.[11]

Two months later, in September, a public garden on the seafront was the setting for a rather hilarious scene. A fisherman, Arthur Elliott, was trying to ride a lady's bicycle in the Steyne quite late at night, 25 past 11.

Difficulties arose in attempting to achieve his superiority over the metallic monster, due to his condition. Well and truly inebriated, Elliott's macabre melee ended in a twisted bundle of man and machine on the ground.

Police Inspector Bristow, who had been discreetly watching the funny antics, attempted to question the collapsed, giggling comedian. When the policeman eventually got some sense from him, it evolved that the bike was not his but one he 'found.'

As a finale he resisted arrest and the Inspector had to summon assistance to take the drunken man into custody.

Before Mr. Harry Hargood, J.P., on the Bench the next morning, Elliott, of Southfield Road, Broadwater was charged with being found unlawfully drunk in the Steyne and fined 5s.

Storms raged in the late Autumn of 1910. On 15 December, the ferocity of the elements was such that beach stones were thrown up onto many parts of the promenade.

The following year, at the beginning of November 1911, storms of even greater severity were experienced. Continuous rough weather damaged part of the Parade. One Monday morning, when the sea was in a particularly turbulent mood at high tide, people flocked to the seafront to watch the spectacle.

The promenade at Splash Point covered in shingle after a storm on 15 December 1910. *Warnes Hotel* in the background.[12]

A close-up of the main entrance to *Warnes Hotel*. The door, opening onto a side street, York Road, can also be seen in the previous picture.[13]

Part of the wooden breastwork to the south of the Bandstand was broken away. A lamp post was forced down under the surge of the weighty waves and carried out to sea before the breakers returned it, throwing it up onto the beach.

In this spate of bad weather, four Worthing fishermen lost their nets, valued at between £60 and £70. A public appeal to replace these nets, which belonged to J.W. Riddles, F. Collier, W. Wells and Steve Wingfield, was launched by John Roberts, honorary secretary of the Worthing RNLI.

A total of £53 was raised, thus alleviating much unnecessary hardship for these fishermen.

One of Steve Wingfield's relatives, a Mr. Wingfield of Littlehampton, brought up this matter of the lost fishing gear at the quarterly meeting of the Sussex Sea Fisheries Committee, held at Brighton Town Hall. Although committee members sympathized with the fishermen they were unable to offer any monetary comfort themselves, but instead, through the press, sought to thank the public for their kind generosity.

The facilities of Worthing's fish market were open not only to local fishermen but also to those from other towns, some a good distance away. For example, on one November morning a Lowestoft steam trawler anchored off the Pier and landed some of its large cargo of herrings by ferry boat. Altogether, some 18,000 fish were sold at the market for a meagre 30s. per thousand, just over one penny for three herrings.

It was not only fish that could produce money from the sea. A bottle, containing a message to be returned for cash, was found washed up on the beach opposite some marshland near the eastern perimeter of the borough.

Discovered by a Mr. H. Blaker, a carpenter living in St. Anselm's Road, Worthing on his way to work at Lancing one morning, it turned out to be a Schweppes mineral water bottle. Its cork was encrusted with barnacles, an obvious sign of long term immersion.

To reach the contents concealed inside, he had to break the bottle carefully, revealing a letter written on headed notepaper of the White Star Line, which read:

On board S.S. *Arabic*
May 27th, 1911
Finch, Captain
Longitude 15° W.
Latitude 51°.

Two ($2.00) Dollars Reward will be paid on demand by the undersigned for the return of this note and the holding for delivery to him of the bottle containing this message.

HENRY D. MASTERMAN,
Elmira,
Chemung Co.,
New York, U.S.A.

Evidently, it had been thrown overboard from a vessel, whose position, according to the information, was some 300-400 miles west of Queenstown.

Excited by his find, Blaker rushed to tell the nearest person – a country man fishing for eels in a marshland stream – about the intriguing instructions.

Fortunately for Blaker, the bottle had broken into only three pieces, and he was able to mend it quite easily. He wrote to the address given and awaited the redemption of the two dollar reward.

A Worthing man who had been in the Merchant Service passed away in October. Henry Finnis, having been a seaman for over half a century since the age of twelve had gradually worked his way up to the post of captain, which he had held for several years. During this exciting career, voyages of varying experiences had taken him round Cape Horn to Valparaiso and as far east as India.

For the last 30 years he was also landlord of the *Running Horse Inn*, Paragon Street, where, as one of the oldest licensed victuallers in the town, he died aged 71.

A small-holder by the name of Saunders eel-catching on marshland to the east of Worthing.[14]

At the funeral, arranged by Mr. H. Hill of Clifton Road, the chief mourners were Henry's three nieces, two sisters-in-law, his sister - Mrs. Piper, his daughter - Mrs. Hutchinson, and his two sons - George and Harry.

As Harry liked his drink too much, George took over running the public house in his father's footsteps. Running a pub was an arduous task: open all day and half the night to satisfy the incessant thirsts of fishermen who worked unsocial hours. As well as his exhaustive work as a landlord he was a crewman on the *Richard Coleman*. Coupled with his livelihood, the additional volunteer work sometimes posed problems as he had to be ready for call-out whenever an emergency arose. George had already notched-up two services on the lifeboat.

Bill Blann junior (pictured right), wearing blue jersey and suit, accompanied by a smart friend.[15]

George Finnis competed in this year's Regatta, where as many as six out of the total of 14 boat races in the fixture were exclusively for licensed watermen. With such a large share of the races, due to the fact that out of 32 Regatta Committee members 12 were watermen, they didn't need to hold their own separate Regatta.

George was successful in three of the events: twice he came second and in the other came fifth. In the first-class three-oared race he teamed up with Jack Burgess and Harry Blann, came second and won £1 10s. cash.

Harry and his brother Bill formed the winning partnership in the first-class pair-oared race and were rewarded with £1 5s. But Bill did not do as well in the solo sculling race. His boat *Mabel Annie*, named after his niece Mabel and his nephew's wife Annie (my grandmother), had not brought him as much luck as he had hoped for. But at least he took the fifth prize of 7s.6d.

Fifty year old Bill did slightly better seated alongside Charlie Collier in the first-class pair-oared race: they came fourth and won 12s.6d.

But, Oh dear! What an embarrassment. Bill Blann junior, now 19 years of age, together with his partner, Fred Searle, not only easily beat his father but, to add insult to injury, actually came first.

This dynamic teenage duo also entered the double sculling race, and again beat all other contenders to take first prize.

In fact most of the watermen, who entered their various rowing or ,sailing matches, received a prize. Presenting the awards at the Town Hall in the evening, Harry Hargood, patron of the Regatta, congratulated the mixed committee on the success of the festival.

"It is pleasing to me," he commented, "to know that the forces had been able to pull together and so hold one really good Regatta. No fouls have been reported and neither have any protests been lodged."

Later in the evening a particularly attractive firework display, held in Steyne Gardens and supplementary to an illuminated promenade concert, completed an eventful day.

These peripheral entertainments were lavish compared to those at early regattas some 40 - 50 years before, when amusements and diversions had been limited to daylight hours.

Entertainment in the town took a big leap forward in 1911. A large, multi-purpose complex, named the Kursall, was built on the seafront, in the huge garden of Bedford House. It was the brainchild of local impresario Carl Seebold, who also ran the Theatre Royal. Encompassing several different forms of entertainment under one roof, it was, in reality, ahead of its time. The main body of the building, called the Coronation Hall, was constructed as a roller skating rink with a stage at the north end and balconies on the other three sides. This main hall doubled as a venue for public meetings and the like. On the first floor in the southern part of the complex, an electric theatre (early cinema) entertained customers, while on the same level was a restaurant. Other facilities included tea rooms and, in a dome-roofed tower, billiards.

On Thursday 22 June, King George V was crowned in London. Here in Worthing, loyalty on this momentous and moving occasion was attested by an address to the King, which read:

'We, the Mayor, Aldermen, and Burgesses of the Borough of Worthing desire to lay before your Majesty an expression of our loyal and dutiful attachment, and one of our sincere congratulations on the Coronation of your Majesty and of your Royal Consort.

'Your Majesty, in ascending the Throne of the British Empire, has inherited a difficult and laborious task, but the support of a loving and loyal people, on which your Majesty may ever rely, will, we venture to hope, lighten the burden.

'We gratefully recall the many occasions on which your Majesty has graciously manifested your active interest and ready sympathy with the Municipal Life of this country, and we fervently pray that your Majesty and our Gracious Queen may, by the Blessing of God, be granted long and happy years to reign over a united and contented people.'

Here in Worthing, coloured decorations tastefully beautified the main thoroughfares in the town centre as well as along the seafront. From Splash Point to Heene Terrace Venetian masts were effectively deployed with festoons of artificial garlands depicting the white and red York and Lancastrian Roses. Banners attached to the street lamp posts were interspersed with foliage wreaths.

In every direction, at villa and cottage alike, the spirit of festive celebration was recognised. With united effort townsfolk of all classes pulled together to present a town of really brilliant appearance. Waving masses of colour impressed the thousands of visitors.

At the main focus of attention, the Town Hall, a luxurious display using electric lights was created specifically for the occasion: the letters G R had been prominently positioned in front of the building, surmounted by a crown; the pillars and other projecting portions of masonry were outlined in colours; and several special electrical designs completed the arrangement.

Across the road in South Street, Jordan & Co.'s entire window space was occupied by a remarkable arrangement of plants and flowers, drawing a continuous stream of admirers, particularly at night when miniature electric bulbs were lit up.

The Kursall, completed in 1911[16]. On the left is the omnibus booking office, and in the foreground is the edge of the fish market.[17]

Outside the newly built Kursall, a huge illuminated device towering above the fascinated crowds conveyed a simple message to the new sovereign — 'Good Luck!' This temporary feature created a most pleasing adjunct to a well-lit building, adding to the effect of the dome-topped turret lined with bulbs.

Conversely, gas design displays outside the Gas Company's office in Warwick Street proved ineffective when exposed flames were hampered by unfavourable weather.

On Coronation morning a large procession formed in the vicinity of the Town Hall in spite of the threatening weather. Headed by the Salvation Army Band and mounted police, the column started off and proceeded up Chapel Road.

Jesse and Annie Blann (my grandparents) stood by the back of the Town Hall on the corner of Ann Street watching the procession. Their two eldest children, Harry, now seven, and Bert, two years his junior, watched with gleeful amazement as the extravaganza passed before their impressionable eyes.

The Mayor and other civic dignitaries, dressed in their robes of office, preceded the Borough Fire Brigade, which was followed by the Worthing Troop of Sussex Yeomanry and a detachment of Territorials, marching in step.

Young Harry's adrenalin ran higher.

"Here they come!" blurted Harry, referring to a body of nearly two dozen men wearing seamen's navy blue jumpers and jackets.

It was the lifeboatmen.

George V Coronation Parade in South Street. Its junction with
Montague Street is in the background.[18]

My uncle Harry Blann (left) playing with his younger brother Bert and
family dog Nell in the back yard of their home at Providence Terrace.

Harry spotted his great uncle Bill Blann at the head of the crew alongside Harry Marshall.

"Hooray for Uncle Bill!" cried the youngster, but although the sound of his voice was deadened by echoing marching music, his great admiration for his idol, marching proudly by, could in no way be diminished.

Close behind the lifeboatmen came the Postmaster, George Stacey, with a strong contingent of smartly uniformed postmen and telegraph messengers.

More music was heard. This time it was the Winter Season Band leading the Holy Trinity Church Lads' Naval Brigade.

By now the head of the lengthy procession had turned left from Chapel Road into Richmond Road.

After the naval brigade came a contingent from the ordinary Church Lads' Brigade, a section from the Boys' Brigade, some Boy Scouts, and the Steyne School Cadets.

1911 Coronation Parade proceeding northward up Chapel Road past its junction with Market Street.

Taken minutes later from the same spot, the procession passing the *Fountain Hotel* (on the left of the picture).[19]

Worthing lifeboat crew, headed by bearded Bill Blann, and followed by Worthing postmen in the town's
George V Coronation Parade marching past the Town Hall at the southern end of Chapel Road.[20]

Worthing Church Lads' Brigade.

134

Boys' Brigade – First Worthing Company.

The last part of the parade included representatives from eight local Friendly Societies, including: the Ancient Order of Foresters, the Sons of Temperance (Sussex District Division), the Buffs, and the Worthing Alliance Slate Club[21]. Worthing Branch of the St. John's Ambulance Association brought up the rear.

From Richmond Road the parade took the second turning left, Grafton Road, to the centrally situated Christ Church which had been designated for an impressive service. Here, after all the marchers had filed in through its western door, there was precious little room left for the general public, despite it being the most spacious church of its kind within the Borough.

A rather striking scene was created inside by the contrasting colours of the various Services against a backdrop of one huge banner unfurled by one of the Friendly Societies.

The Rev. C. J. Hollis had been selected to deliver the address. He pointed out that they were but one of countless congregations, both in these Islands and in our Colonies, that were united in the same spirit. They were as one in loyalty and devotion with our fellow citizens of Canada, Australia, New Zealand, India and South Africa.

From the different continents of the world came the self-same cry, "God Save the King!"

Knowing that Worthingites would echo it, Rev. Hollis proclaimed, "God Save our King and Queen!"

After the congregation had united in singing the National Anthem, the church organist, Mr. Carnell, played his own composition of a Coronation March as the church emptied. The parade re-formed in Grafton Road and made its way south.

On reaching the seafront, the men turned left and marched along in the direction of the Pier. Opposite the Pier the march turned up South Street and progressed the short distance to the Town Hall.

The atmosphere in this central area must have felt electric. A huge crowd of people had braved a sharp shower of rain and were buzzing with expectancy, excitedly awaiting the next item of the day's programme.

Members of Christ Church Choir, having walked from their church near the Town Hall down Chapel Road looking angelic in their surplices, lined up neatly in an area cordoned off on the wide expanse of road fronting the Town Hall.

Coronation Day Parade 1911 making its way south down Grafton Road.

Approaches to South Street thronged with eager Worthingites and visitors alike. Many had secured vantage points in upper storeys of neighbouring buildings, some even on rooftops. At least a dozen photographers focused their cameras on the animated scene.

With the arrival of the parade, the Mayor and his municipal colleagues took up their positions on the Town Hall steps where a projecting platform had been set up for his Worship.

After the Salvation Army played the Coronation March, the public were invited to join the Mayor in singing the hymn 'O God, Our Help in Ages Past.' There followed a rousing rendition of the National Anthem, stiring many a humble patriot.

One such person, Bill Blann Junior, overcome by euphoria, prematurely called for cheers for the King, unaware that this item was scheduled for later in the ceremony.

Then local Territorials, H Company 4th Batalion Royal Sussex Regiment, fired a Feu de Joie. Captain Sim's loud but abrupt command was heard and the sound of a volley echoed round the town. This was repeated three times, with a few bars of the National Anthem being played between each salvo, after which the soldiers remained in the firing position with their rifle butts pressed firmly into their shoulders until the last chords of God Save the King melted into the distance.

Lifeboatmen and postboys in the Parade moving along the seafront, past the junction with Montague Place.[22]

Coronation Day 1911. Territorials, positioned between the Town Hall and the South Street fountain, fire a 'Feu de Joie.'

A Royal Salute followed, and again the National Anthem reverberated around observers on the rooftops. The Mayor now called for three rapturous cheers for the King and Queen from the loyal crowd. The band playing Rule Britannia brought this small but impressive affirmation to a close.

It was now nearly noon and many in the crowd walked down to the fish market to the east of the Pier where mortars and anvils were fired and Boy Scouts demonstrated their skills.

By this time, the inclement weather necessitated the postponement of three other outdoor events: a children's tea, an aquatic festival and a firework display. But thankfully one part of the celebrations that remained unaffected was a dinner for old folks at the Kursall, facing' the sea to the east of the Pier.

A happy gathering of nearly 500 guests dined in the aptly-named Coronation Hall, a magnificent venue with a stage at the north end surrounded by a white ornamental proscenium which contrasted admirably with the rich red and gold curtains. A balcony lining the two sides and the southern end was packed with visitors watching the elderly Worthingites seated at two long rows of trestle tables enjoying themselves.

To protect the splendid Canadian rock maple floor, the Kursall's owner, Mr. Seebold, insisted that it be covered with a thick layer of sawdust, which in turn was covered with planks.

Aged between 65 and 90, the guests relished an appetising meal of beef and mutton joints (roasted or boiled), potatoes (baked or boiled), spring cabbage, carrots and turnips; and for sweet there were the traditional plum puddings, jellies and various pastries, fresh fruit in the form of bananas and oranges followed by coffee or tea. Twenty townsfolk volunteered to carve the joints, and 70 ladies acted as waitresses, thereby providing a prompt and excellent service.

Old Folks' Dinner in the Coronation Hall at the Kursall, photographed from the eastern balcony looking north towards the stage.[23]

Whilst they were eating, the Theatre Orchestra on stage played a selection of light melodies to complete the relaxed, joyful atmosphere amidst gaily hung colourful decorations in keeping with those outside in the main roads.

Mineral waters were supplied in generous quantities, but each of those who preferred more potent liquids were furnished with a pint bottle of light dinner ale.

Special Coronation mementoes were distributed to the guests: teapots portraying the King and Queen were given to the women; and similarly adorned tobacco boxes, filled with tobacco paid for by the Mayor, were handed to the old men.

At the conclusion of the dinner the Mayor led grace and prayed that King George V would reign over his loyal subjects for a far longer period than his predecessor, the late King Edward.

King George, like his father, Edward, and his grandmother, Victoria, took a great interest in the works of the Royal National Lifeboat Institution and his continued prestigious patronage was to be of capital benefit to the Society.

Old Folks' Dinner in the Coronation Hall at the Kursall, photographed from the stage looking south towards the entrance.

Footnotes

[1] The New Theatre Royal on the west side of Bath Place opened in 1897, having been converted from what was the New Assembly Rooms. Competition from cinemas forced the closure of the Theatre in 1929; and the building was subsequently demolished and replaced by the present Woolworths store.

[2] Beach Parade was also known as the Faggot Walk. The wall in the picture is the southern boundary of the Beach House Estate.

[3] This photographic postcard was purchased from Spencer's Photo Stores, 24 Chapel Road (a stones throw from the Town Hall) at 3.30 p.m. on the same day as the photograph was taken.

[4] The lifeboat crew are in the foreground of this photograph.

[5] The *Fountain Hotel,* with its wall-hung sign, is seen on the southern corner of Chatsworth Road. A small coastguard detachment is in the foreground, followed by the fire brigade and bowler-hatted dignitaries.

[6] Worthing Lodge was later demolished, and the Rivoli Cinema was built on the site. Its auditorium was destroyed by fire in 1960; and the front of the building, housing the foyer, was pulled down in 1984 to make way for a dual carriageway through the town.

[7] Another Worthing connection had been established when a William Hayden served on HMS *Bellerephon* in the 1870's and 1880's on the North American Squadron. His great nephew, Phil Hayden, lives in Worthing today.

[8] I have located Willy Kiernander's daughter-in-law, Freda, who now lives in Derbyshire.

[9] Charlie Lee had served in the Russian War when he was a highly-spirited and adventurous young man. Whilst crewing a merchant vessel that was transporting stores and British troops in the Bay of Balaclava, he and a fellow shipmate managed to sneak ashore one night. They found their way into the trenches, but were taken prisoner, and the next morning they were taken before the commanding General for questioning, whereupon they were warned that they were liable to be shot. In the face of this terminal threat, Charlie cheekily retorted: "Well, we were ashore, and we thought we must go and see some of the fun." They were ordered to return to their ship at once. Charlie Lee's great grandson, Charles Lee, lives in Worthing today.

[10] This is a rare shot of the *Richard Coleman* with sail rigged.

[11] An interesting postcard produced by Walter Bros. of South Street. Bathing machines can be seen close to the water's edge on the far right of the picture. To their left, at the top of Steyne Gardens, stands the Boer War Memorial, erected in 1902. Moving left of the centre of the photograph is a large white board bearing the words 'Kursall Garden', on the site of today's Dome Cinema.

[12] On the right of this exposure, captured by G.W. Tuft, is a Nestles Chocolate vending machine.

[13] The *Warnes Hotel* is now under serious threat of demolition following a fire which gutted the building in 1987, after being purchased by developers.

[14] This marshland was made into a boating lake and pleasure park called Brooklands in the early 1960's. Mr. Saunders' granddaughter, Mrs. Ann Tugnett (nee Bashford) lives in Worthing.

[15] Photographed at Edwards & Son's Excelsior Studio.

[16] The Kursall, a magnificent and unique Edwardian entertainment complex which was renamed the Dome during the Great War, survives today. It is thanks to the hard-working efforts of all of Worthing's conservationists that the building is now listed with the Department of the Environment as being of historical and architectural importance. But, unfortunately, it could still be under threat. The 'Save the Dome' Campaign fights on!

[17] This photograph was published as a postcard by J.H. Kirk of 1, Ann Street.

[18] Photographed by Edwards & Son of 20, New Street.

[19] Two pictures taken by a photographer of Spencer's Photo Stores of 24 Chapel Road; and showing the *Fountain Hotel,* which is still there today. This postcard was purchased by some people whose identities are known only as Annie, Alice and Jim, who are standing in the crowd near the junction with Market Street, and posted to a Mrs. Holden, who lived near Midhurst.

[20] The sign 'Gentlemen', affixed to the north wall of the Town Hall in Ann Street, refers to a basement lavatory that provided many a timely convenience for generations of Worthing males.

[21] Worthing Alliance Slate Club was established in 1906. Their motto was 'United we stand.' Non-profit making slate clubs were run in pubs for the benefit of weekly subscribers. When unable to work through sickness, they drew benefit. The landlord looked after the subscriptions; then once a year, just before Christmas, the money was divided equally among the members.

[22] This photograph taken by W.J. Knowles of 23 Warwick Street shows Harry Marshall, wearing a white cap cover and a lifeboat badge, heading the lifeboat contingent. Alongside him marches Bill Blann. Sporting a white tufty beard is Frank Burden in the row behind. Next to him are two more of the Marshall brothers, Fred and Mark. According to some old writing on the back of the photograph, the spectator indicated by a cross, and apparently dressed in bright garb, was called Frankie.

[23] Reproduced from a damaged postcard.

A view from the back of the Kursall looking north east across its garden. Originally part of the grounds of Bedford House (the building fenced off at the end of the garden), it is now a Southdown bus company building fronting Bedford Row. On the opposite side of the road is Bedford Hall (part of this tall Greek-style building can just be seen), now the Sports Bar of *The Thieves Kitchen*.

Looking east along Warwick Street, which is today a pedestrian precinct. This view shows its junction with Bedford Row on the right. On the far corner the significant marble pillar remains today – although the shop is now a dry cleaners. Premises containing Bostel Bros. Electricians on the near corner has changed radically and is now part of the *The Thieves Kitchen*. Shopfronts on the left of the picture have been altered over the years but most of the upper storeys have remained unchanged.

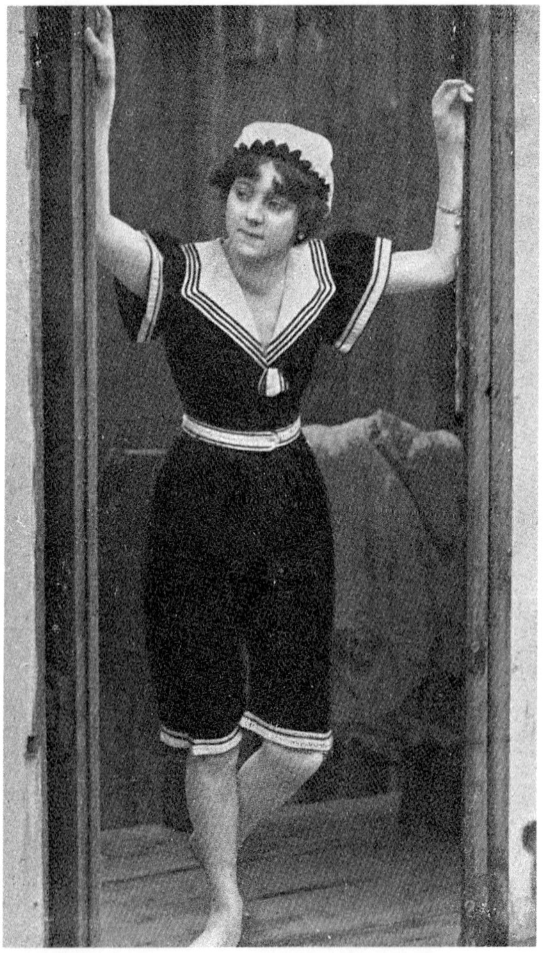

Chapter 8

A Vital Role

1912

Owing to the nature of its foreshore, Worthing has never been an easy place from which to launch a lifeboat. There was great danger whenever the Worthing lifeboat had to be launched for services at high water with a heavy sea running. Two horses harnessed immediately in front of the lifeboat with a third horse leading were used to pull the boat into the water. All could have been imperilled. The lead horse particularly, was at risk from being caught by the rolling breakers or from being sucked-in by the swirling current.

Such an accident could have resulted in broken legs or the drowning of a horse, as had been experienced at some other stations, or even the loss of men's lives.

Eight lifeboat stations that experienced similar threats at high tide were supplied with launching poles (an invention which was the brainchild of Lieutenant Garthside Tipping, a former District Inspector) in a determined effort to combat this danger. About eight stations each received a pair of these 26 feet long poles, which were fitted to either side of the boat carriage using strong swivel brackets.

Horses pulling the *Richard Coleman* into the sea. Note the haul-off warp being taken to the lifeboat.[1]

An application by the Worthing Station for the supply of a pair of launching poles was granted. After taking delivery they were fitted and tested.

With the novel gear in use, only two horses instead of three were required to back the lifeboat into the sea. These two horses were no longer in front of either the lifeboat or the carriage. As each pole was attached by a specially-designed sliphook it could be released instantly by the horse's rider pulling a rope, thus freeing the steed from the outrigger, and enabling the horseman to get himself and his workhorse clear of the carriage as soon as their work was done.

The outrigger itself was about five feet to the rear of the ring in the chain, bringing the horses about level with the two large wheels, instead of in front of the boat, where they had been unnecessarily vulnerable. The purpose of the jutting out horse launching poles was to avoid a collision between the horses and the spoked wheels.

When the assistant surveyor of the RNLI, Mr. Green, came to instruct our crew in the use of the new invention, Coxswain Harry Marshall was ill and missed the launch, his first absence in 22 years. Second Coxswain Bill Blann took charge.

When the lifeboat was re-housed, the two poles had to be removed to get the boat inside. And so for future launches of this nature it was to be necessary to fix the poles in position after the *Richard Coleman* had been brought out onto the road; losing a minute or two in precious getaway time, but gaining about six or seven minutes on the actual launch using the new equipment.

At the annual meeting of the Worthing RNLI, members were appreciative that the request for horse launching poles had been met. The cost of this expensive new equipment, and also of two new carriage wheels, was met by head office. Any exceptional expenditure exceeding £5 was always defrayed by headquarters and therefore in this particular year the branch received considerably more than they remitted.

The meeting, held on a Saturday afternoon in March 1912, attracted an exceptionally large and influential attendance, on account of the presence of two members of Parliament — Sir Godfrey Baring, Bart., a private secretary to the Board of Trade, and Major Campion, member for the Division.

A change of venue this year. Instead of using the Town Hall, a local hotelier offered more comfortable facilities. Luxury surrounded the gathering: Mr. G. H. Warne placed the spacious lounge of his *Warnes Hotel* at the disposal of the committee. The hotel, an imposing building on the east side of the Steyne Gardens and facing the sea, had been converted from the individual dwellings that had comprised York Terrace.

Worthing's premier *Warnes Hotel* fronting both the seafront and Steyne Gardens.[2]

The meeting heard that the Institution now boasted four steam lifeboats as well as five auxiliary motor lifeboats in its national fleet. But they were expensive: £2 - 3,000 each; more than double the cost of a pulling-and-sailing self-righter like the *Richard Coleman*. Yet only a few years earlier the average cost of a lifeboat had been about £750.

With the rising costs of ever-improving lifeboats the financial burden on the Institution was always increasing. With the discontinuance of the Saturday Lifeboat Movement, which left an annual shortfall of about £20,000, the RNLI was having to fight even harder to maintain its standard of income.

During the year, British lifeboats saved 540 people. An average of more than one life for each of the 458 lifeboat services; while 147 were rescued by shore boats and others, making a total of 687.

Answering the suggestion that a government department could be set up to take over lifeboat rescue work from the RNLI, Sir Godfrey said that that would be disastrous. Lifeboat work requires flexibility of administration and that would be impossible under a public body. By asserting that the organisation should be left as it was and that voluntary efforts could be relied upon to do the work, he won the hearts of the assembly.

Society, and with it the quality of individual characters, was changing. Even in 1912 it was sometimes inferred that the advancement of a comparatively luxurious lifestyle resulted in Englishmen losing some of their old hardiness and pluck in the face of danger. But that could not be said of lifeboatmen!

A Worthing man's personality, that of our local lifeboat chairman Harry Hargood, had not changed in all his long years of drumming up support for the Institution. A typical example of his wit and humour entertained guests as he revealed the following tale.

When a new lifeboat had been launched at Ramsgate, he, as a member of the RNLI executive, had assisted at the naming ceremony. Later a local fisherman had asked his permission to name his own fishing boat after his (Mr. Hargood's) good lady, Elizabeth Mary.

"Of course, if you so wish it," had been the reply. But sometime afterwards, Mr. Hargood confessed to feeling shocked when he had received the following telegram:

'Elizabeth Mary gone to pieces: sold remains for 10s., all she was worth.'

The committee was sorry to lose its long serving, ardent honorary secretary, Mr. John Roberts. It was partly due to his deep interest in the welfare of the branch that Worthing was able to claim that it was one of the best-equipped and best-supported branches in the South of England. The latter part of this statement is still true today. Threats of his resignation over the past three or four years had been countered by sufficient persuasion to put it off, but that persuasion was no longer forthcoming and with great regret his resignation was accepted after 14 years in this important office. The meeting concluded with a vote of thanks for the chairman.

A destructive storm hit Worthing on Monday afternoon 4 March. It proved to be one of the worst in the early 20th century. Heavy showers during the day were followed by a thunderstorm which began at about 5 p.m. Strong winds during the day increased to a violently powerful gale as the evening advanced, creating havoc all night.

High seas lashing the Bandstand shelter and covering the Parade with shingle, 5 March 1912.[3]

The shingle-strewn wooden platform surrounding the Bandstand shelter, after the storm.[1]

Marine Parade (looking west) flooded on 5 March 1912. The hoarding in the centre is on the corner of South Street.[1]

Hundreds of tons of shingle were thrown up by the swelling sea onto the Parade at high tide. Between Worthing and Lancing the coast road was blocked, and early morning mail vans from Brighton had to make a detour by taking the upper road through Sompting.

Two market gardener's vans which attempted the perilous seafront route were abandoned when they stuck fast in several feet of shingle. At Navarino Corner at East Worthing the sea pushed inland for about 200 yards, flooding several roads. Occupiers of some of the houses on the north side of Brighton Road to the east of the *Half Brick Inn* found their gardens flooded sufficiently deeply to enable boats to float with ease. The sea had been driven in with such a force that even a 'To Let' sign outside one of the houses was carried a distance of several hundred yards, lifted over a five foot hedge, and left on the lawn of another house.

Along Worthing seafront, the visitation was evident: Splash Point and the Beach Parade (also known as the Faggot Walk) suffered a good deal of damage; one of the groynes opposite Beach House was considerably knocked about; the timber planking around the bandstand was forced up; much of the seafront road was flooded, the water extending part way up South Street and Bath Place; while the promenade itself was thickly covered with shingle along its entire length.

The subject of sea defences came to the forefront of public debate during March. Plans for three new groynes east of Ham Road, submitted to the General Purposes Committee by the Borough Surveyor, were adopted by a slim majority after much argument.

These controversial plans were for the construction of more groynes angled in a south easterly direction and longer than the traditional ones angled in a southerly direction, but many of those who knew the beach well spoke out against the new proposals.

One James Churcher, a builder, of 70 Ashdown Road, who had studied sea defence, commented that since the Corporation had started erecting groynes at a south eastern angle a large amount of beach had been washed away. "Standing at the Pierhead I have watched the waves strike against the new groynes opposite Beach House. A volume of water is drawn five or six feet in the air and when it falls it takes the beach round the toe of the groyne and carries it right away to the east," remarked Churcher.

Conversely, the old groynes from Heene Road to Splash Point constructed about 40 years earlier when the Parade was made, did the job they were built to do – every groyne retained the beach and prevented it from being washed away.

Fisherman E.B. Edwards of 6 York Road was totally against the south east pointing groynes. He was concerned that boats could strike the piles that run out so far on the sands, thus endangering lives. "Our strongest gales are from the south west which cause a heavier sea than any other point on the compass; and these long groynes, laid down on the south east angle, have to take all the weight of these heavy seas that come from the western ocean."

Worthing had had some long groynes some years before: one under the Pier and another opposite the Fish Market. The latter groyne had run out about 50 yards from the toe of the beach and had been planked-up. Seaweed had piled against the groyne emanating an offensive smell. At that time Councillor Patching had asked Edwards' advice.

"Take the planks off, sir, and see what nature will do," Edwards had replied.

The planks had then been removed and the nuisance eradicated. Later, the piles had been dug up and the long-toed groyne opposite the Fish Market dispensed with altogether, as was the similar groyne under the Pier.

Edwards was now being asked his opinion on the south easterly angled groynes. "Long before they are worn out the sea will knock them down if they are planked up. Ask any of our old established watermen and you won't find one who will say that the groynes are put down the right way."

Harry Marshall, the lifeboat coxswain and a licensed boatman of many years standing, said: "Down at our stand, opposite *Stanhoe Hotel*, there is more beach at the present time than I can ever remember, and we have been at that stand ever since the first Jubilee. The groynes run north and south, and fill themselves – they couldn't do better; and so are all the groynes along the front. The beach in front of the town was never better than it is now. But when you come to groynes east of Splash Point, that's where the trouble begins; they are all on the south east angle, which I think is altogether wrong, because instead of retaining the beach, they only scour it away. The south groynes break the force of the sea coming in, and keep the beach; but these new groynes don't keep the beach at all, because our usual winds are south west, and the beach is carried away. That's my opinion, and I believe you'll find that pretty nearly every man along the Front thinks the same as I do about it. There was talk at one time of putting these long groynes down in front of the town. I'm precious glad they never did that, but if they were to, we could never run our boats ashore, and they would probably drown half the boatmen."

A councillor by the name of Baker tried to rescind the resolution regarding the proposed construction of the controversial groynes. He attempted this by submitting a resolution to overturn it, but on the vote it failed to get a majority.

The story of the bottle washed up by the sea and found by a Mr. Blaker in 1911 took on another episode in March. The bottle which had evidently been put in the sea about 600 miles west of Worthing and had floated about in the ocean for some seven months before being discovered had been returned to a Mr. Masterson in New York in accordance with the instructions found in the letter.

Blaker subsequently received the promised reward of two dollars. Masterson then wrote to the Worthing Gazette asking for back copies of the newspaper which carried details of this matter, stating that: 'Newspapers in two different cities in this State who learned of the incident have stories about it, with large display heads. Everyone here who heard of the matter considered the recovery of the message from the sea a very unusual occurrence.'

What a curious ending to such a strange affair!

The pleasure steamer *Worthing Belle* began its season of Sussex coastal cruises during the Easter holidays. Having been overhauled during the winter months in a dry dock at Southampton, the brightly-coloured vessel with its smoking funnel stood prominently at Worthing Pier when it loaded its cargo of fun-loving holiday makers.

The saloon paddle steamer *Worthing Belle*, 180 foot long, 193 tons gross.[4]

And now to switch from a joyful trip to a disaster of international magnitude. In the wake of the sinking of a large vessel in the Atlantic various charity events were staged in Worthing to raise cash for the dependants of the huge number of people that drowned. The world famous 'unsinkable' liner *Titanic* collided with an iceberg in April.

On Thursday 11 July, three months after the national disaster, distress signals were seen from Worthing seafront out over the Channel. This was rather surprising because it was a delightful summer evening with no movement of air to stir the surface of the sea.

Three white rockets were sighted at 8.40 p.m. by the duty coastguard, Wm. Robert Deadman. He conferred with Harry Marshall, the lifeboat coxswain, who had also seen them, and together they estimated the flares to have been about 10 miles out into the Channel.

Harry ordered the immediate firing of the lifeboat gun. Two loud bangs signalled an emergency call-out. Fishermen and boatmen who made up the trained lifeboat crew came running, some in pairs and others alone.

The familiar sound of the mortar aroused considerable excitement among a large number of people on the seafront, some strolling along the prom and others listening to the Season Band. No sooner had the maroon gone up than the chairs around the bandstand were deserted. Everybody was running towards the lifeboat house.

There was no time to lose. Lives could be at risk somewhere out there on the Briny.

A large number of eager helpers dragged the *Richard Coleman* out of the boathouse on its carriage. Once horsed, it was drawn eastward along the seafront road to its customary launching position by the Pier. Here they expeditiously pushed the lifeboat into the sea. It was now 9.15 p.m. and high water.

Deserted seats around the Bandstand.

Our lifeboatmen pulled simultaneously and the *Richard Coleman* glided with ease through the calm waters, unlike the more familiar stormy conditions that the rescuers were used to on these occasions. There was not even the faintest of breezes to make it worthwhile raising canvas.

This one element – complete lack of air movement – distinguished this one service from so many others.

Seeing their plight in the 'Doldrums', the motor boat *Pegaway* drew near to the lifeboat just south of the Pierhead, and its owner, Mr. C. G. Fairer, offered to tow the lifeboat out to sea.

The Bandstand and its shelter viewed from the beach.

The *Richard Coleman* being drawn along Marine Parade past its junction with New Street.

With a hawser connecting the two craft they travelled in a south-south-easterly direction out into the Channel. About one mile out, the *Richard Coleman* displayed a blue light. Some of the huge crowd spectating from the Pier and the Parade reckoned that there was an answering signal out at sea, but this was not corroborated by the lifeboatmen. Quite soon the lifeboat disappeared in the darkness out of sight of the shore watchers, leaving the distinct lights of various fishing smacks and other craft to be seen in the Channel.

Some of the massed onlookers left the vicinity of the seafront after 11 o'clock to wend their way home, excited by the events they had witnessed. But many remained behind, vigilantly scanning the blackness for any sign from their lifeboatmen. Together, they were very supportive, not only of the crew but also of each other in their communal purpose.

For nearly two hours, the motor boat chugged away, drawing the powerful-looking rescue craft. It must have seemed a strange and ironical sight! A lifeboat virtually disabled by lack of wind when strong wind was most often the cause of shipwreck and the lifeboat being called out.

A further irony became apparent when, just after 11, the *Pegaway* itself nearly became disabled. It ran short of petrol and had to return towards land, leaving the lifeboat to continue its search alone.

Dependent once more on the whims of the wind, the lifeboat crew hoisted sail. Thankfully it fluttered a little, using the slight breeze that prevailed out here in the Channel.

At half past midnight they came across the Brighton fishing smack *Lord Roberts* and hailed her crew.

When the fishing boat fell in with the *Richard Coleman* the Brighton skipper told Coxswain Marshall that they had not only seen the rockets but had also heard the firing of a gun, between 8.30 and 9.00 p.m., which they had taken to be a distress signal as well. The skipper pointed abeam. "Oi'd say it were about eight mile yonder way."

Invigorated by this further confirmation, Coxswain Marshall ordered his crew to sail further out to sea until they were about 15 miles from England and right in the track of big liners, several of which passed them.

The lifeboat cruised about in search of a distressed vessel or even some wreckage. After heading towards mid-Channel for six hours, a new day dawned. They searched a wide area and even approached quite close to the Owers Light ship.

But they found nothing and eventually abandoned the search. Assisted by a freshening breeze, the tired lifeboat crew sailed the *Richard Coleman* back to terra firma.

It was quite some time before they approached Worthing. Just before 6 a.m. the returning lifeboat was sighted in the fresh dawnlight some distance out at sea, sailing home in a direct line with the Pier, the Southern Pavilion of which was used as a landmark.

They had been out all night and didn't set foot on the beach until 7 o'clock in the morning. Many of the watchers had also been up all night, maintaining an all-night vigil on the beach. Wearily, but nevertheless eagerly, they awaited news from the lifeboat crew.

Harry Marshall, his heavy boots now feeling like lead weights, expressed the opinion that there had probably been a collision somewhere in mid-Channel. Whilst trudging up the beach with the lifeboat he managed to point out to a doubting person that the distress signals would not have been fired without good cause as there was a heavy penalty for the wrongful use of rockets.

One possibility was that two fishing boats may have collided and that one of the crews had sent up distress rockets before the true extent of the damage had been realised. It was thought by some that, not wanting to risk a heavy fine, the two fishing boats may not have waited to explain.

It took the crew and volunteers half an hour from the time of beaching to return the *Richard Coleman* to its quarters in readiness for the next emergency.

In some respects it was unfortunate that the lifeboat crew's long 10 hour search had resulted in an anti-climax. But, had they not attempted to solve the maritime mystery of the distress rockets, the public would have, without doubt, criticised our lifeboatmen, as was the case over the *Zadne* affair in 1894.[5]

The launch cost the RNLI dearly, a total sum of £45 1s.9d., but those who supported the charity did not begrudge the outlay, as there had been at least a possibility of people being saved. Our lifeboat crew had executed their vital role of protecting the lives of sailors.

The bulk of the costs involved immediate payments made to those who crewed, launched or hauled-up the lifeboat: each of the 12 lifeboatmen received 25s., the regulation amount laid down by the RNLI for an extended night service during the summer; while a total of 66 assistants were rewarded with the sum of 7s.6d. per man; and the signalman was allowed 8s.9d.

For the use of the horses, an amount of £4 16s. was paid out, being the cost of eight horses at 12s. each. Just one other expense was listed: 2s. under the section for 'Allowance to Messenger', which I presume must have been the cost of notifying the Shoreham Lifeboat Station not to launch its boat when Worthing had already done so.

Bill Blann, the regular assistant coxswain had not been available for this service. His vacant position was filled by Steve Wingfield who was normally the bowman and who had been on 11 services before. Steve's relative, George Wingfield, in turn acted as bowman on this, his ninth service. Among the rest of the crew was another member of the Wingfield family, Tom, who had been afloat on nine lifeboat rescue missions.

The Marshall family had experienced many services between them, with Harry, the coxswain, having notched up the most – 14 in all. His two brothers, Fred and Mark, had previously been on 12 and seven services respectively.

George Benn, another veteran, had been out a total of 10 times on service, while Fred Collier had taken part in nine rescue launches. The other members of the crew on this occasion were Jack Burgess, F. Hutchinson, George Finnis and William Cousins.

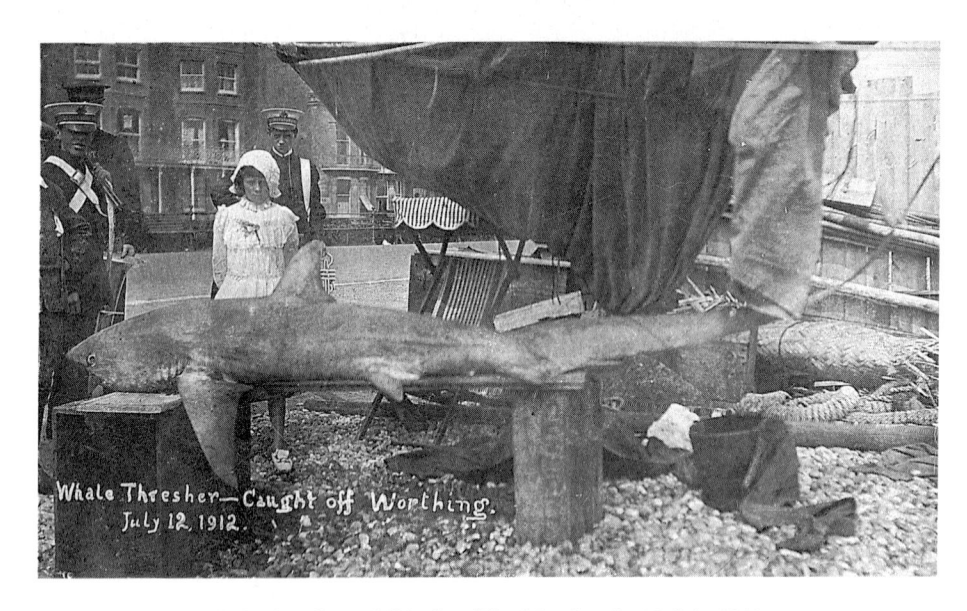

Whale thresher exhibited on Worthing beach, 12 July 1912.

Later on the same day the lifeboatmen returned from their search, a Worthing fishing boat they had passed in the Channel returned from its working trip. Among the catch was an unusual fish of giant-like proportions. It was a whale thresher which had accidentally got caught in their nets off Worthing. The fearsome fish was displayed at one of the fishermen's stands at the top of the beach on a makeshift bench of planks of wood placed across two wooden crates. An old canvas sail was hung around the prize to conceal it from the view of curious promenaders, while one of the fishermen sat in a deck chair, accepting coins from the inquisitive for a glimpse of the strange phenomenon. Although it was a rare occurence in these waters, it was not the first to be caught here. In the 19th century, the occasional odd one had got tangled up in fishermen's nets, had been brought back to Worthing and had been exhibited here for a short while on the beach.

Other strange things had appeared on Worthing beach from time to time. For example, 19 months earlier, on 11 December 1910, a torpedo had been washed up by the tide just east of the lifeboat house. The Royal Navy was informed and a detachment sent to Worthing to disarm it and take it away.

July 1912 was a significant month: there was the lifeboat launch and search which was immediately followed by the display of the whale thresher. Later in the month, several boatmen from two families of fishermen were in trouble for not being licensed to ply for hire.

A torpedo on Worthing beach, 11 December 1910.

It would seem that the Hackney Carriage Inspector was responsible to Worthing Corporation for policing our inshore waters, for the inspector gave evidence before the Magistrates Court which convicted each defendant.

The inspector, Walter James Butcher, the man who had retired from the position of signalman for directing the lifeboat ashore, and who for many years supplied the horses for launching the lifeboat, was now in the situation of bringing to justice some of the watermen that he knew so well.

Butcher, together with a policeman, P.C. Wiseman, saw boatman John Elliott and his son at sea with five people in the unlicensed boat *Kia Ora* (a Maori term meaning good health). One of the passengers, a lady, was seen to hand Elliott some silver, and his son said, "Take for four!"

In court, Elliott said that he had had a licence for 44 years but was sorry that he had let it go.

The second case was brought against Arthur Elliott for carrying passengers in the boat *Phyllis Irene* without a proprietor's licence.

Thirdly, Charlie Wingfield was summoned for committing a similar offence with his boat *Charlie* on 3 July.

It would seem that there had been a tendency among some boatmen at this time not to bother to apply for a licence. In an attempt to try and halt this trend, the defendants in each of the three cases were fined 10s. inclusive of costs.

One of the most exciting and memorable incidents of 1912 was the lifeboat rescue of some Italian sailors during one of the dreadful summer storms, just 26 days after the previous lifeboat service that had involved an all-night search for the source of distress rockets. It was Tuesday 6 August, the day after Bank Holiday.

It was a wild and tempestuous day. A severe gale, somewhat unusual for this time of year, had been sweeping the Channel since the day before.

At about 7 o'clock in the morning Coxswain Harry Marshall, who had been scanning the Channel's horizon from the lookout turret in the lifeboat house, spotted two vessels in danger of coming ashore. From this moment a watch was kept on them. Harry sent word to the stables to warn them to keep some horses available and ready at a moment's notice. Walter Patching, the new honorary secretary of the Worthing RNLI, joined Harry at the boathouse, and all morning they observed the approaching vessels until, at 1.30 p.m., signals of distress were seen flying from one that was driving down. Instantly, the secretary authorised the launch of the *Richard Coleman*.

Boom went the maroon, quickly followed by a second airborne explosion.

People recognised this double signal to call out the lifeboat in emergency and there was a general rush towards the Parade.

Not a moment was lost in getting the lifeboat out of her quarters.

Whipping up a heavy sea and blasting the seafront at 70 m.p.h. the wholesome south-south-westerly gale tore at everything in its path, even rocking the normally secure lifeboat on its carriage, as the horses pulled it eastward along the seafront road.

The force of the gale was so strong that one could scarcely stand against it!

'White horses' riding on the crest of the huge waves racing shoreward presented a grand spectacle. As each wave crashed violently on the beach with a deafening roar, it surged slowly back into the sea, sucking shingle with it, into the open jaws of the following wave. Each wave action remodelled the contours of the beach before being swallowed into the sea once more.

With the tide at three hours' flood and the forceful gale prevailing, the launch from the beach to the east of the Pier was one of the most dangerous for many years, yet, by the same token it was one of the most exciting for the watching public.

On the Pier, the hauling rope, which was kept there for emergencies, was brought into use. One end was dragged over the railings and along the beach to the lifeboat where Bowman Steve Wingfield connected it to the bow. When it was made fast, Coxswain Marshall gestured towards the Pier, indicating that his crew were ready. Then scores of eager men, waiting lined up on the Pier in the driving rain, heaved the thick rope onto their shoulders and began to tread the decking, slowly moving seaward.

The distressed barque was closing in. Barely a mile from the Pier now!

On the beach, helpers struggled to get the *Richard Coleman* into the water. In the melee one of them was knocked down by the violently uncaring sea and hurt, but fortunately not badly.

Even with the aid of the towline the heaving sea consistently threatened to turn the boat broadside. If this had happened, it would have been cast back on the beach and its crew flung into the breakers. At length, with the help of the many volunteers on the Pier, the *Richard Coleman* was successfully hauled out away from the beach at 1.45 p.m.

As if the heavy rain was not enough, enormous billows repeatedly struck the lifeboat when in the troughs of the sea and completely drenched the crew.

The *Richard Coleman* putting to sea, being towed by the haul-off warp from the Pier.

The *Richard Coleman* under sail passing the Pierhead on a rescue mission, 6 August 1912.

As soon as the crew were able they hoisted sail and sped rapidly away in a south-easterly direction making for the disabled barque. A loud cheer went up from the watching crowd, but the wind direction and the din from the storm prevented the sounds of encouragement from reaching deserving ears.

Meanwhile, the wind had veered towards the west, and the furthest of the two observed vessels, which was some six or seven miles due south of the Pier, managed to get away under its own power.

The vast crowd of spectators now focused their attention on the distressed vessel, which could be seen some three to four miles off, unmanageable and drifting at the mercy of the wind and tide.

Time after time the huge waves encountered filled the lifeboat.

Despite the hazardous conditions, splendid progress was made under the guidance of its efficient coxswain, Harry Marshall. It took an hour for the *Richard Coleman* to reach the iron-hulled barque, which was being subjected to a severe battering by enormous waves, and by now was off Southwick. All of her sails had been torn to shreds by the screaming wind, but the Italian national flag remained, still flying upside down as a recognised distress signal.

As the Worthing crew arrived they found the Littlehampton lifeboat *Brothers Freeman* there, just leaving with nine of the barque's sailors aboard.

By skilful handling, the Worthing boat was worked round to the leeside of the ghost-like craft. Now with an additional danger from collision, the coxswain, his assistant, and the bowman each took the precaution of affixing themselves to the lifeboat by a lifeline.

Bowman Steve Wingfield, his life at great risk, managed to secure a rope to the barque.

Two sailors were then persuaded to leave the ailing ship. Risking life and limb, they had very narrow escapes from falling into the mountainous broth.

The remaining three crew, including the captain and his mate, refused to leave, in the hope of reaching Newhaven. So the Worthing boat stood-by for about six miles until they saw the Shoreham tug *Stella* arrive at the scene, whereupon Coxswain Marshall decided to return home.

Waiting anxiously on Worthing Pier for the *Richard Coleman* to return, 6 August 1912.

The Worthing lifeboat crew tacked westward, but when they were off Worthing Pier, the crashing breakers rendered it too dangerous to come ashore between the groynes. So they dropped anchor, and the boat stayed in this position for an hour and a half.

Very few of the onlookers understood the meaning of a small red flag which the lifeboat now displayed in her bows, and many questions were asked on shore. It denoted that there were rescued persons on board, and this was further emphasised when Coxswain Marshall semaphored the news to a coastguard on the Pier.

At 5.30 p.m., when the tide had ebbed, signalman Wakeford on the shore sent up a white rocket, meaning that it was safe to come in, and the lifeboat answered at once with a green light.

Excitement was now most intense as preparations were seen to be made by the lifeboat crew to come ashore: the anchor was hauled in, the oars got out and the boat was soon on the beach amidst tremendous cheering.

Return of the *Richard Coleman* and crew with two rescued sailors on board, 6 August 1912.

They were heartily greeted by the large crowd still waiting for them near the Pier, by now grown in size, amounting to some thousands of eager spectators. Lining the sides of the Pier and on the beach, and in blinding squalls of rain, they watched our weary, weatherbeaten lifeboatmen clamber out of the boat.

The rescued men were most exhausted and, being only scantily clad, had suffered from exposure. On realising that the two shipwrecked sailors only spoke Italian, a Mr. M. Lowther ran and got Mr. L. Ferrari of the Imperial Restaurant to act as interpreter for the two Europeans. It evolved that their names were Chiesa Romolo and Martoio Raimondo, and that both were bachelors. It was ascertained that they were in need of some attention. First aid was rendered by Lieutenant A. Dean Willcox of the National Reserve (Worthing), who took them to the *Pier Hotel* where Mr. Howell and his nephew gave assistance.

Afterwards, Chief Coastguard Officer Goldfinch took charge of the foreign sailors, one with his head bandaged, and put them up at his house. Whilst they were there, they were attended by Dr. Lockwood.

The next day the men, apparently none the worse for their experiences, were given fresh clothes and boots by their coastguard host, and later left for Newhaven.

In the meantime, Lieut. Willcox telegraphed the Italian Ambassador in London to notify him of the fate that had befallen some of his countrymen.

It transpired that the Italian barque *Andrac* of Genoa, en route from Rochester to Bahia in Brasil, had got into difficulties between the Owers Lightship and Littlehampton earlier in the day. The 1060 ton vessel, loaded with cement, encountered an exceptionally severe gale, which ran her aground two miles off Littlehampton. In the extremely heavy sea she refloated but the mighty wind ripped her sails apart and rendered her unmanageable, leaving her at the mercy of the howling elements to drift with the gale.

After the Littlehampton and Worthing lifeboats had rescued 11 of the 14 crew, the Shoreham paddle tug *Stella* arrived towing the Shoreham lifeboat *William Restell*. Securing a towline on the disabled barque in this uncontrollable sea was a hazardous ordeal.

It was now the task of the third lifeboat in danger's hour to manoeuvre alongside the rolling wreck. Four of the lifeboat crew perilously boarded the swaying craft and helped to make fast the tow-line from the tug.

The barque had been spotted by people on Brighton seafront at 5 p.m., and just one hour later it was off Newhaven being towed into harbour by the steam tug with the Shoreham lifeboat behind.

The storm-damaged barque *Andrac* being towed into Newhaven Harbour by Shoreham's paddle-steaming tug *Stella*, 6 August 1912.

Therefore, the team of three lifeboats ably assisted by the tug *Stella* had now effectively rescued all the 14 Italian seamen.

Later, the Shoreham coxswain, Captain Charles D. Tracy, painted his eye-witness impression of the tug towing the *Andrac* eastward past the cliffs at Peacehaven, making for Newhaven, with the *William Restell* being towed behind the barque.

Captain Tracy gave the picture to a Mr. Oliver Jones, a long-serving secretary of the Ipswich RNLI branch, who eventually, many years later, sent it to Alderman H. L. Frampton, whose wife was chairman of the Worthing Ladies Guild of the RNLI.

Alderman Frampton had been one of those who had braved the stormy weather to crouch on the Pier and watch the hazardous exploits of our lifeboatmen on 6 August 1912. He wanted Worthing to add this item of local history to its permanent collection of pictures, but the Library and Museum Committee declined it on the grounds of 'insufficient local interest.'

As Worthing didn't seem to want it, it was offered for sale to benefit RNLI funds.

Those Worthing lifeboatmen who so bravely risked their lives in the *Andrac* rescue were paid the basic sum of 10s. each, but the secretary, Walter Patching, wrote this recommendation in the lifeboat log:

'My committee are of the opinion that having regard to the severity of the gale, the question of a slight additional recompense to the acting crew is worthy of consideration.'

Coxswain Marshall later said, I have never known such high seas, and in my long experience of lifeboat work I have never before had a life-line attached to me; but even in these conditions the *Richard Coleman* behaved splendidly.

Harry commanded 12 crew, five of whom were comparatively new to active service on the lifeboat. Bill Blann junior experienced his very first lifeboat rescue at the age of 20, while his uncle, 54 year old Harry Blann (my great grandfather), had been out only three times before. Jo Street and James Groves were only on their second mission, and for Jack Burgess and Steve Wingfield junior it was their third.

Steve's father was an experienced bowman: he had logged 12 services. George Wingfield, from the same family, had experienced nine service launches, one less than George Benn. The other three accomplished crew were the three Marshall brothers and Assistant Coxswain Bill Blann.

Seventy one volunteers who helped to launch and haul up the lifeboat shared £10 13s.; and an extra 2s.6d. was awarded to the one who was knocked down by the sea and suffered minor injuries. Our signalman received 5s.6d., and eight horses were hired for 9s. each, bringing the total expenditure on this rescue mission to £21 3s.

Several weeks afterwards, a holidaymaker paid tribute to the Worthing lifeboatmen in a holiday competition run by the *British Weekly*. The entry, which was about a trip to Worthing, won third prize. After recording first impressions of Worthing, the contribution from Mr. C. E. Powell of Dublin continued:

'The wind was very rough, and the waves were rolling grand and strong. On Bank Holiday it was worse, and the next day worse again, so no one was surprised when someone called, There's a boat driftin' in!

'We watched with great anxiety. All at once two shots were fired. The German invasion! I said to myself — but it was the lifeboat summons. In a few minutes her brave crew were ready and off; the sea was tremendous. It was a trying time, and no one said much.

'But after several hours, back they came, bringing one or two poor foreigners with them; some others had been taken by another boat.

'Sometimes in Ireland we say the English are cold, but never again will I be saying it, for the noise of the cheering which welcomed the brave crew back rings in my ears yet.

'Again the troublesome lump rose in my throat. Not home sickness but fellow-feeling caused it this time.'

'God save Ireland and England too.'

Footnotes

[1] This postcard was published by Luff of Worthing. Luff's sweetshop was in Montague Street, and later in Broadwater Street West.

[2] The Boer War memorial on the left of this picture was erected in 1902.

[3] Photographed by Edward & Son of the Excelsior Studio.

[4] Built by Messrs Barclay, Curle & Co. of Glasgow in 1885, originally as the *Diana Vernon* for the North British British Steam Packet Company. Powered by a 110 h.p. single cylinder steam engine, she was employed on their Holyloch and Gareloch service from Craigendoran. In 1901 she was purchased by Mr. J. Lee of Shoreham and renamed *Worthing Belle*.

[5] See chapter 15 of 'A Town's Pride' for the *Zadne* affair.

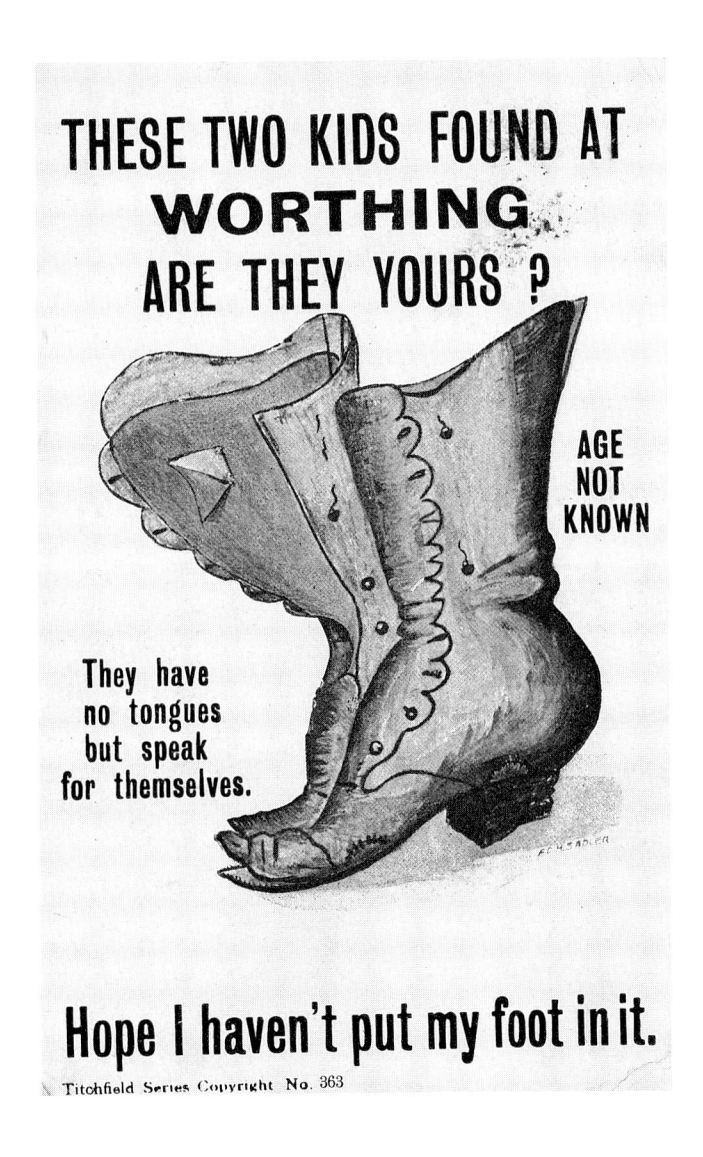

"When I am kissed, though I scream very soon
Dont think I object to An-Ice (s) cream Spoon".
EXAMPLE OF AN ICE CREAM SPOON, AND AN "I SCREAM SPOON".

Chapter 9

A Severed End

1912-13

The month of August, 1912 proved to be a bad time for boatmen and fishermen. Excessively bad weather, uncharacteristic of our summers, plagued the livelihoods of our fishermen. At least 124 fully equipped lobster pots were washed away in the sea, incurring a total loss of £15 10s. for six fishermen: Bill Blann, Fred Wakeford, William Wells, Steve Wingfield sen., Steve Wingfield jun., and another Steve Wingfield from a family of the same name.

In the temporary absence from the town of the Mayor, Alderman E.C. Patching, J.P., an appeal to the charitable was circulated by the Deputy Mayor, Alderman J.G. Denton, and the full sum was raised to reimburse our fishermen.

When the Mayor returned to Worthing he identified himself with a general appeal for the town's watermen, for whom the season had been very unpropitious. They had to face the winter months with but slender provisions for themselves and their families. The boatmen, who were generally considered by townsfolk to be uncommonly civil and hard-working men, depended upon fee-paying visitors coming here during the summer. But the weather this summer had been unusually unkind to boating: high winds and copious rainfall effectively banned the pursuit of pleasure in this direction.

Typically, the Annual Regatta had to be postponed because of the disastrous weather, and was eventually held on Tuesday 3 September. Even then it was dogged by inclement elements, for although the weather appeared fine to start with, attracting large numbers of spectators to watch the afternoon's events, the wind soon began to gust strongly from the south-west, and many patrons departed from the seafront, leaving but few to witness the finish of events.

The occasion had been organised by the Joint Committee of the Town Regatta and the Watermen's Regatta. Representatives of the latter were Steve Wingfield (vice-chairman of the joint committee), Harry Belton (sailing judge and starter), Jack Burgess, F. Collier, the three Marshall brothers Fred, Harry and Mark, Fred Wakeford, Wm. Wells, Tom Wingfield, Steve Wingfield sen., and Steve Wingfield jun.

Despite the unfavourable conditions the watermen's races featured some excellent rowing and some challenging sailing.

Towards the end of September some wreckage was found washed up on the coast between Littlehampton and Worthing. The son of Willy Kiernander found a capstan bar near the *Half Brick Inn* bearing the name *Magic*. Another piece of timber was painted with the words '*Magic*, Faversham.' As for the wreck of the vessel itself, which was a victim of the recent rough weather, it was discovered in about 10 fathoms of water, five miles south-west of Portobello, between Brighton and Newhaven.

Let's put the bad weather into perspective. In the month of September, 2.71 inches of rain fell in six days, more than the average of 2.46 inches for the month since 1852 when Worthing's meteorological records began. The clouds released the heaviest downpour on Sunday 29th when a colossal 1.43 inches was collected.

From January to September, rainfall was more than 40% above average at 25.49 inches compared with a mean of 18.09 for the same period in any year since 1852.

The weather improved by the second weekend in October, but not before one of our fishermen had all his six nets swept away whilst herring fishing. As luck would have it, they were found a few days afterwards quite by chance, by waterman Jack Burgess.

He had hired one of his boats to a fishing party who'd gone off to the wreck of the *Indiana*, a popular habitat for fish and eels.

When Jack went to the beach the next morning to check the boat, he was annoyed to discover that two pairs of oars were missing, and upon further examination found that the craft now leaked.

He and another boatman took one of his boats out to sea to search for the missing oars. They were nowhere to be found, but whilst on the look-out for their own property the watermen came across the fishing nets which had previously been lost.

That Sunday afternoon, when Jack took a party out fishing, a big conger eel that was hooked put up a fight and struggled violently before it could be landed in the boat. It was one of the largest fish of its kind seen at Worthing, reported to be 5 feet 10½ inches long, 21 inches round, and weighing 45lbs.

Seventeen days later, on Wednesday afternoon 30 October, a resounding boom stopped townspeople in their tracks. It was the lifeboat gun being fired: just once, indicative of a quarterly practice. Jack Burgess and other watermen along the seafront hastily assembled at the lifeboat station, while sightseers and townsfolk excited by the mortar signal gathered on the Parade.

Apparently, the task of hauling the *Richard Coleman* over the beach met with some difficulty on this occasion; but the launch itself was a success in the heavy running sea, thanks to the helpers marching down the Pier pulling the haul-off warp. Some of the large crowd of interested spectators approached too close and were drenched by the spray, much to the amusement of the other onlookers.

The magnitude of the crowd on the beach was recorded in a photograph taken from the Pier by Mrs. Ernest Ellis, a copy of which was subsequently sent to each member of the lifeboat crew.

Launching the *Richard Coleman:* the crew pulling on their oars, assisted by the hauling-off rope.

Worthing, together with other towns along the Sussex coast, took the brunt of a gale which swept most of the country on Boxing Day 1912. Coinciding with high tide, the powerfully unstoppable combination of elements repeatedly pummelled the sea defences, and provided an amazing spectacle to those who braved the weather.

Splash Point, at the eastern end of the Parade and opposite Warwick Road, was swamped with sea-water and shingle as huge waves pounded against the breastwork and shot up into the air.

To the east of Splash Point, the Beach Parade, or Faggot Walk as it was more commonly known, was almost impassable with a continual barrage of high waves and shingle sweeping over it.

Huge waves pounding Splash Point, and casting beach stones over the asphalted Parade.

A woman clutching a shawl-wrapped baby attempts to pass along the shingle-strewn Beach Parade.

The crests of the waves were riding so high that it was said that the landing stage at the southern end of the Pier was completely submerged, whilst the high sea rolling underneath the structure sent showers of water up through the narrow gaps between the deck planking, time after time.

When the storm subsided, townsfolk living along the seafront were thankful that it had passed. What a Christmas for them to remember!

Worthing Pier lashed by ferociously powerful waves.

Four weeks later, on 22 January 1913, a meeting of Worthing seafarers was held at Highworth[1], a Victorian villa which housed the offices of a local partnership of solicitors, 60 yards west of the (old) Town Hall. It was the annual meeting of the Worthing Fishermen's and Watermen's Association. Secretary Frank Dean submitted the balance sheet which showed that £126 11s.6d. had been distributed in the past year (1912) among 23 recipients, leaving a balance of £359 14s.9d. in their Post Office Savings Bank account.

Officers and the committee were re-appointed *en bloc* for the coming year.

Six weeks on, and another maritime meeting took place in the town - the annual meeting of the Worthing RNLI. Held in the lounge of *Warne's Hotel* on Wednesday afternoon 5 March, the session was supported by a large gathering of subscribers and supporters, who welcomed highly complimentary observations by Admiral of the Fleet, Sir Gerald Noel, who addressed the assembly.

This distinguished officer remarked that the Worthing Lifeboat Branch and Station were notably among the most perfectly managed in the Kingdom.

Speaking on the general work of the Institution, he explained that an expensive change was now being undertaken, by supplying motor lifeboats wherever it was possible.

In moving a vote of thanks to Sir Gerald, Mr. W. R. Campion, M.P. for Lewes, congratulated Worthing on its successful work for the Institution. "It was a matter for congratulations that the lifeboat system in England, although voluntary, was so thoroughly efficient. Sussex was the largest recruiting county for the Navy, and one of the best recruiting counties for the Army. The result, indirectly, was that Sussex people, perhaps more than those of any other county, went to far distant parts of the world, and Sussex residents had therefore a keen interest in anything connected with the sea, because the sons and daughters of Sussex went so far abroad."

The Mayor, Alderman Robert Piper J.P., in seconding, declared that the town owed a lot to the RNLI, for 19 years earlier, when Worthing was recovering from an outbreak of typhoid, they had an event in the town that day such as they had never seen before. The RNLI had put on a marvellous demonstration of lifeboats, helping the Council to show visitors that the town was once again healthy. An example of town and lifeboatmen working together for common good.

The committee's report, read out by the chairman, Harry Hargood, contained some items of particular interest. The new launching poles which had been fitted to the carriage had proved a great success and were a source of safety going through the large crowds which assembled whenever the boat was launched for service or exercise. The poles kept people clear of the large carriage wheels.

The parent Institution in London bore the cost of the poles, together with the costs of wreck services, stores, etc., which altogether amounted to £112 3s.6d. for the year.

During quarterly practices the collecting boxes were passed around the crowds of spectators, but it was the rule not to do so when the lifeboat was being launched on service. But at the incident involving the *Andrac,* a lady had begged Mr. Hargood so intently to have a collecting box out among the crowd that he was ashamed to say he had hauled down his colours and surrendered. This greatly amused his audience, comfortably seated in the hotel lounge. The rule, for once, had been broken, and the lady had not been gone long before she came back and wanted another box. Before she had finished she had collected £10 on behalf of the Institution. On hearing of this woman's spirit, members cheered.

The sum of £80 had been forwarded to head office. Mr. Hargood reminded his captive audience that in contributing to the funds of the local branch of the lifeboat service, they were also helping to maintain lifeboats in places where there were no funds available locally.

For instance, westward along the Sussex coast, there was a lifeboat at a strategic point, Selsey, which was frequently called upon to go to the rescue, but the total amount raised there was less than £5 a year.

At Shoreham, also, where there were very few rich people, they did not raise anything like enough to cover expenses.

At Dungeness they got no subscriptions at all!

Among the many generous and consistent supporters of the RNLI had been the late Alderman Captain Cortis, who had the distinction of being Worthing's first mayor. In his will he bequeathed the magnificent sum of £1,000 to the Institution's head office in London, showing his high regard for their beneficent operations.

The great amount of work put in by Mr. Hargood to inspire Worthingites to take an interest in the Lifeboat Institution was truly appreciated by the committee in London.

The Worthing Station was held in high regard: not only did it remit one of the largest amounts of money from the South of England to the parent Institution in London; but it was held in great esteem by the Institution's chief inspector, who, on his last visit, had paid a very high compliment to the coxswain for the excellent condition in which he had found everything.

In Mr. Hargood's opinion, it would have been impossible to find anywhere round the coast with a more efficient coxswain or one who took a greater pride in the boat than Harry Marshall, who had a highly capable second coxswain, Bill Blann, and two very able crews.

Seventeen days after the annual lifeboat meeting it was Easter Saturday; an exceptionally ferocious storm expended its violence on the south coast.

At Worthing, this great storm created havoc on the seafront and damaged the Bandstand shelter to the west of the Pier. But worst affected was the Pier itself.

'Easter Island'. The Pier pavilion and jetty after the great storm of 22 March 1913.[2]

Montague Street looking west from its junction with South Street.

High tides and severe gales had, over the years, combined many times, and were notorious for causing damage and destruction to groynes and the promenade. But this latest uncanny combination of the elements culminated in the biggest, most spectacular conquest of them all ever seen here at Worthing.

By Sunday morning all that was left standing of the Pier was its pavilion and landing stage, marooned like an island in the sea.

On the Saturday afternoon there had been no indication of what was to come. Rain poured down, but no one guessed what was to follow. Even at 7 o'clock in the evening there was no sign of a tempest. But soon after eight the wind began to increase, and within an hour its velocity was reckoned to be nearly eighty miles an hour.

It was dangerous to walk in the streets!

People in Montague Street experienced considerable difficulty in walking along, as the wind blew furiously and whistled round the many turnings in an unpredictable way. Several ladies tried to make their way to the Kursall on the seafront, but found that the force of the gale at the corner of South Street simply blew them back again.

The hoarding which hid the vacant site at the junction of Marine Parade and South Street, where the *Royal Hotel* had been gutted by fire in 1901[3], was in danger of being blown down. A policeman was positioned there at 9 p.m. to warn passers-by to keep clear. The raging winds rocked the wooden panels, causing them to creak, as though they would come down at any minute.

A high sea was threatening the Pier, and it was deemed necessary to close it to the public at the same time, 9 o'clock. Huge waves were thrown up over it, but no-one thought that the sea would be stronger than the stout ironwork.

Fishermen along the seafront were getting anxious about their boats and tackle stored at the top of the beach. So at about 10 o'clock, they began to move these across to the other side of the Parade, against the railings.

The sea began to look upon the promenade with angry eyes.

Huge waves rolled up the beach and over the asphalt. The sounds of smashing glass and splintering wood could just be heard, muffled by the thundering of shingle being thrown about.

Part of the bandstand shelter went! The relentless sea was advancing!

The delightful Kursall entertainment complex on the seafront.

Hundreds of sightseers exploring the tangled wreckage of Worthing Pier, Easter 1913.

167

A view, looking north, of the Pier's remains.

Debris-scattered promenade and flooded road, between the Pier and the Bandstand.

Damaged shelters adjacent to the Bandstand.

Wrecked wooden bungalows on the beach between Lancing and Shoreham.

More wooden bungalows in a terrible state of collapse, Easter 1913.

Enlisting the help of some of the many bystanders, boatmen hauled their craft down from the Parade and into the road. Everywhere was strewn with beach stones and water.

The time was now 11.30 at night, and the tide was at its highest point.

Moonlight reflected on the advancing waves, giving them a silvery hue, but when the moon hid behind cloud, the evil sea turned to a dull and dirty grey.

Although the wind had dropped, angry waves kept surging on, driven by an invisible force.

Huge seas repeatedly enveloped the Pier in showers of spray, until, a rapid succession of exceptionally large waves rocked the structure.

It began to twist. The screeching sound of metal on metal filled the atmosphere. Crash upon crash could be heard as the piles fell away and onto the sea bed.

Nothing on the main promenade section of the Pier was spared.

Suddenly, the electricity manhole cover at the corner of Bath Place and Marine Parade flew up in the air. An extensive flash of light lit up buildings close by momentarily, as the town was plunged into darkness.

Early next morning, at daybreak, the angry night tide had receded, exposing a twisted mass of metal on the sand, where a proud Victorian structure had previously stood. Many people flocked to see its remains and some took away manageable pieces as momentoes.

Some of the boatmen, including Jo Street, discovered a windfall of pennies among the wreckage on the sand, where amusement machines had crashed down in the night and broken open. Filling their pockets with coins they delighted at the find.

Eastwards along the beach, decking planks were strewn as far as the promontory at the *Half Brick Inn,* Ham Road.

A few miles along the coast, between Lancing and Shoreham, scores of wooden bungalows had been damaged, many beyond repair.

On the Monday morning, the paddle steamer *Worthing Belle,* which called regularly at the Pier, carried a larger than usual number of passengers from Brighton to see the spectacle. She ventured as close as she dare before returning eastward.

News of the disaster travelled fast: this same day, London papers carried illustrations; and at Worthing, about half a dozen movie cameramen were at work on the beach filming the scene of destruction.

Worthing was inundated with sightseers, and one restauranteur reported that on this particular Monday his takings were the highest ever.

The loss to the Pier company shareholders, caused by one night of havoc, must have been in the region of £15,000.

Footnotes

[1] Highworth was demolished in 1988 to make way for the Montague Shopping Centre. I commissioned a model of Highworth, which was made by local craftsman Ted Bayley; and I have lent it to the former occupants of Highworth – Malcolm, Wilson & Cobby (solicitors). It is on public display in their reception room at 3, Liverpool Terrace.

[2] This view was taken after the Pier debris had been removed. According to information written on the back of this photograph, it was taken by an anonymous amateur using a box camera, showing his great friend, Fred Hoad, with a telescope looking back to Brighton. They had both walked from Brighton to see the island pier, and then walked back again. Apparently, they later enlisted together in 1914, but Fred tragically died in 1917, hurrying to catch a boat home for a week's leave.

[3] A covered shopping mall, called the Arcade, now occupies the *Royal Hotel* site.

Looking north towards Broadwater from the railway bridge c.1913. Trees have since been felled and the road widened to form a dual carriageway.

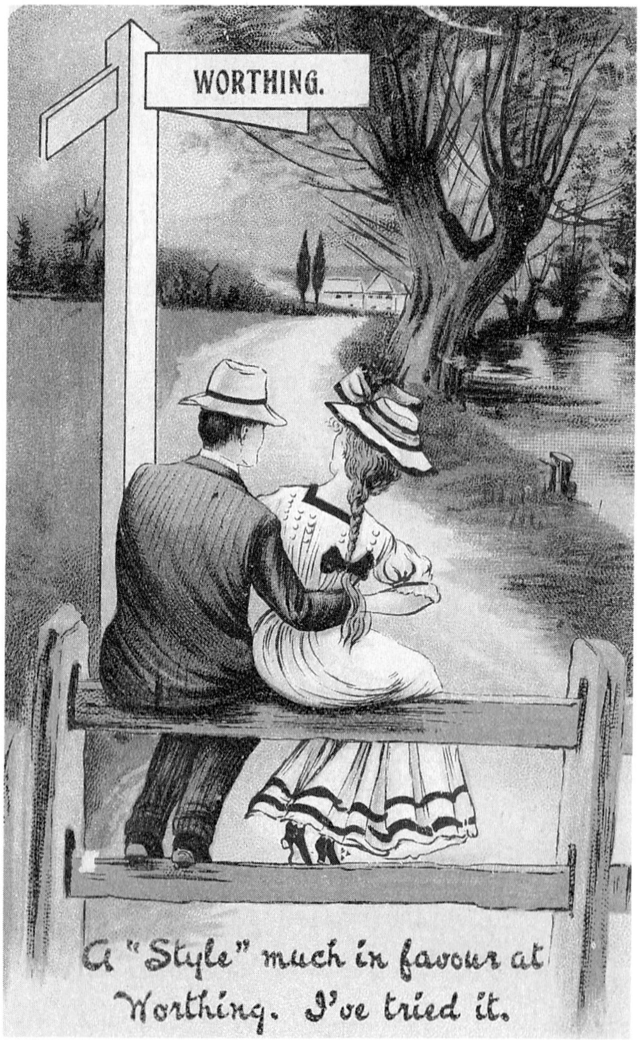
WORTHING.
A "Style" much in favour at Worthing. I've tried it.

Chapter 10

Pulling Together

1913-14

The sweeping away of the Pier created difficulties for our lifeboat launching here at Worthing. Two important facilities had been lost: protection from the attacking elements of wind and sea; and the capacity to position a haul-off rope and men. Without these it would be like turning the clock back to the early days. It was imperative that arrangements be made to enable the lifeboat to be launched at any time, without delay, should an emergency arise.

Using the initiative and comradeship for which they were renowned, our lifeboat crews and committee members pooled together their various ideas.

Very quickly, it was decided to install a temporary lifeboat warp. Firstly, the committee purchased some new ropes; and then the lifeboatmen anchored the new warp in the sea opposite West Street, just east of the lifeboat station.

By 3 o'clock on Easter Sunday, the afternoon following that calamitous night, facilities were ready for any impending launch of the *Richard Coleman*.

As the saying goes, Worthing was always prepared!

This new launching system and the resourcefulness of the lifeboat crew were tested on Friday morning 6 June, when the lifeboat was launched for inspection by the District Inspector, Lieut. Keppel Foote. Conditions were ideal for the purpose: a south westerly wind blew strongly and waves broke heavily on the beach.

To make matters even more difficult for the launch, the Easter storm had deposited extra shingle along the beach, imposing a great strain on the horses and men in getting the lifeboat over the ridge and down to the water. The wheels of the eight ton carriage and boat sank deep into this loose shingle.

Even though the *Richard Coleman* took the full force of the strong wind in this exposed position, the experienced lifeboatmen proved equal to the task and managed to get her off with very little delay by both rowing and pulling on the temporary warp. Excited onlookers breathed a sigh of relief as the oarsmen pulled her out into the open sea. Many spectators, including several experts, believed that in the event of a gale raging, it would be impossible to get the boat off at all.

After a severe testing, our clever crew emerged successful, and came in for a word of appreciation from Lieut. Keppel Foote, who was highly pleased and well satisfied. After many years of visits, this was his last inspection at Worthing: he was about to retire from the RNLI.

At the 89th annual meeting of the National Institution, held at this time, Lord Mersey pointed out that the Institution has in its service a body of men whose qualifications for their work have made the lifeboat service of this kingdom a model to the countries which have any corresponding service.

It was appropriate that, at this time, the RNLI came into possession of the very craft used by Grace Darling in her splendid deed of heroism — a coble 21 feet long and six feet across. Since its inauguration, the Lifeboat Institution had been instrumental in saving 51,000 lives at sea.

It was reported in the Worthing Gazette that on several occasions at Worthing, passengers from Brighton on the pleasure steamer *Worthing Belle* enjoyed the novel experience of a trip round the 'island' that was left supporting the Pier Pavilion. It seems to me that the skipper, Capt. John Trenance, could have been taking a risk in the shallow water on the landward side of the 'island'.

Then, on Tuesday 9 July, for the first time since the Easter disaster, the *Worthing Belle* embarked passengers from the Pier head. From here they were conveyed to the beach in small motorised craft, courtesy of local boatmen, for a penny fare each person.

The 'Island Pier', photographed from Messrs Pashley Brothers' aeroplane at 1,300 feet on 6 September 1913.[1]

The use of motor boats had advanced irresistably over the past two years. Registered pleasure boats at Worthing now numbered 116, an increase of four. Yet, ironically, the actual number of licensed boatmen had diminished from 79 to 45, as fewer crew were needed for motorised vessels than for sailing boats.

These figures were a significant indication of the trend – employment of watermen with sailing skills was waning.

One Worthing boatman who consistently refused to license his craft was James Gilham Davis, who contended that the Local Government Board had no jurisdiction over the foreshore, and that compelling men to take out licences stopped trade.

He was, of course, wrong. In reality, under the Charter of Incorporation, the Borough of Worthing extended to low water mark. Davis had been flouting the Corporation for years. The last time was on Monday 7 July when the Corporation Inspector, Walter James Butcher, saw Davis's boat leaving the shore, containing seven passengers under the charge of Charles Stubbs, who was not a licensed boatman.

The passengers, one of whom was a pretty young lady from Walton-on-Thames, paid 6d. each for the pleasure trip. Davis was subsequently summonsed before the Magistrates Petty Sessions, sitting at the Council Chamber on Wednesday 23 July, on a charge of 'suffering passengers to be carried in an unlicensed boat.' He was fined £1 10s. inclusive of costs, with an order that he should be imprisoned for 14 days on default.

This year it was left to Worthing watermen to provide that essential attraction in a seaside town – the Regatta – as the Town Regatta had been abandoned, severing a link which had lasted 64 years, the first Regatta having been held here on 22 August 1849.

Lack of financial support had led to the cancellation of not only this year's Regatta but also of other spectacular displays, held in recent years but now to become just bygones.

Now the watermen were called upon to substitute their fixture for the more comprehensive enterprise. For as soon as the decision was made known that there would be no Town Regatta, the watermen banded together and formed a committee.

In addition to obtaining sponsorship from prominent residents and tradesmen in the town, the committee enlisted the support of several well-known people, including the Duke of Norfolk. Monday 25 August was the date appointed for the fixture, and for once it turned out to be a brilliantly fine day.

All along the beach were groups of onlookers. Nearer the Pier, the scattered groups compacted into a large mass of hundreds of expectant spectators. Some even paid the customary Pier toll, were rowed out to the landing stage, and took up vantage points on the island Pier head.

Crowds along west beach, which happens to be lined with seaweed.

In all, 10 events were staged during the course of the afternoon: one sailing race and six rowing competitions, which were open to all licensed watermen of Worthing; two amateur rowing contests; and climbing the greasy pole. Note that it was climbing the greasy pole, and not walking it. In previous years, the pole had been affixed horizontally to the Pier deck, and had extended over the sea. This year, with the Pier gone, the pole was erected vertically on the beach, secured by guy ropes.

Competing boats started in a line from where the Pier once stood, raced westwards to some anchored buoys, turned, and raced back again for the finish.

Members of the Wingfield family fared particularly well. They won five races, and were runners-up in another two. In two events, they even walked off with three out of the five prizes awarded for each race.

Small wonder that both the chairman and the honorary secretary of the committee were both Wingfields.

In the pair-oared race for amateurs, J. Wingfield teamed up with F. Worley[2], but they were both beaten to second place by A. Dean and A. Friend – I wonder who that was?

A total of £85 10s. was distributed in cash prizes to all the winners. The watermen received so much encouragement that it was felt certain that they would continue to organise their own fixture in future years.

Excellent work had been done by the Fishermen's and Watermen's Benefit Association during the previous year of 1913. To relieve two dozen needy members, the association paid out £122 18s., leaving £232 14s.6d. in the kitty. During that year, the Association's numbers decreased, on account of four members passing away.

The number of fishermen employed in the fishing industry generally was diminishing because of the increasing number of large steam trawlers, from home and abroad, that now plied the seas. In the whole of the Sussex Sea Fisheries District there were approximately 560 registered fishing boats and about 14,000 men employed in the industry.

Owing to the very unsettled weather during the first four months of the year, the various fisheries were adversely affected. When the fishing boats had been able to get out, the trawlers had done fairly well, but for the smaller craft, fishing had been a virtual failure.

During the month of June, however, conditions improved, and, furthermore, as a result of large shoals of mackerel visiting the English Channel local fishermen were able to secure extensive catches. Although they were of excellent quality, they were sold cheaply because of their abundance.

It was a difficult and erratic life being a fisherman: it tended quite often to be all or nothing. If the catch was sparse, there was little to sell; and when the haul was enormous, the fish fetched very low prices. In some cases the fishermen had to almost give them away. It could almost be a no win situation.

Fishermen continued to be favoured with good hauls of fish, well into July, at the peak of what must have been the best mackerel season for years.

The same applied to the herring fishery on this part of the coast: it too was considered the best herring season for some years. Fishing for sprats also proved to be very productive in 1913.

When it came to counting out the fish, fishermen all along the south coast mostly used one particular method. They were accustomed to 'keep a tally': one fish was thrown into a basket for every 100; and when the counting was finished, they looked into the basket to see how many hundred had been registered – that was called the 'long hundred' of the fishermen, which was said to represent a hundred and twenty.

Fishermen on the beach early on Monday 15 September spotted an unusual sight in the Channel – a waterspout. It was first noticed at about a quarter to seven, some two miles out, rather to the west of the Pier head. At the time, a light shower of rain was falling, whilst out to the east, the sun shone, creating a crystal clear atmosphere.

One observer described the waterspout as 'descending in a clearly defined thin arched column from a great height, and the impact with the sea was so great that the sea was churned into masses of foam, from which masses of spray could be seen rising into the air.'

At first the spout was stationary, then it appeared to move towards the shore, and it was last seen moving rapidly in the direction of Beachy Head.

Two months later, during a severe storm, on Tuesday 11 November, another unusual phenomenon visited Worthing. It happened shortly before ten o'clock in the evening, and took the form of a miniature whirlwind, which stripped leaves from the trees during a torrential downpour, accompanied by thunder and lightning.

This year saw the passing of a popular Worthing fishmonger. Mr. T. Davis, from a well-known local family, died in September, aged 64. Twice married Davis was highly esteemed by those who enjoyed his friendship. His late father, Tom, had run the fish shop in Montague Street before him, and had been a boat owner as well as a bathing machine proprietor.[3]

Thoughts of a barque which had been involved in a collision on the south coast a quarter of a century earlier in 1889 had not faded. Worthing folk often recalled the casks of petrol and wooden wreckage washed ashore from the *Vandalia*[4] which had eventually grounded off Brighton. A piece of the jib-boom had been found by William Churcher of 7 Buckingham Road, and fashioned into a pair of candlesticks.

After William died, his son Fred acquired the tiller of another even earlier wreck, the schooner *Theresa*[5], which had come ashore opposite St. George's Church at East Worthing in 1883. Fred's hobby was collecting pieces of timber from wrecked vessels and old windmills, much of which was of excellent quality and ideal for shaping into ornamental items. The well-known Worthing turner, F.J. Randell, undertook work for Fred; and the tiller was to be next to receive his attention.

Remarkable variations in the weather were witnessed in January 1914. In one week alone, the temperature plunged 20 degrees Fahrenheit. A thick, white frost made the roads slippery, necessitating the services of Corporation employees to sprinkle grit on the thoroughfares. Ponds froze, enabling locals to participate in the pleasures of skating, but not for long. The temperature soon rose again, and the ice thawed.

In February, rain descended and strong winds struck the town. During this bad weather, a series of high tides was exceptionally rough. Although the heavy swell brought up a quantity of stones onto sections of the Parade, no actual damage was caused. During the dismal third week of February, it rained every day, and the sun shone for only nine hours.

Once more the great groyne debate dominated local feelings. At the annual meeting of the Worthing RNLI, on Tuesday afternoon 24 February, a serious warning was issued by Mr. Hargood regarding the proposed alterations to the angle of the groynes. "On Worthing beach," he declared, "between Splash Point and the Coastguard Station, there was now the finest accumulation of shingle that even the oldest inhabitants could remember."
"Pointing due south, these sea defences had done their job well, and it would be foolhardy to construct south easterly angled groynes as some suggest, because the coast would no longer be safe for our boatmen," Mr. Hargood continued.
"It would be almost impossible to launch the lifeboat!" exclaimed the chairman, "and the Institution would have to seriously consider closing down the lifeboat station!"

Reconstruction of Worthing Pier, photographed from the 'Island Pier' on 27 February 1914.

An alteration to the groyning system would also finish the sailing club, and destroy the town's fishing and boating industry. Mr. Hargood knew what he was talking about, for over a period of nearly 50 years he had kept a close eye on the coastline, and he urged the town council to maintain the existing system of groyning.

At the meeting, the new Inspector for the Southern District praised the Worthing Station. Based on his 18 years experience of lifeboats around Britain, Lieut. Basil Hall, R.N., stated that of all the lifeboat stations with which he was familiar, he knew of none in better order than that at Worthing.

An old familiar face reappeared on the committee this year. John Roberts, who had served for many years as honorary secretary before stepping down and being replaced by Walter Patching, consented to take care of the finances of the branch, and was elected honorary treasurer.

Rebuilding Worthing Pier was a lengthy task, work had continued since the previous year, and by February, the upright piles and the steel girders to support the decking had reached the halfway point, where this time, a short stretch of the Pier was made wider to give it extra stability in severe storms.

A few weeks after this meeting, the Worthing lifeboat crew began experimenting with oil to calm the heavy seas. They started a series of trials using the viscous liquid as a means of quietening troubled waters.

The use of oil had been so successful at Bridlington that the Chief Inspector of Lifeboats had recommended tests at other stations. Worthing, one of the first to be chosen, was selected for the trials in the Southern District.

The Bridlington Quay lifeboat crew had used it constantly when running for the beach with the drogue out, having achieved beneficial results, claiming definite calming of the water even in a breaking sea. Subsequently, the Inspector supplied the Worthing station with one small bag and three tins of oil for trials.

When the Worthing crew made their first experiment, accompanied by the honorary secretary Walter Patching, a high wind was howling with what seemed like hurricane force, rendering the sea so heavy that the severe conditions abounding proved an excellent test.

"This is the sort of weather to launch a lifeboat!" exclaimed Jesse Blann, spectating on the seafront this Saturday morning, watching the huge breakers as they rushed, tumbling over each other in their eagerness to reach the shore.

It was indeed a wild day, and the sea presented an awe-inspiring spectacle. "Just the kind of weather for a lifeboat launch," repeated Jesse mockingly, smiling incredulously at Harry Marshall standing by his side.

Harry's reply was received without astonishment, "We are about to launch!"

Blowing strongly and viciously from the south west, the gale was bringing ashore large breakers as the lifeboat was successfully launched near the lifeboat house. Stout horses employed to pull her down the beach, although accustomed to the task of facing the billows, reared and plunged, nearly unseating their riders.

Use of the temporary warp, anchored on the sea bed, was essential to get the boat off in these conditions. Standing in a line down the centre of the boat, the crew worked with a will, hand over hand at the hauling off rope, which passed through the bullring (a pulley fixed to the bow), to a capstan or a chain buried in the beach (called a frap); and soon the sturdy craft was a safe distance from the dangers of the shore.

Further out, however, the lifeboatmen who had now taken to their oars, were met by a tremendous running sea.

From the beach, the progress of our boat, was watched with considerable interest by crowds of onlookers. But they could not see in detail what was happening.

A small bag of coarse canvas, tied with ropes and containing oakum soaked with half-a-gallon of thick oil, was towed over the weather quarter by a lanyard five or six fathoms long.

The oil oozed out slowly through the pores of the canvas to spread itself over and smooth the waters. A decided calming of the surface was visible to the crew, but the boat did not reap the full benefit from it, owing to a very heavily running cross sea. It was an ideal day for this sort of test: the wind being so violent and the waves so turbulent that the *Richard Coleman* was constantly awash.

Worthing lifeboat crew hauling out the *Richard Coleman* using a temporary warp
near the lifeboat house, during March 1914, to test the use of oil on the sea.

However, Walter Patching and Harry Marshall were both of the opinion that all that the Bridlington crew laid claim to was correct. The oil had a wonderful effect on the sea, and Worthing was able to send a very satisfactory report to head office.

It was largely in consequence of this report that a Lieutenant Hall took with him to Whitby a large quantity of oil, which was used with marked effect during a famous rescue. The Tynemouth lifeboat saved all 50 people, crew and nurses, aboard the hospital ship *Rohilla*, wrecked on the Yorkshire coast.

Reconstruction of Worthing Pier. Photographed on 8 April 1914 when the last section was being built.
(To the left of the picture is the halfway point).

During the following month, news reached Worthing that one of the local steamboats, the *Worthing Belle*, was to be taken out of service from its regular trips along the Sussex Coast. The owner of the steamer, Mr. Reid, had sold it to a company who proposed to run it across the Bosphorus. The paddle steamer's skipper, Captain J. Trenance, together with Worthing inhabitants was saddened by this disclosure, as the *Worthing Belle*[6] had for some years been the most popular steamer to call at Worthing Pier. She was the last of the privately-run ships to compete with the growing activities of Messrs P. & A. Campbell of Bristol, some of whose fleet of White Funnel paddlers were regular summer visitors.

Building work had been going on for a year to reconstruct the pier, which had been wrecked on Easter Saturday 1913. At last it was complete. Worthing was once more the proud possessor of a promenade platform linking the Victorian Pier Pavilion with land.

The last stages of reconstructing the Pier: decking planks and guard rails being positioned.

A grand gala opening was prepared. The Mayor, Alderman R. Piper, J.P., in conjunction with Alderman J.G. Denton, chairman of the Pier Company, had managed to persuade the Lord Mayor of London to perform the opening ceremony. His famous ceremonial coaches with coachmen and footmen in all the pomp and dignity of their office were to provide a spectacle. It was arranged for the coaches to be sent down overnight in advance of the civic dignitary, who was to arrive in the middle of the appointed day, to be guest of honour in a procession from the railway station, through the town, to the new Pier.

Through the columns of local newspapers, the Mayor of Worthing appealed to townspeople to hang colourful decorations on shops and houses along the designated route.

To decorate the line of the route itself, an order was placed with a well-known London firm for a similar scheme to that adopted here in Worthing when King George V and his Queen were crowned.

The first visible indication of the preparations was the appearance of Venetian masts in Chapel Road.

The Town Hall and Chapel Road decorated for the re-opening of the Pier in 1914.

When the big day arrived, the Lord Mayor of London, Sir T. Vansittart Bowater, Bart, travelled down on the train in a specially provided carriage. His wife, Lady Bowater and their daughter came too, accompanied by the deputy chairman of the railway company, Mr. C. C. Macrea.

Just before 12.30 p.m., the train pulled under Broadwater Bridge and into Worthing station. The Lord Mayor, in his uniform of office arrayed with a wealth of gold braid, stepped onto the platform, where he was escorted by some pupils from Wykeham House School into the waiting room, which had been strikingly transformed to feature a series of choice prints of old London that belonged to the stationmaster, Mr. W. M. Mullinger. Here, the civic visitors were formally introduced to pillars of local society, including those representing Worthing Corporation and the Pier company, together with local member of Parliament Major W.R. Campion.

After a dull, grey morning the sun popped out from behind the clouds just as the guest-of-honour appeared on the station steps, but its welcoming influence was short-lived as cloud shielded it from view once more.

At this moment, a fanfare of trumpets filled the air, played by three members of Mr. Cramer-Suckley's band positioned on the opposite side of the flag-adorned approach road. After taking in the momentous scene that had been laid on for him, the Lord Mayor proudly descended the steps from the station to the road, and smartly climbed into a waiting carriage followed by his wife and daughter. In groups of four, the local civic dignitaries walked to six other carriages lining the road and seated themselves comfortably inside.

With several contingents of troops and artillery, a procession formed, led by the band of the Royal Garrison Artillery, and moved off in splendid formation passing huge, swelling crowds of enthusiastic sightseers, who had to be restrained by policemen to keep the road clear.

Soldiers marching and horses trotting, the parade made its way down Chapel Road, watched all the while by never-ending throngs of excited townsfolk. For the locals it was a day they had been looking forward to for some time: not only for the fantastic atmosphere created by the sight of a procession and the beat of a military band, but also because they knew that their Pier was once more complete and majestic-looking.

Everyone was enthralled by the marching troops. The air abounded with patriotic fervour emitted by the soldiers' band.

Arrival of the Lord Mayor of London at Worthing Railway Station, 29 May 1914.

The Lord Mayor's Parade crossing from Railway Approach[7] by the foot of Broadwater Bridge to Chapel Road.

Lord Mayor's procession in Chapel Road, passing its junction with Market Street.

The Parade going past the Town Hall and the decorated fountain.

Two photos, in sequence, of the Lord Mayor's Parade passing down South Street, 29 May 1914.

A close-up of one of the carriages in the Lord Mayor's procession.(Warwick Street junction is in the background)

All the way to the Pier, a brilliant display of colour brightened the thoroughfares, elaborately decorated by Messrs. Brock & Co.

When the party arrived at the Pier entrance, emblazoned by the motto 'Welcome to Worthing's new Pier', a fanfare of trumpets burst forth once more as the officials alighted from their conveyances.

The Pier, standing so upright with the unpredictable sea lapping gently around its metallic knees, looked strong and robust. Just a year ago the entire promenade section had been torn down and swallowed by tumultuous waves. Gradually, by the hands of efficient, skilled workmen under the guidance of expert engineers, the new structure had risen slowly from the saline water to reveal an even greater splendour.

Foundations and sub-structure were now much stronger than a year ago, strong enough to support this wider version, which allowed for the future erection of a pavilion at the landward end, which was now 84 feet wide. For most of its length it had a width of 36 feet, while half way along, the width had been extended by a further 24 feet over a distance of 80 feet to allow for a bandstand to be built with an enclosure for outdoor concerts.

For this special day the Pier was hung with colourful streamers and flags. The civic dignitaries walked in procession along the decking of well-seasoned hardwood planks towards the pavilion, passing lines of well-disciplined young people on the way: Steyne School Cadets under the command of Captain Bennett; 1st Worthing Troop of Boy Scouts, under Assistant Scoutmasters G.V. Paine and S.S. Hills; Captain F.J.R. Mountain commanded 1st Worthing Boys Brigade; the Church Lads' Brigade was in the charge of Captain Pitt; and the Holy Trinity Naval Brigade was commanded by Captain Waller.

As the guests of the day entered the Pavilion, a packed assembly arose, while the public figures took seats on the stage where an abundance of plants had been arranged for the occasion.

Wearing a long, white dress, the Mayor's little daughter, Joyce Piper presented the Lady Mayoress (her mother) with a delightful bouquet of carnations. In turn, little Miss Piper was kissed by the Lady Mayoress and then by the Lord Mayor, arousing much applause from the gathering.

Arrival of one of the coaches at the Pier entrance for its re-opening, 29 May 1914.[8]

In procession on the Pier, 29 May 1914.

Lord Mayor's procession outside the *Warnes Hotel*.

The Town Clerk read an address to the Lord Mayor which was in volume form, of dark blue Morocco with the Borough's coat of arms embossed in silver gilt.

After a series of speeches the procession re-formed and made its way to the *Warnes Hotel* amid crowds of excited onlookers.

Outside the premier hotel, local artillery and Territorials formed a guard-of-honour as the nobility entered. Nearly 180 guests, including mayors and council chairmen from many south coast towns, advanced along an extensive corridor, which was attractively draped with flowers and foliage plants, and seated themselves in the handsome lounge where a commemmorative luncheon, which included boar's head, was served.

While the meal progressed, the Royal Naval Ladies' Orchestra conducted by Madame Florence Sidney entertained the company. Toasts and more speeches followed the meal. Alderman Denton acknowledged the generous way in which the debenture stockholders had allowed the Pier directors to divert money subscribed for a new pavilion scheme to the rebuilding of the Pier, and said they still hoped a shore-end pavilion would come, as well as a windbreak down the centre, both of which were much needed. Worthing was most honoured to entertain the Lord Mayor of London, and the guests felt priviledged to have a man of such importance seated in their midst.

After lunching, Sir Vansittart asked everyone present to raise their glasses and join him in drinking "Success and prosperity to the new Pier."

Feeling the effects of the heavy meal, one of the guests made a hasty exit to stretch his legs. It was Mr. Harry Hargood J.P. He crossed the road to the prom where he strolled westward past the magnificent Pier.

Coming across Harry Marshall maintaining his boat the *Jolly Sailor* at the top of the beach with fellow waterman Bill Blann, Harry Hargood, the traditional and much-respected representative of the watermen stopped for a chat.

Looking at the iron structure of the Pier before him, Harry mused on how different in mood it could be. Sturdy, firm and robust enough to withstand stormy conditions; yet right now its colourful decorations above deck, coupled with the whispered lapping of water around its legs conjured a quite different picture. The impressions it radiated were versatile. It could emit an almost feminine charm while retaining its masculine strength.

"This is the beginning of a new era for the town. You mark my words!" declared Harry Hargood.

"Worthing sure 'as got a lot to be proud of right now," insisted Harry as the two fishermen looked up from their stooping positions in the boat.

"Aye, an' it's 50 years come next March our lifeboat's bin under the RNLI banner," exclaimed Bill.

Looking the magistrate straight in the eye, Harry declared, "And its down to you. You've inspired townies alongside us seafolk, with one common aim – saving lives with the lifeboat: them to raise money, and us to man it."

Beaming triumphantly across his neatly-moustached face, the lifeboat chairman looked pensively into the air, as if wanting to pluck words from the sky, and pronounced in his diplomatic way: "Pulling together I would call it!"

"Yes, pulling together," he re-affirmed.

The Royal Naval Ladies' Orchestra, which played at the celebration luncheon, 29 May 1914.

Footnotes

[1] Cecil Pashley was only the second person in the country to hold a flying licence. From Shoreham he taught many people to fly.

[2] A Frank Worley owned the well-known fried fish shop which operated in North Street. Demolished in the 1980's to make way for a dual carriageway, only a few of the historic buildings in North Street/High Street now remain.

[3] There are many references to the Davis family in my book 'A Town's Pride'.

[4] For the *Vandalia* story read chapter 10 of the book 'A Town's Pride'.

[5] Details of the wreck *Theresa* can be found in chapter eight of 'A Town's Pride'.

[6] The Turkish company who acquired the *Worthing Belle* renamed her the *Touzla*. In 1914, as a gunboat, she became an enemy ship and was 'sunk' by ships of the allied fleet during the Dardanelles Campaign. In fact, she was only damaged, was then beached, and after the war she was saved and returned to her former ferry duties, until 1926 when she was broken up.

[7] This end of Railway Approach is now blocked by the Teville Gate shopping centre and multi-storey car park

[8] According to the sender of this postcard, which was sent to a Mrs. Monk at Bletchley in Buckinghamshire, one of their party of visitors, a little girl called Doris, is just inside the Pier entrance sitting on her daddy's shoulders – marked with an X.

A postcard of Worthing by the sea produced in 1909 with inset views of the pier entrance, the ornamental water park (now drained and called Homefield Park), East Parade, The Broadway, and West Beach

Mayors of the Borough

1900 - 1902   Councillor Francis Edward Ovenden
               (Deputy Mayor: Alderman Frank Parish)
               (Mayor's Chaplain: Rev. C.G. Coombe M.A.)

1902 - 1904   Alderman Edward Thomas Cooksey

1904 - 1906   Councillor James White

1906 - 1908   Alderman Frederick Ceasar Linfield J.P.

1908 - 1910   Councillor James Gurney Denton

1910 - 1912   Alderman Edward Cunningham Patching

1912 - 1914   Alderman Robert Piper

Worthing lifeboat crewmen   1901 – 1914

Steve Bacon
George Belton
George Benn
Bill Blann (second coxswain)
Bill Blann junior
Harry Blann
Frank Burden
Jack Burgess
Frank Collier
Fred Collier

William Collier
Fred Collins
William Cousins
William Curven
J. Elliott
George Finnis
James Groves
F. Hutchinson
Arthur Marshall
Fred Marshall

Harry Marshall (coxswain)
Mark Marshall
George Newman
Jo Street
William Wells
Charlie Wingfield
George Wingfield
Steve Wingfield (bowman)
Steve Wingfield junior
Tom (Jumbo) Wingfield

Signalman up until 1909 : Walter J. Butcher. After 1909 : Fred Wakeford.
Horse contractor up until 1909 : Walter J. Butcher. After 1909 : Mr. B. Haslett.

Worthing Fishermen's and Watermen's Benefit Association Committee

A. Beck
F. Beck
George Benn
W. Benn
Tom Blann
Robert William Charles (trustee)
Tom Clark
Dr. A.H. Collet (auditor)
Golding Bird Collett (trustee)
T. Davis

Frank Dean (secretary)
Ed Edwards
E. Haylor
W. Lucas
John Roberts (trustee)
J. Searle
J. Tester
W. Verrall (auditor)
James White (president and treasurer)

Worthing Branch RNLI Committee members
(mentioned in this book)

E.G. Amphlett J.P.	Harry Hargood J.P.	Alderman E.C. Patching
J. Andrews	(chairman)	F.W. Patching
E.W. Bennett	Mrs. Hargood	Walter G. Patching
J. Brown	Rev. C.J. Hollis	George Piggott
Mrs. Latham Brown	Admiral Leicester Keppel	A.A. Ralli
L.W. Burnand	Chief Coastguard Officer T.	John Roberts
J.R. Denton	Lester	R. Selway Chard
A. Buckland Dixon	G.H.P. Livesay	F.B. Tilt
Alderman G. Ewen Smith	Mrs. Livesay	F.J. Timms
Rev. W.B. Ferris	J. Long	Alderman J. White J.P.
R.J. Fry	E. Meagre	Miss Wigham
W.H.B. Fletcher	Alderman F. Parish J.P.	H.R.P. Wyatt J.P.
F.C. Gates	Rev. J.O. Parr	
M. Goodman	Miss Parry	

Swimming Club officers

J.M. Head
E.A. Paine (captain)
F.P. Twine (honorary secretary)

Built in the Edwardian era

1901 The Broadway, Brighton Road – a row of shops erected in the fashionable Neo-Tudor-Baroque style of the period.
1901 Methodist Church, Steyne Gardens
1903 Congregational Church, Shelley Road
1908 The Tabernacle, Chapel Road – built by Henry Charles Child, whose great grandson Terry Child has a keen interest in the town's history.
1908 Museum and Public Library, Chapel Road – now the Museum and Tourist Information Centre.
1911 Kursall – now the Dome Cinema. Purchased by Worthing Borough Council in 1969 for redevelopment, but following a campaign waged by conservationists it was listed by the Department of the Environment in 1989 as a building of historic and architectural importance. Its future is still uncertain.
1912 Salvation Army Citadel, Crescent Road
1914 The Picturedrome, Union Place – a cinema opened for Mr. C. Seebold on 29 January. Today the Connaught Theatre.

Demolished in the Edwardian Era

1901 Royal Hotel, Marine Parade destroyed by fire – now the site of the Arcade.
1910 Navarino Windmills, Ham Road

Guests at the Lord Mayor's luncheon at Warnes Hotel to celebrate the re-opening of Worthing Pier, 1914 included:

Mrs. Allerton
Mr. Allingham
Mrs. Aston
Alderman Baker
Mrs. Banfather
Lieutenant Barker
Mrs. A. Barker
Miss Barnett
J. Barnett
H.J. Barnett
H. Barnwell
Mrs. Berwick
E. Blinkhorn
H.W. Bowen (City Surveyor)
Lieutenant H.C.B. Bowles
Councillor Brackley
Councillor Brake
R.J. Brewster
Councillor L.W. Burnand
Cyril Campbell
Major W.R. Campion, M.P.
H.R. Carter
W. Cash
J. Chaplin
Councillor Ellen Chapman
Robert W. Charles
W.W. Chilton
Councillor Chipper
H.W. Clarke
Mrs. G. Coe
H.N. Collet
Captain G.S. Constable (Mayor of Arundel)
Alderman J.G. Denton (chairman of the Pier Company)
A. Denyer
H.W. Doll
J.B. Dore, J.P.
Councillor Duffield
W. Dyball
Councillor Ellis
W.H. Elsworth
Alderman J. Every, J.P.
Rev. S.S. Farrow (the Mayor's Chaplain)
J.M. Forsey
Miss Marian Frost
Councillor Gardiner
H.H. Gardner
J.T. Godwin
Councillor Goodall
Dr. W.A. Gostling
F. Grace
Councillor G. Gravett
H.J. Gray
Councillor Greenyer
Lieutenant-Colonel A. Henty, J.P.
E. Henty, J.P.
Mr. and Mrs. J. Hill
Captain E.H. Hills, R.N.
Captain H.F. Holman
Alderman Humphery
Councillor Jackson
Mrs. Knight
H. Lake
Mrs. Langton
Alderman E.H. Leeney, J.P. (Mayor of Hove)
B.R. Leftwich
C. Lewis
Alderman Linfield, J.P.
Dr. J.R. Lunn
T.J. Lyne
C.C. Macrae
F. Martin
F.C. Mason
Captain E.H. Mathews
Lieutenant-Colonel Maltby, J.P.
E.L. Mansergh
Rev. J. Mayles
J.W. Mills
S.L. Moffatt
Colonel Neale
Dr. Nicholls
F.J. Norman
Councillor Norris
A.W. Oke
A.C. Osborn
Charles Paine
L.S. Palmer
Councillor Parsons
G. Pilgrim
H.B. Piper
A. Pope
G. Porter
Mr. and Mrs. W. Powell
C.F. Pycroft
S.S. Pyle
Frank Roberts
E.M. Rodocanachi
M.W. Shanly
Arthur Shelley
Mrs. Smyth
H.E. Snewin
Rev. C.G. Squirrell
G. Stacey
Dr. Strong, J.P.
A. Stubbs
Councillor Taylor
W. Thomas
S. Thornely (Clerk to West Sussex County Council)
T.M. Tolputt
R. Tomlin
Mrs. Tulloch
P. Twine
W.F. Verrall
Denis Wade
A.F. Walter
Alderman J. White
Councillor J.F. Whyte
Dr. Wilshaw
Councillor Winchester
Captain A.E. Wood (City Marshal)
Mrs. Wright

By the same author

Rob Blann set out to write a trilogy about the townsfolk of Worthing and their lifeboats.

A TOWN'S PRIDE – Victorian Lifeboatmen & their Community
price £9.95

EDWARDIAN WORTHING – Eventful Era in a Lifeboat Town
price £12.95

the third is under preparation.

Worthing Lifeboat Watercolour Print
'A Town's Pride' – Limited Edition

Commissioned for the front cover of the book 'A Town's Pride', this unique watercolour is a true-to-life portrayal of the Worthing lifeboat *Henry Harris* and crew returning from the wrecked steamship *Indiana* on 1 March 1901.

A Victorian photgrapher captured this exciting scene in monochrome. Beautifully enhanced by the Southwick artist Richard Marsh using characteristic colouring, the result is remarkable.

This is the only known painting of the Worthing lifeboat, whose crew, held in high esteem by their national executive, were indeed the town's pride.

Limited to 850 copies, each one is signed and numbered by the artist, and comes complete with a list of the crew members and their ranks.

price £25

Part of the proceeds from each book and painting sold will be donated to the
Royal National Lifeboat Institution.

Available from the author and publisher:-
Rob Blann
349 Tarring Road
Worthing
West Sussex
BN11 5JL

Please add £1 per item for U.K. postage and packing.

Sussex 225A   8314